Making Sense with Offenders

The Wiley Series in Offender Rehabilitation

Edited by

Clive R. Hollin
University of Leicester, UK

and

Mary McMurran
East Midlands Centre for Forensic Mental Health, Leicester,
& University of Leicester, UK

Young Offenders and Alcohol-Related Crime
Mary McMurran and Clive R. Hollin

What Works: Reducing Reoffending
Guidelines from Research and Practice
Edited by James McGuire

Therapeutic Communities for Offenders
Eric Cullen, Lawrence Jones and Roland Woodward

Addicted to Crime?
*Edited by John E. Hodge, Mary McMurran
and Clive R. Hollin*

Making Sense with Offenders:
Personal Constructs, Therapy and Change
Julia Houston

Making Sense with Offenders

Personal Constructs, Therapy and Change

Julia Houston
Shaftesbury Clinic, London, UK

JOHN WILEY & SONS

Chichester · New York · Weinheim · Brisbane · Singapore · Toronto

Other Wiley Editorial Offices

John Wiley & Sons, Inc., 605 Third Avenue,
New York, NY 10158-0012, USA

WILEY-VCH Verlag GmbH
Pappelallee 3, D-69469, Weinheim, Germany

Jacaranda Wiley Ltd, 33 Park Road, Milton,
Queensland 4064, Australia

John Wiley & Sons (Asia) Pte Ltd, 2 Clementi Loop #02-01,
Jin Xing Distripark, Singapore 129809

John Wiley & Sons (Canada) Ltd, 22 Worcester Road,
Rexdale, Ontario M9W 1L1, Canada

Library of Congress Cataloging-in-Publication Data

Houston, Julia.
    Making sense with offenders : personal constructs, therapy and
change / Julia Houston.
        p.   cm. — (The Wiley series in offender rehabilitation)
    Includes bibliographical references and index.
    ISBN 0-471-95415-2 (case). — ISBN 0-471-96627-4 (pbk.)
    1. Prisoners—Mental health. 2. Personal construct therapy.
3. Prisoners—Mental health services. 4. Criminals—Mental health.
5. Criminals—Mental health services. 6. Criminals—Rehabilitation.
I. Title II. Series.
RC451.4.P68H68 1998
616.89'14'086927—dc21   97-33472
                                                                            CIP

British Library Cataloguing in Publication Data

A catalogue record for this book is available from the British Library

ISBN 0-471-95415-2 (cased)
ISBN 0-471-96627-4 (paper)

Typeset in 10/12 pt Century Schoolbook by Mathematical Composition Setters Ltd, Salisbury
Printed and bound in Great Britain by Biddles Ltd, Guildford and King's Lynn
This book is printed on acid-free paper responsibly manufactured from sustainable forestry,
in which at least two trees are planted for each one used for paper production.

To: Mike, Conor and Kate

Contents

About the Author

Julia Houston   Forensic Psychiatry Services,
Shaftesbury Clinic, Springfield University Hospital
Glenburnie Road, London SW17 7DJ

Julia Houston is a Chartered Clinical and Forensic Psychologist at the Shaftesbury Clinic Medium Secure Unit, Tooting, London, UK. She has extensive experience in the clinical assessment and treatment of a wide range of offenders, particularly those described as 'mentally disordered' and those who have committed sexual offences, and has used PCP to inform her clinical practice over the past ten years.

Foreword

One of the aims of this series is to encourage readers to become familiar with the full range of therapeutic approaches relevant to working with offenders. While it is true that treatments based on cognitive–behavioural principles are currently capturing the attention of many practitioners, there are many other approaches to consider. For example, the last book in this series took as its central topic the applicability of therapeutic communities with offender populations.

This book considers the applicability of personal construct theory to both understanding offending and working with offenders. It offers an overview of the theory and, with case examples, shows how the theory can be applied in forensic practice. We are sure that this book will be welcomed by those working in the field and we are pleased to have it as part of our series.

Clive Hollin
Mary McMurran

Series Preface

Twenty years ago it is doubtful that any serious consideration would have been given to publishing a series of books on the topic of offender rehabilitation. While the notion of rehabilitation for offenders was widely accepted 30 years ago, the 1970s saw the collapse of what we might call the treatment ideal. As many other commentators have noted, the turning point can be pinpointed to the publication of an article titled 'What Works—Questions and Answers about Prison Reform', written by Robert Martinson and published in 1974. The essential message taken from this article was that, when it comes to the rehabilitation of offenders, what works is 'nothing works'. It would be stretching the case to say that Martinson single-handedly overturned the rehabilitative philosophy, but his message was obviously welcomed by a receptive audience. As writers such as Don Andrews have suggested there are many reasons why both the academic community and politicians and policy-makers were more than willing to subscribe to the 'nothing works' philosophy. (Although the evidence suggests that the public at large did not buy completely the need to abandon rehabilitation.) Thus the 1970s and 1980s saw a return to hard sentencing, the predominance of punishment, and the handing out of just deserts to those who transgressed the law of the land. Throughout this period of rehabilitative nihilism a small group of academics and practitioners kept faith with the rehabilitative ideal, led perhaps by Paul Gendreau and Robert Ross, and slowly began to look for new ways to argue the case for rehabilitation. The turnabout, when it came, was dramatic. Through the development of a methodology for statistically reviewing large bodies of research, called 'meta-analysis', unequivocal evidence was produced that rehabilitative programmes did work. The view that 'nothing works' is simply wrong: rehabilitation programmes do have a positive effect in reducing recidivism. The effect is not always large, although sometimes it is; nor is it always present, although on average it is. However, it is there and that cannot be ignored.

Since 1990, armed with these findings, there has been a remarkable resurgence of the rehabilitative ideal: practitioners have eagerly attended conferences, seminars, and training courses; researchers are working not to make the case for rehabilitation, but to improve and refine techniques for working with offenders.

This series aims to provide a ready source of information, for both practitioners and researchers, on the developments as the renewed emphasis on rehabilitative work with offenders gathers pace. We are keenly looking forward to its continued unfolding, and we hope that in time practitioners and researchers will also eagerly await each new volume.

Mary McMurran
Clive R. Hollin

August 1997

Preface

Like many clinical psychologists, my first (and very brief) introduction to Kelly and personal construct psychology (PCP) was through a single lecture whilst an undergraduate. These vague memories were resurrected when, as part of my clinical psychology training, I worked with Paul Devonshire at Broadmoor Special Hospital, where there is a long tradition of both the clinical and research use of PCP with 'mentally abnormal' offenders. I found that using the PCP perspective opened up a whole new dimension to the assessment and treatment of this complex client group. In particular, this approach appeared to me to provide information over and above that which could be obtained from a standard interview assessment plus psychometric/personality testing, i.e. an understanding of the unique way in which each individual made sense of their world and their offending. Over the years I have found that the PCP approach has continued to help make sense of 'deviant' behaviour which is otherwise often frustrating and difficult to comprehend. Trying to see the world through the eyes of an offender and keeping in mind the view that an individual behaves in the way *which makes most sense to them* has, I think, enabled me to work more effectively with those offenders who do want to change, and to understand the resistance of those who are more ambivalent.

When Clive Hollin first suggested the idea of writing a book about the use of PCP with offenders, this therefore seemed like an opportunity to share my enthusiasm with other clinicians. My own struggle through the rather complex and abstract language with which Kelly set out his theory meant that one of the primary aims of this book is to demonstrate that PCP can be an accessible theory which has wide applicability to clinical work with an offender population. The book aims to inform the reader about the clinical application of PCP to offending behaviour and therefore add to the understanding of individuals who commit offences, and also to enable readers to use the approach practically to inform their own clinical work, as an adjunct to their existing theoretical orientation.

Despite my initial enthusiasm, actually completing the book was a far more difficult task than I had naively anticipated. I would therefore like to express my heartfelt thanks and gratitude to the many people who have contributed to this process in different ways. In particular, I am indebted to my colleague and co-author on Chapter 4, Chris Evans, who not only has guided me through grid analyses over many years, but has also somehow made time to read drafts of substantial sections of the book and helped to direct and clarify many of my ideas. Throughout most of the writing of the book I was also fortunate to work with Maggie Hilton as Head of Forensic Psychology, who was particularly supportive. I would very much like to thank her and others who have taken time to read drafts of chapters and provide helpful comments: Ronald Blackburn, Paul Devonshire, David Sperlinger and David Winter. Clearly the gaps that remain are entirely my responsibility. I would also like to thank Clive Hollin, Series Editor, for his continuous support, guidance and encouragement, and Wendy Hudlass and Lesley Valerio of John Wiley & Sons. Thanks are also due to Sandy McLaren, who saved my sanity by typing the references and some of the figures, and Pauline Thomson and Andrea Cohen who have assisted with grid analyses. Finally, I would not have been able to see this through without the encouragement and very practical support from my family, particularly from my husband Mike who has been so tolerant throughout, and to whom I owe a very special thank you.

In order to preserve anonymity, the specific details of case examples described in the book have been changed.

PART I

The Theory and Practice of Personal Construct Psychology

The first part of this book introduces the theory of personal constructs and examines PCP perspectives on the aetiology of deviant and offending behaviour (Chapter 1). Subsequent chapters describe the PCP approach to assessment and treatment (Chapters 2, 3), and highlight the issues which are particularly pertinent to working with offenders, such as resistance to change and the understanding of guilt and hostility (in both the traditional and the Kellian sense). Chapter 4 provides a step-by-step account of the use of repertory grids. Although this technique is by no means an essential part of working with a PCP perspective, grids can provide an illuminating insight into the way in which an offender views the world, as illustrated in Part II. Although clinical examples are used throughout the book, readers who are unfamiliar with personal construct psychology may find it helpful to read some of the more detailed case examples in Part II in conjunction with these first four chapters.

CHAPTER 1

Personal Construct Psychology and Offending

This opening chapter begins by reviewing some of the recent developments in therapeutic work with offenders. These have primarily been cognitively oriented, and emphasise the importance of addressing the way in which offenders appraise the world. The central concepts in personal construct psychology (PCP) are then described and illustrated by examples of the ways in which offenders construe the world. The PCP perspective on the aetiology of deviancy and offending is examined and factors which may be relevant in the development of socially deviant construing are discussed. The chapter ends by considering what the PCP approach has to offer the clinician working with offenders.

Introduction

Historically, researchers have long been interested in the ways in which offenders make sense of their own behaviour. Sykes & Matza (1957) analysed the ways in which delinquents attempted to justify their antisocial behaviour, and noted the importance of cognitive factors. They described five main ways in which offenders neutralise or justify their criminal behaviour: *denial of responsibility* (offending is a consequence of a disrupted childhood or being drunk), *denial of injury* (their behaviour is not harmful), *denial of the victim* (the victim deserves it), *condemnation of the condemners* (focusing attention on authority figures who disapprove), and *appeal to higher loyalties* (the needs of others, such as peers, are more important). Agnew & Peters (1986) see 'acceptance of neutralisations' as a predisposing factor for offending, and although it has still not been demonstrated that these neutralisations necessarily precede deviant acts, as opposed to being *post hoc* rationalisations, this framework of justifications is still commonly used in clinical practice (e.g. Salter, 1988).

Interest in cognitive approaches to offending did not really develop further until the 1970s. Ross & Fabiano (1985) attribute this delay to the earlier prevailing sociological theories of offending, which rejected any explanation of criminal behaviour that failed to view the offender from a social, political or economic context. They also noted that there had previously been no attempt to integrate knowledge about relevant cognitive factors into a coherent body of knowledge. This changed with the advent of cognitive–behavioural therapies, which emphasised the central role of cognitive factors in the development and maintenance of emotional and behavioural problems (Beck, 1976; Meichenbaum, 1977). A variety of authors applied this model to the understanding of offending. Jurkovic & Prentice (1977) argued that persistent delinquents were limited in their understanding of social behaviour and their capacity to assume the role of others, and therefore had difficulty in predicting or anticipating the behaviour of others. Other authors have described ways in which the thinking and perceptions of offenders differ from those of non-offenders, particularly in relation to their abilities for perspective-taking and problem-solving (Sarason, 1978; Duguid, 1981). One of the most influential cognitive explanations of offending behaviour in the 1970s was Yochelson & Samenow's (1976) analysis of 'The Criminal Personality'. The authors used case studies of recidivistic offenders to describe 52 'thinking errors', which they suggested characterised the thinking patterns of offenders. These included impulsiveness, perfectionism, concrete and compartmentalised thinking, and failure to put oneself in the position of others. However, the methodology of their research typified the problems of early attempts to demonstrate the role of cognitions in offending. Authors often made generalised observations which were untested, and the small number of empirical studies were carried out only on particular groups of offenders. Noting these limitations, Ross & Fabiano (1985) systematically reviewed the research literature to determine whether there was any empirical evidence to suggest that offenders differed from non-offenders in their cognitive functioning. They particularly focused on *social cognition*, i.e. 'that facet of thinking and perception which allows one to make inferences about others, to take the perspective of others, to understand the perceptions others have of oneself, and to understand social phenomena' (p. 34).

The authors reviewed studies of the link between offending and a range of social cognitive abilities, including self-control/impulsivity, concrete thinking, self-esteem and locus of control, problem-solving and social perspective-taking. They also reviewed the effectiveness of treatment programmes which included a cognitive training component. Ross & Fabiano (1985) concluded that many, *but not all*, offenders show inadequacies in their development of a number of cognitive skills, which may limit their ability to function effectively in a prosocial manner. Furthermore, many treatment or rehabilitation programmes that included some technique expected to have an impact on the offender's thinking, were effective in reducing the recidivism of adolescent and adult offenders. That is, effective programmes addressed not only the individual's behaviour, vocational or interpersonal skills, but also 'his cognition, his expectations, his understanding and his appraisal of the world and his values' (Ross et al., 1988, p. 30). Subsequent outcome studies have provided further support for the inclusion of cognitive training as an essential component of effective interventions with offenders (Ross et al., 1988; Izzo & Ross, 1990).

Ross & Fabiano (1985) do not suggest that cognitive inadequacies are a *cause* of crime, as they are neither necessary nor sufficient for offending behaviour to occur. Cognitive deficits may contribute to the development and maintenance of offending in some individuals, but it is not possible to say to what extent. The cognitive model is therefore not a theory of crime, but 'a model for rehabilitation' (p. 142), and as such, not incompatible with other sociological models of offending behaviour which emphasise the role of environmental factors. In other words, the causes of inadequate social–cognitive development may well be the same factors which have been viewed as criminogenic by some authors, such as absent or inappropriate parental models, erratic or excessive discipline, poverty and inadequate schooling (Haney, 1983).

The work of Ross and colleagues (Ross & Fabiano, 1985; Ross et al., 1988, Izzo & Ross, 1990) has subsequently influenced the nature of treatment services provided to offenders. In the 1970s institutionally based behavioural approaches were predominant (e.g. Hoghugi, 1979). However, in his comprehensive review of psychological interventions with offenders, Blackburn (1993) notes that interest in applying cognitive–behavioural methods grew throughout the 1980s. He emphasises that such interventions include a range of approaches which all share the view that cognitions affect behaviour, and use both verbal and behavioural methods to alter cognitive processes. In the early 1980s social skills training was used to increase an offender's social interaction and communication skills and therefore help to prevent reoffending (Hollin & Henderson, 1984). With problems of violence and aggression, Novaco's (1978) anger management programme is still widely used clinically, although there are only a few reports in the literature about its use with an offender population (e.g. McDougall et al., 1987). This approach involves the identification and restructuring of cognitions about anger, the use of positive self-statements (e.g. 'I'm not going to let this person wind me up') and training in coping skills. A review of studies by Levey & Howells (1990) suggested that anger management is useful in managing disruptive behaviour in institutions, and a national anger management course is now operational in many UK prisons (Towl, 1995). However, the major developments in cognitive–behavioural treatment with offenders in the latter half of the 1980s and in the 1990s have been with young offenders, high-risk adults on probation (Ross & Fabiano, 1985; Ross, et al., 1988; Izzo & Ross, 1990) and with sex offenders (Murphy, 1990; Marshall & Barbaree, 1990a; Marshall, 1992; Beckett, 1994).

There are therefore increasing numbers of outcome studies which suggest encouraging results when using cognitive–behavioural interventions with offenders. Such interventions are 'therefore clearly here to stay' (Blackburn, 1993, p. 363). However, as Blackburn goes on to discuss, there are still uncertainties about the exact relevance of specific techniques and targets in such interventions, and also about the functional relationship of cognitive deficits to criminal behaviour. While raising a note of caution about applying a variety of techniques in a haphazard manner (Kazdin, 1987), he suggests that multi-faceted treatment (although not yet demonstrated to be more effective than single-component interventions) is perhaps an ideal for clinical practice, given the heterogeneity of offenders.

WHAT IS PERSONAL CONSTRUCT PSYCHOLOGY?

Personal construct theory (PCT) is a theory of personality, developed in the 1950s by George Kelly, a psychologist who disagreed with some of the assumptions of Freudian and behavioural psychological approaches. One of his essential beliefs was that people are active agents interacting with the world around them, rather than simply passively responding to either predetermined events in their childhood or their environment. In essence, PCT (G. Kelly, 1955; reprinted 1991) is a theory about how people make sense of the world around them. Kelly suggested that all individuals actively interpret or *construe* events in the world, and then behave in ways which are consistent with their own particular view of the world (*construct system*). Personal construct *psychology* (PCP) describes the way in which this theory applies to an individual, based on the following underlying principles:

- The explanation for any individual's behaviour lies within that individual.
- People are active in the world and not passive recipients of events going on around them.
- Change is always possible—no one is the victim of their own history.

Working clinically with the PCP approach with offenders therefore involves trying to understand how the client's unique view of the world contributes to the development and maintenance of their offending behaviour. The clinician using the PCP approach with offenders does not condone the client's behaviour, but assumes that understanding their perspective on this is a prerequisite to setting realistic goals for change. The approach provides specific techniques for assessing construing (see Chapter 2) and suggests means of therapeutic change (see Chapter 3). However, in keeping with the theory itself, working with a PCP perspective does not necessarily involve one specific way of working. It is more of an approach to understanding people and seeing the world from their perspective. PCP can either be used alone or as complementary to other therapeutic interventions, as 'one tool in an armoury of possibilities' (Dalton & Dunnett, 1992, p. 149).

CENTRAL CONCEPTS IN PCP

Before considering the PCP perspective on offending, the central concepts and processes involved will be described. There are four key concepts which are important in understanding PCP.

The Process of Construing

The process of construing is one of the central concepts in PCP, and one of the main aims of this book is to explore how people who commit offences construe the world. Construing refers to how people interpret events, and *constructs* are personal discriminations that individuals make between people, events or situations. G. Kelly (1955/1991) defined 'personal constructs' as *'an awareness of how two things are alike in a way that differentiates them from a third'*. Construing is not the same as thinking, as it involves the notion of contrast, and of making an active interpretation or discrimination. For example, if a person described herself and her mother as 'trustworthy', in direct contrast to her father, then the discrimination 'Trustworthy vs Not trustworthy', is a construct which that person uses. This construct contributes to their view of the world, i.e. it is part of their construct system.

People as 'Active Scientists'

Kelly suggested that individuals are active in the sense of anticipating events by making hypotheses, and testing them to see whether or not they fit into their existing construct system. He therefore saw people as scientists, who acted in ways that were consistent with their existing view of the world or amended their view if the results did not turn out as they had expected. For example, if a person believes that their work colleagues are honest, then they might leave some money out on their desk. If it then gets stolen, they may change their view, and may subsequently hide personal possessions and money. Many offenders have the opposite expectations, i.e. that other people are not to be trusted and are out to get the better of them. There may be a certain reality to this within their particular peer group or subculture, and treatment may involve encouraging them to test and amend their expectations in a different setting, such as in therapy.

Constructive Alternativism

G. Kelly (1955/1991) used the term *constructive alternativism* to describe the notion that all events in the universe are open to different interpretations which are, in turn, subject to revision or replacement. He emphasised that individuals experience the universe in different ways, depending on the interpretations that they make. Since events are open to interpretation this means that the individual has a 'choice' in terms of how they see themselves and the world around them. PCP therefore offers hope of change, in that no one need be stuck in a particular way of thinking or behaving because of previous events in their life. Although a person might not choose to change their way of thinking, feeling or behaving, the option for change is there. Kelly summed this up by saying 'No one needs to paint himself into a corner; no one needs to be completely hemmed in by circumstances; no one needs to be the victim of his biography' (G. Kelly, 1955/1991, Vol. 1, p. 11).

PCP as a Universal Theory

G. Kelly used the term *reflexivity* to describe the concept of PCP applying to everyone and all behaviours in all situations. In other words, it is not a theory that just explains disorder or deviance. It is an approach which can be used to understand why one person may hit out in an argument, whilst another would walk away. Clinicians using PCP should be able to apply the approach to themselves and their own behaviour just as easily as to that of their clients, and this book therefore ends with a reflexive look at the use of the PCP perspective by clinicians.

THE PSYCHOLOGY OF PERSONAL CONSTRUCTS

G. Kelly elaborated the above assumptions and set out his theory very formally. Button (1985) provides a particularly clear exposition of the theory, and Dalton & Dunnett (1992) clarify this for those who are completely unfamiliar with the approach. The central assumptions of the theory are presented in a statement called the *fundamental postulate*, and 11 subsequent *corollaries* elaborate specific aspects of the theory, describing the nature of construing. These provide the framework for understanding an individual's personality.

The Fundamental Postulate

A person's processes are psychologically channelized by the ways in which he anticipates events.

This abstract statement is fundamental to the whole theory. It states that a person is active in their construing, and that this process operates through a structured network of pathways (i.e. the construct system), which enables them to anticipate future events. It implies that people do not react to the past but rather behave in relation to their anticipation of the future. For example, people who have been sexually abused as children anticipate future adult relationships in different ways, depending on how they construe their past experience. PCP proposes that it is that anticipation which determines their ability to successfully establish and maintain future adult relationships, rather than the effect of the abuse *per se*. People check how much sense they have made of the world by seeing how well their understanding enables them to anticipate it in future. The way a person goes about making sense of the world is therefore a reflection of their individual personality (Bannister & Fransella, 1986).

The Corollaries

The 11 corollaries are statements which describe the nature of construing, and expand the theory in more detail. G. Kelly's (1955/1991) original statements were written in very abstract language to avoid the theory being limited in time and culture (see Appendix I). However, this language has also tended to make PCP less easily accessible, and the corollaries are therefore clarified below;

1. *Construction corollary:* A person anticipates events by noticing patterns in their experiences, and then putting these into a meaningful order or categories. This involves an awareness of similarity and difference between events and experiences, for example whether things are pleasant or unpleasant, whether people are helpful or not. The contrast is termed a construct (i.e. 'Pleasant vs Unpleasant', 'Helpful vs Not helpful').

2. *Individuality corollary:* People differ from each other in their interpretation of events. While this seems common sense, Dalton & Dunnett (1992) note that it is the central feature of the philosophy of constructive alternativism, and the basis upon which the approach is termed *personal* construct psychology.

3. *Organisation corollary:* People make sense of their world by developing a system which links events together and orders them into a hierarchy. In other words, constructs are interrelated in a way unique to each particular individual. This makes up that person's personal construct system, their own particular way of seeing the world. Figure 1.1 illustrates the way constructs link together, with some constructs being more abstract or *superordinate* (i.e. higher up in the structure) and others being more concrete or *subordinate.* This system is continually being amended by the individual to make it fit best with their experience.

4. *Dichotomy corollary:* A person's construct system consists of a finite number of bi-polar constructs. Therefore when a person uses a term (e.g. 'caring'), there is always an implicit opposite (e.g. 'not caring'). This is not necessarily the semantic opposite, but may be unique to that person. For example, an individual with an alcohol problem might possess a construct in which the opposite pole of 'likes a drink' is 'boring'.

5. *Choice corollary:* People choose between the poles of their constructs when deciding how to behave in any situation, e.g. whether to act in a 'Caring' vs 'Not caring' way. They will choose ways of construing which make most sense to them, i.e. which *elaborate* their construct system. This either occurs by 'defining' their construct system (i.e. confirming their previous experience) or 'extending' this (i.e. being more adventurous and exploring new

Figure 1.1. The organisational hierarchy of constructs

areas). What people choose to do is determined by their need to be able to anticipate events so that their world is predictable. Therefore some offenders may continue to choose to offend (defining their existing construct system) as that makes for a more certain and predictable future.

6. *Range corollary:* A construct is only applicable to a finite range of events or situations, and this is termed its *'range of convenience'*. Constructs applicable to offending behaviour (e.g. 'Planned vs Impulsive') will not necessarily be applicable to victims (e.g. 'Child vs Adult'). This is important when designing repertory grids (see Chapter 4).

7. *Experience corollary:* As a person goes through life meeting new situations and experiences, their existing hypotheses and expectations are challenged and the person may amend their construct systems accordingly. An individual's construct system is therefore continually subject to revision. However, change can also be very threatening, and many offenders (and others) therefore ignore the implications of their experience, distorting or ignoring the facts.

8. *Modulation corollary:* Constructs are more or less *permeable*, depending on the extent to which they apply to or make sense of new events. This is important in understanding how a person changes their construct system. A construct is *impermeable* if it only has limited applicability, i.e. only applying to very specific past events. For example, consider a client whose previous therapist (construed as 'trustworthy') had agreed to keep all information confidential. The permeability of the client's construct 'Trustworthy vs Not Trustworthy' would determine how able they were to trust a new therapist in a different setting who could not agree to total confidentiality.

9. *Fragmentation corollary:* In order to maintain continuity between apparently different experiences (e.g. how a person behaves when they are in a meeting at work and with family at home), there are relatively permeable, superordinate constructs in any construct system, which apply to a wide range of events and situations (e.g. 'Professional vs Personal'). This means that a person's construct system is often 'fragmented', i.e. their construing of some areas of their experience may appear inconsistent with their construing of others.

10. *Commonality corollary:* So far the difference between individuals has been emphasised, but people can also share similarities in construing when they interpret experiences in similar ways. People who form groups on the basis of similarity (e.g. sex, religion, special interest) show some similarities in their construing, even

though there may be many other differences between them. This is important in relation to offenders, as although they often show a lack of similar construing to other people in society, they are likely to share similarities with each other.

11. *Sociality corollary:* Finally and crucially, we cannot successfully relate to other people without understanding their way of construing the world. In other words, a person's ability to take part in meaningful social experience and interaction depends on their ability to construe the constructions of others. This is something which is lacking in many offenders, who have little empathy for their victims or other members of society. There is therefore often much emphasis on perspective-taking and victim empathy in treatment programmes. However, if that work is to be set within the context of a meaningful therapeutic relationship, the clinician must also understand (but not necessarily agree with) the construction processes of the offender.

TYPES OF CONSTRUCTS

In order to assist clinicians to construe the constructions of their clients, G. Kelly (1955/1991) provided a number of *professional* or *diagnostic* constructs. These are important ways of thinking about an individual's construing, and subsequent chapters explore their use in the PCP assessment and treatment of offenders.

Core and Peripheral Constructs

G. Kelly (1955/1991) used the terms *core* and *peripheral* constructs to describe the significance of specific constructs for a person's view of themself. Core constructs are those which are essential to a person's sense of identity, for example the notion of being male or female, a parent or not a parent, or belonging to a particular profession, culture or religion. Other core constructs may relate to the type of person an individual sees themself as being, such as caring, ambitious, or trustworthy. Peripheral constructs relate more to preferences or activities (e.g. 'enjoy watching sport') and can be altered without major implications for a person's view of themself.

The way in which a person's core constructs are interrelated forms that individual's *core role structure* and change to one construct therefore implies change in others. Douglas Kelly (1992) outlines four principal components which make up the core role structure. First, the *identity* component defines oneself in relation to the membership of key groups, and roles within these. For example, people may define themselves by their marital status, occupation, age or leisure interests. For some offenders, this may include seeing themselves as members of a particular peer group, which has a delinquent or deviant identity. The second component is *descriptive*, or the sort of person an individual considers themself to be. People usually try to achieve consistency between their view of themselves and their behaviour, and the former will therefore shape the latter. The view which some offenders have of themselves may help to make sense of behaviour which is otherwise difficult to understand, such as seeing themselves as 'tough' or 'able to hold a drink'. A third component of a person's core role structure is *predictive*, and enables them to anticipate how others are going to react to them. For example, a person who sees themself as aggressive or tough is more likely to expect others to react to them with fear or challenge, and may behave accordingly. Finally, the *evaluative* aspect of a person's core role makes a judgement about the acceptability of the kind of person one is. An estimation of self-worth or self-esteem is made by comparing our perceived self with our ideal. Some offenders are well aware that their behaviour is problematic or that it causes them distress, and consequently tend to have lower self-esteem. However, for others their offending may be a way of increasing self-esteem (at least temporarily), or even entirely congruent with their 'ideal self'.

A person's core role structure is therefore crucial in determining their behaviour, as they will want to behave in ways which are consistent with this. This involves actively resisting any challenges to this view of themself, as this would lead to a sense of uncertainty and unpredictability. If many of the constructs in a person's construct system are interrelated, any change to one is likely to be threatening to the system as a whole. Therefore, as discussed earlier, for some offenders the consequences of their behaviour may be perceived as less threatening than the implications of behaving in a different way.

Tight and Loose Constructs

One important way of describing an individual's way of construing the world is in terms of how tight or loose their construct system is. If a person's construing is tight, their constructs are all interrelated and lead to unvarying predictions. For example, they may always construe other people who are 'sociable' as also being those who 'enjoy drinking alcohol'. This therefore implies a close association in that person's view of the world between those two behaviours. A person whose construct system is tightly organised is therefore someone whose view of the world is rather rigid and inflexible, who always makes the same predictions without trying anything new. In contrast, in loose construing, individual constructs bear little relationship to one another and there is no consistency or predictability in the way the person applies them. Such an individual appears to make inconsistent decisions and it is difficult for others to predict their behaviour.

Most people have a balanced construct system, in which there is a structured hierarchy of constructs. A construct system which is either too tight or too loose can cause problems. There is a large body of work which suggests that schizophrenic thought disorder is related to a construct system which is too loose (Bannister, 1960, see Chapter 10). Loose construing has also been found in emotionally disturbed boys (Reker, 1974) and some (but not all) alcoholics (Chambers & Sanders, 1984). On the other hand, people whose construct system is very tightly integrated may only have a limited repertoire of ways to anticipate events and subsequently behave. Such individuals may therefore have difficulties relating to other people, as they are unable to make fine discriminations between social behaviours, may be poor at predicting how other people are likely to behave, and will have difficulty adjusting to novel situations. Although studies have failed to find a consistent association between tight construing and violent offending (Noble, 1971; Howells, 1983), tight construing has been demonstrated in those police officers whose response to stress involved breaking the law or being violent, compared to those who reacted in other ways (Winter, 1993).

Preverbal and Submerged Constructs

No one is aware of all of their constructs all the time, and constructs exist at different levels of cognitive awareness. A person is aware of their own *verbal* constructs, for example, the importance to them of whether or not people are 'honest'. In contrast, a *preverbal construct* is one which continues to be used even though it has no consistent word label. Constructs do not need to be verbal; babies and infants can make discriminations between experiences and people who cannot speak still form such concepts. Preverbal constructs are likely to have been formed in childhood and to be expressed in actions rather than words. Fransella (1995) suggests that preverbal personal constructs are often to do with dependency, and the therapist should not expect a person who is using preverbal constructs to behave like an adult. The *submerged pole* of a construct is another form of construing at a low level of cognitive awareness, and is the pole which is less available for application to events. For example, a person who maintains that they never get angry, or that they do not dislike anyone, is submerging the negative poles of constructs. Many sex offenders initially maintain that they are easily controlled by their victims, submerging the poles of constructs which relate to dominance and control. G. Kelly (1955/1991) suggested that this type of construing might serve the purpose of enabling the person to avoid construing themself at the 'submerged end'. One of the aims of therapy might be to make such constructs more accessible and verbal, and to facilitate the person's ability to use both construct poles in an adaptive way. Button (1985) suggests that this process could be seen as the client achieving insight.

PROCESSES OF CONSTRUING

As discussed previously, PCP proposes that individuals continually make hypotheses about the world based on their existing construct system. These hypotheses are then either supported (*validated*) or not (*invalidated*). In the latter case, the individual needs to revise their existing constructs to take into account the new experience. Normally, this process of construing occurs in a cyclical manner, by one of the following processes.

Dealing with Incompatabilities; Dilation and Constriction

Dilation and constriction are the terms used by G. Kelly to describe the processes that occur when a person broadens or narrows their perceptual field, after being faced with apparently incompatible thoughts or events. For example, a man who goes on to sexually abuse young boys after himself being the victim of similar abuse has to justify this to himself. He may initially do this by *constriction*, i.e. a process of tightening constructs and narrowing one's focus. This may involve tightening the construct of 'Harmful vs Not harmful' to apply only to physical harm, thereby convincing himself that both his own victimisation and subsequent offending did not cause harm. In contrast, *dilation* is an expanding process, in which the person sees new links between events or aspects of their life, broadening their view of the world. In the case above, a dilating process would involve broadening the construct about harm to include the notion of emotional as well as physical harm. Dilation often therefore leads to reorganisation of the construct system. Both of these processes may be useful in treatment at different times, depending on the way the person is construing (see Chapter 3).

Making Choices: The CPC Cycle

The CPC cycle is Kelly's description of the process by which choices are made about how to act. For example, consider the choices available to a client with a drink problem who wants to relieve stress. First, the range of possible ways of viewing the situation is considered (*circumspection*). This may involve talking to friends, going for a walk, exercising, relaxation or other anxiety management techniques, or drinking alcohol. Second, one particular alternative is decided upon (*pre-emption*), e.g. drinking alcohol to relieve stress vs not drinking alcohol to relieve stress. Finally, the choice is made of which way to act from those alternatives (*control*). If the person decides not to drink alcohol at that point, they then go back to the circumspection phase to consider an alternative.

G. Kelly (1955/1991) described impulsivity as the result of a foreshortened or non-existent circumspection phase. This is supported in part by the work of Thomas-Peter (1992) with psychopaths. However, being stuck in the circumspection phase can also cause difficulties for an individual, who endlessly considers all possibilities without being able to pre-empt a situation and decide on one alternative.

Developing New Constructs; The Creativity Cycle

This describes the process of developing new ways of construing, and is a continual process of loosening and tightening constructs. In other words, when faced with a new situation or when looking at an event from a different perspective, it is initially important to be open and flexible about different possibilities (i.e. to construe loosely). However, in order to test out the different hypotheses, the individual needs to be more focused and consistent in their predictions (i.e. construe tightly). Different options can then be tried and tested, one of which is hopefully validated, at which point construing can be tightened again.

Revising Hypotheses; The Experience Cycle

As described earlier, one of the key concepts in PCP is that people are 'active scientists', continually making and testing out hypotheses about the world, and revising their view accordingly. The Experience Cycle (G. Kelly, 1970), describes the process by which this occurs, and a person functioning in a healthy way will complete this without difficulty. The first stage (Anticipation) involves formulating a prediction about a particular event. The person then fully involves themselves in that anticipation (Investment phase) before actively experiencing the event (Encounter phase). They then assess how the encounter has gone, bearing in mind their initial prediction (Confirmation and Disconfirmation phase) and make any necessary revisions to their way of construing (Constructive revision phase). For example, a man with a previous conviction has to decide what to tell potential employers about this. He may initially predict that if he minimises the seriousness of his offence, then it will not count against him in an interview (anticipation). He therefore prepares what he is going to say in the interview (investment) and duly attends (encounter). If he gets the job he is likely to decide that he took the right strategy (confirmation), and does not need to revise his construing for future occasions. However, if he does not get offered the job, he needs to reassess his initial prediction, and change his way of construing. Successfully completing the Experience cycle would therefore require the man to make a different prediction at his next interview (e.g. that he would be more successful in interview if he was either more honest about his offence, or if he concealed his offending from potential employers).

The Process of Change; Constructs of Transition

Although constructs ideally need to be revised if they are not supported, in reality this does not always occur. This is understood in PCP terms by considering what happens to construct systems when they undergo change, and recognising that the notion of change may be very threatening for an individual. To most clinicians, the notions of threat, aggression, guilt or hostility are understood as emotions or behaviours. However, G. Kelly (1955/1991) used very different definitions of these and other terms to describe the process of change in an individual's construct system. These are particularly pertinent to working with offenders, in relation to the understanding of guilt, resistance to change, and the experience of being a therapist. These notions are revisited in Chapter 3 when discussing the application of the PCP perspective to working therapeutically with this client group.

Kelly defined *guilt* as 'the awareness of dislodgement of the self from one's core role structure'. As discussed earlier, the core role structure refers to the system of constructs that deals specifically with the self, and relevant constructs are those by which people evaluate aspects of their own behaviour. Therefore for offenders to feel guilt about their behaviour requires this to be incompatible with the kind of person that they always thought they were. If a person has a self-image which involves seeing themselves as 'an armed robber' or 'aggressive', then they will not feel guilty about behaviour which is compatible with that. Other offenders feel no guilt because they construe their behaviour in such a way as to make it consistent with a positive view of themself, such as a child sex offender who convinces themself that they are 'educating' the child.

Resistance to change can be understood in terms of Kelly's definition of *threat,* i.e. 'the awareness of an imminent comprehensive change in one's core structure'. In other words, people are threatened when their major beliefs about the nature of their personal, social and practical situation are invalidated and the world around them appears to become chaotic. Although the clearest example of this is with someone who has experienced a traumatic event, Kelly emphasised that change for the better can also be threatening. People going through therapy are therefore also likely to experience threat, as they begin to change the way in which they construe themselves. For offenders, the realisation that their beliefs about themselves and the world may not be valid, is extremely threatening. They have the choice of avoiding the threat by finding ways of discounting the new evidence, or amending their core constructs.

A related concept is *fear*, or 'the awareness of an imminent incidental change in one's core structure'. Although this change may still be unpleasant, it is not as drastic as threat, as the degree of potential change is not so great. Some offenders, as with other clients, may therefore experience fear at the start of treatment, which then turns into threat as they realise the extent of the necessary change. Similarly, it is also relevant to consider Kelly's definition of *anxiety*. He defines this as 'an awareness that the events with which one is confronted lie mostly outside the range of convenience of one's construct system'. In other words, people become anxious when they are confronted with things that are unknown and therefore not subsumed by their construct system. Again, for an offender, contemplating change requires them to think about themselves and the world in a new way, and is likely to provoke anxiety in both the traditional and Kellian sense.

Kelly also uses the term 'aggression' in a completely different way to our usual understanding, defining this in terms of what is going on solely inside the individual, without automatically assuming negative intent or consequences. *Aggressiveness* is 'the active elaboration of one's perceptual field', in other words, an active and positive attempt to be adventurous in one's construing, such as a work colleague who is always wanting to challenge existing procedures. It is therefore not always negative, and can potentially be very creative. However, from the point of view of other people around them, this can sometimes be a very uncomfortable process, which may be perceived as a personal attack.

Finally, Kelly's notion of *hostility* is particularly relevant in understanding the behaviour of many offenders. He defined hostility as 'the continued effort to extort validation or evidence in favour of the type of social prediction which has already been recognised as a failure'. In other words, people are likely to become hostile when they are in a situation in which they have been shown to be wrong, yet they cannot cope with the idea of abandoning their beliefs. This is because they can see no alternative way of viewing the situation and are potentially faced with a sense of chaos. In this position people are likely to become hostile in terms of trying to bully others into behaving in ways which confirm their predictions. For example, the childhood experiences of some offenders have led them to believe that everyone will reject them. When faced with a clinician who does not do this, they will go out of their way to try to provoke this, which can be very uncomfortable. Problems occur when the hostility continues and the attempts to extort the evidence become increasingly drastic. Hostility can be further understood in terms of a person 'distorting the data to fit their hypothesis' (G. Kelly, 1969a), a pattern which, as seen in Part II, is observed in the construing of many offenders.

The Relationship between PCP and Cognitive Approaches

Over the years, of all the attempts to align PCP with another orientation, that of the cognitive approach has most frequently been suggested (Neimeyer, 1985, 1986; Goldfried, 1988) and most cognitive theorists acknowledge the influence of George Kelly (Beck et al., 1979; Ellis, 1979). It is fair to say that in terms of assumptions about human nature, PCP has more similarities with social cognitive approaches than with any other theoretical orientation. Dalton & Dunnett (1992) place PCP (together with Bandura's (1977) social learning theory) in the middle of a bipolar construct of 'Freedom vs Determinism'. This reflects Kelly's (1955/1991) view of the construct system as providing a person with both freedom of decision (because it allows the person to deal with the meaning of events) *and* limitation of action (because they can only make choices from the existing alternatives in their construct system).

Both PCP and cognitive approaches are concerned with the processes by which people appraise themselves, other people and the world around them (see also Figure 1.2). The more recent cognitive approaches which use the term 'schema' to describe a hypothesised *structure* of cognition (e.g. Beck & Freeman, 1990, Layden et al., 1993) are particularly less dissimilar than the earlier approaches which focused only on the *content* of an individual's core beliefs (e.g. Ellis, 1979). However, there are also essential differences between the two approaches (see Figure 1.3), and personal construct theorists still differ about the appropriateness of their alignment. Neimeyer (1985, 1986) suggests that those who favour some degree of integration with cognitive approaches may be taking the pragmatic view that this is the only way for PCP to have a wider influence on psychology. His work has illustrated that, as long as the essential differences between the two

Both PCP and cognitive approaches:

- Are concerned with the way in which the individual appraises or makes sense of the world and explores the construction of meaning and action
- Accept that constructions can be highly idiosyncratic and not known to the client
- Emphasise the importance of individualised assessment and treatment strategies
- Use a collaborative style in therapy, and focus on client-defined goals and targets (Aveline & Shapiro, 1995)
- Aim not only to change what clients say to themselves, but also to alter the underlying structures which maintain construing or cognition (Goldfried, 1988)
- Use many similar techniques to help reassess those constructions, and suggest tools for 'thinking about construing' (see Chapter 3)

Figure 1.2. Similarities between PCP and cognitive approaches

approaches are born in mind and PCP retains its own identity, there can be benefits from cross-fertilisation and dialogue between cognitive-behavioural and personal construct therapists.

PCP	Cognitive approaches
Problematic constructions of clients seen as alternative constructions of reality	Problematic cognitions of clients seen as distorted or irrational
Concerned with the *viability* of the client's view of the world	Concerned with the *validity* of the client's view of the world
Has a holistic view of the individual	Distinguish between thought, feeling and emotion
Provides techniques for assessing construing	Provide techniques for assessing thinking
Provides a formal theory of personal constructs to describe the structure and process of construing	Do not have a consistent theoretical framework to describe the ways in which cognitions link together

Figure 1.3. Differences between PCP and cognitive approaches

THE PCP PERSPECTIVE ON OFFENDING

Despite the fact that one of the earliest and classic case studies using PCP was of the construing of an arsonist (Fransella & Adams, 1966) the subsequent application of the approach to understanding and working with offenders has been suprisingly limited. Most published work has investigated the nature of construing in different types of offenders and explored how this can contribute to an understanding of their behaviour (e.g. Needs, 1988). Some authors have also used PCP to understand the aetiology of deviance (Scimecca, 1985; Brennan, 1992; D. Kelly, 1992). However, first the PCP perspective on the definition of offending will be considered.

The Definition of Offending Behaviour

George Kelly (1955/1991) did not specifically comment on offenders or offending, but if he had, he would probably have emphasised the importance of understanding the meaning of the behaviour for that individual. There are a number of ways of defining offending and anti-social behaviour. The Concise Oxford Dictionary defines an offence as 'an illegal act; a transgression or misdemeanour' (1990). The legal definition is simply that which is against the law. Antisocial behaviour, which encompasses a wider range of problematic behaviours than that represented by formal convictions, is that which goes against the social and cultural norms of society, and which has a harmful impact, either directly or indirectly, on other people. However, these are all definitions that have been made by other people—the police, Courts, or other members of society, and the individuals subject to those definitions may not necessarily agree. If this is not at least acknowledged, it can hinder the clinician trying to work with an offender in treatment or rehabilitation. The first question therefore asked by the clinician taking a PCP perspective would be '*What is the meaning of that deviant, antisocial or offending behaviour for that person?*' As emphasised earlier, this does not require the clinician to agree with or condone the behaviour of the client, only to understand their way of construing.

The Aetiology of Deviancy

The PCP perspective on the aetiology of deviancy uses the same general framework to understand why some people offend, as it does to account for why others do not. As discussed previously, G. Kelly (1955/1991) saw people as endeavouring to bring a chaotic world under some control through imposing a predictive and meaningful structure on to it, via the individual's construct system. Later authors have applied this idea to the understanding of deviant or offending behaviour, although they have focused primarily on delinquency.

Scimecca (1985) came from a background of radical criminology, in which structural and cultural determinants (such as poverty and class) are seen as 'causing crime', because people are shaped by the conditions under which they live. He suggested that powerless individuals would necessarily see less opportunity for resisting criminal behaviour, and would be more likely to construe alternatives which take this notion of reality into account. Brennan (1992) placed greater emphasis on the notion of deviant identity. He suggested that in understanding deviancy it is important to understand the way in which the notion of being 'deviant' is an integral part of that person's own self-image. His hypothesis was that deviancy may represent for some people 'a quest for manageable relationships in a world of chaos' (p. 39), i.e. it is their way of seeking predictability. Deviant behaviour therefore represents a kind of thwarted or uncreative aggression, in which the person repeats the same patterns of construing despite continual invalidation, showing a lack of sociality with others. Consistent with the view of Scimecca (1985), Brennan suggested that the choice of deviant behaviour is made by individuals when this makes most sense to them, and confirms their previous experience (i.e. elaborates and defines their construct systems). This is more likely to be the case when their identity is one of being deviant. Brennan's (1992) framework is consistent with the 'self-presentation' approach to delinquency, which also sees delinquency as a non-pathological and rational social identity, purposefully chosen by young people as it makes sense to them in terms of their circumstances (Reicher & Emler, 1986). However, Blackburn (1993) noted that this approach does not adequately account for the heterogeneity of delinquents, nor indicate why only some delinquents go on to offend in adulthood.

Douglas Kelly (1992) also examined the importance of the person's view of themselves in his PCP perspective on deviance, again focusing particularly on delinquency. However, he notes that any theory which purports to explain why some people offend should also explain why others do not, and puts the emphasis on understanding human conformity rather than deviance. For example, why would a person who needed money hand in cash that they had found, even if they were not likely to be caught? He suggests that although criminal behaviour is socially deviant, it is psychologically normal, and can be understood by using the same psychological principles which explain any other behaviour.

D. Kelly (1992) uses the notion of core role structure to examine the question of why most people *don't* offend. He suggested that there are three main reasons. First, offending is not something which is compatible with most people's core role structure. Offending would cause a fundamental challenge to most people's self-image, and raise many questions in relation to the kind of person they thought they were.

Offending would also present a major challenge to the predictability of most people's world. The need to avoid this, together with the accompanying guilt, leads most people to conform to the norm. Secondly, for most people, being a member of the group called 'society' is something which is valued, and again part of their core role structure. When other members of a group to which we belong become aware that we have violated norms, D. Kelly suggests that we experience a sense of shame. It is not the membership of the group *per se* that is important in determining the degree of shame, but rather the importance we attach to being a member of that particular group. Thirdly, there is a set of formal rules and laws which impinge on us, and for which there are formal sanctions if broken. A person may lose their job, friends and family, as well as their freedom, all leading to a loss of role and identity. A need to avoid such powerful sanctions again imposes a powerful influence on most people not to offend.

D. Kelly therefore argues that most people resist the temptation to offend because of the powerful effects of the personal, social and judicial consequences on 'an otherwise viable core role structure'. The key to his argument lies in the word 'viable', as he suggests that for many offenders, their delinquent behaviour begins at a time when their core role structure is shaky. For example, adolescents who are experiencing conflicts at home and school may find that delinquency provides them with positive benefits (the focus of attention, status with peers, positive self-esteem and membership of a delinquent group). D. Kelly does not suggest that this holds true in every case, but seeks to illustrate how offending may provide a means of resolving rather than creating a core role crisis.

The above models are consistent with studies that have emphasised the contribution of personal morality and fear of loss of status or social respect to the understanding of why people do not offend (e.g. Tyrer, 1990). The PCP models of deviancy are also consistent with other models which relate delinquency to the enhancement of self-esteem (e.g. Kaplan, 1980). Although there is no empirical evidence to suggest that there is a consistent *causal* link between self-concept and delinquency, the lack of an adequate theory of self-concept has meant that such studies have differed in terms of what they are measuring and the way this is done (Blackburn, 1993). Whilst conclusive evidence is therefore lacking, it is likely that self-concept may be an important contributor to the development and maintenance of a particular *individual's* offending.

Having said the above, not all offenders consider themselves to have a deviant self-identity. Some individuals who offend may have a strong core role structure with a positive self-image, but convince themselves that they will not get caught. For example, an individual who commits professional fraud and 'white collar' crime may construe themselves as someone who is able to outwit others, and may decide that the material gains obtained from breaking the law outweigh the risks and consequences of getting caught. For such individuals, although they may not have a deviant self-identity, the content of their construing may be socially deviant (i.e. lack commonality and/or sociality with the rest of society).

Socially Deviant Construing

G. Kelly (1955/1991) defined a 'disorder' as 'any personal construction which is used repeatedly in spite of consistent invalidation' (Vol. 2, p. 193). As will be illustrated throughout the book, this holds true for many offenders. They acknowledge that their behaviour leads to problems for themselves and others, yet do not seem to change. A healthy functioning adult is able to cope with the invalidation of their hypotheses by revising their constructs and testing out new ones (i.e. successfully completing the Experience Cycle). In contrast, some offenders *ignore* evidence that their hypotheses are being invalidated, as change involves too much threat. As outlined above, they may continue to offend despite the negative consequences, as offending is part of their deviant self-identity and leads to a more predictable world than the anticipation of non-offending.

However, offenders who do not have a deviant self-identity have to construe themselves and their behaviour in a way which enables them to *avoid* being invalidated. The construing of these offenders is often socially deviant in two important aspects. First, it may differ markedly from the way in which most other people in society view the world (i.e. show a lack of commonality), for example paedophiles who construe children as capable of consenting to sexual contact with adults (Chin-Keung, 1992). Secondly, some offenders may be unable to construe the construction processes of other people (i.e. show a lack of sociality), which is essential for successful social relating. This deficit has been demonstrated in a number of different clinical populations, including psychopaths (Widom, 1976).

The development of healthy and/or deviant construing begins in childhood. Dalton & Dunnett (1992) describe how, from an early age, babies and infants begin to make discriminations between their experiences, such as what is 'pleasant' compared to what is 'unpleasant'. They carry out their own experiments to see what is predictable about their world, and soon learn to elicit responses from others. A child's later sense of self-worth is determined by their sense of being validated by their carers, ranging from interest and encouragement, to feeling wanted, loved and included. Social interaction with a wide range of people is also important in order to experience different possibilities and choices in the world, and to note comparison and contrast. The discrimination between 'self' and 'others' is an important one, and further contributes to a child's self-image. Clearly, therefore, children's experiences as they are growing up are crucial in determining the ways in which they construe the world as adults.

In contrast to the above, the childhood experiences of many offenders leave them with ways of construing themselves and others which set the scene for problems in adulthood. The PCP understanding of the effects of physical and sexual abuse on later relationships and the construing of adult survivors has been considered by a number of authors (Cummins, 1992; Clarke & Llewelyn, 1994; Harter & Neimeyer, 1995). Some adult survivors of abuse may have great difficulty in construing alternative, non-abusive ways of relating to those outside the family. A woman may ignore evidence of affection from others and choose a relationship with an abusive partner, and a man may behave towards his female partner in the same way as his father did towards his mother (Dalton & Dunnett, 1992). Some individuals may protect themselves from the repetition of pain in relationships by avoiding intimacy altogether, and many believe that the damage to their 'self' is irreparable. For some such individuals, deviant or offending behaviour may provide for a more predictable world, consistent with their previous experiences.

Winter (1992) details further the ways in which the development of socially deviant construing can occur. For example, a child who has been repeatedly abused or rejected by adults is likely to experience invalidation of their hypothesis that adults can be trusted. A person may therefore alter their construing either to attempt to adapt to a traumatic event or because their previous way of construing has been constantly invalidated. In addition, individuals whose *deviant* patterns of construing are constantly *validated* will also maintain this way of viewing the world. For example, children who grow up in a family where violence is the norm, will base future hypotheses on the assumption that violence is a legitimate means of relating to others. There are therefore a number of different pathways by which an offender may come to construe themselves and their behaviour in a different way to most of society, and/or to have difficulty in construing the world from the perspective of others.

CLINICAL APPLICATIONS OF PCP WITH OFFENDERS

There are a number of factors which combine to make clinical work with people who have committed offences particularly challenging, and different from work with other clients who have mental health problems. Some aspects of the PCP approach may therefore have to be modified in order to reflect those differences. For example, PCP was originally used therapeutically with clients whose problems were primarily of the neurotic type, with whom the therapist was able to be relatively 'client focused' in assessment and treatment. In contrast, when working with people who have committed offences, the consequences of a recurrence of their 'problem' may be directly harmful to other people, and therefore the therapist needs to be more directive in both assessment and treatment (see Chapters 2 and 3). It will still be important, where relevant, to assess the dangerousness of a particular client in the standard nomothetic way, or to maintain the approach to assessment which the courts expect. The PCP approach can be used as an *additional* framework with which to gain a greater understanding of the way in which a particular *individual* client makes sense of the world.

Other factors which contribute to the challenging nature of the work with offenders are, however, those which make the PCP approach an ideal framework with which to approach the treatment and rehabilitation of such clients, and are discussed further in Chapter 3. First, in many settings offender clients have not referred themselves for help, and may not consider that they have a problem, only accepting that their behaviour is illegal. Some dispute the law, justifying their behaviour in different ways. Such clients do not necessarily think they need to change, and may be ambivalent and/or resistant to doing so. The clinician working with offenders sometimes faces antagonism and hostility, and has to be prepared for high levels of recidivism. Although some clinicians are in a position to refuse to take on such ambivalent clients for treatment, others, such as probation officers, may not have the luxury of refusing a supervision order. The PCP approach is one which enables the clinician to understand the client's offending from their perspective, and therefore to set appropriate and realistic goals. Personal construct psychology offers the following:

- *A framework for understanding how offenders see the world.* To work effectively with offenders it is important to be able to see things from their point of view. This is not the same as excusing or condoning their behaviour, but does reflect an empathic approach rather than a punitive one.
- *An understanding of why many offenders show an apparent failure to learn from past experiences.* It can be a great source of frustration to clinicians working with offenders that patterns of offending are repeated, despite the consequences. An understanding of the

offender's construct system may provide clues as to why previous prison sentences or probation orders have failed to have deterrent effects.

- *An understanding of resistance to change.* By understanding the implications of change for one's core role, the PCP approach enables the clinician to make sense of resistance, rather than viewing this as a wilful antagonism towards treatment.

- *A collaborative way of working with a client, in which they take some responsibility for the process of change.* This is not an approach in which the clinician is seen as the expert who has all the answers, or as the one who is responsible for the success or failure of change.

- *The provision of an opportunity for the person to change,* and a hopeful approach in that no one has to be the victim of their own history.

- *Techniques for understanding how people construe the world, and for measuring change.* These are explored further in Chapter 4.

PCP therefore offers a framework within which to consider the personal meaning of offending for individuals. Offenders are judged by other people as deviating from cultural, social and legal norms. However, from their own perspective, their behaviour usually makes sense, and is compatible with their view of the world. The challenge for the clinician is to enable the individual to recognise the link between their view of the world and their offending behaviour, to point out options for reconstruing, and to help the person achieve that process.

SUMMARY AND CONCLUSIONS

Recent developments in the treatment and rehabilitation of offenders have recognised the importance of including a component which addresses the way in which these clients appraise themselves, their behaviour and the world. Although there are currently different views among personal construct theorists about the appropriateness of aligning PCP with cognitive approaches, this book takes the approach that it is possible to use PCP as an *additional* and *complementary* theoretical framework with which to work with offenders. The very nature of this client group means that standard nomothetic assessment and treatment approaches are also important, but the PCP perspective provides a greater understanding of the personal meaning of offending to any particular individual.

Recent theories of crime have also recognised the limitations of relying on one theoretical approach, and have integrated elements from different perspectives (e.g. Farrington, 1992). Although different authors have proposed PCP models of deviance (Brennan, 1992; D. Kelly, 1992), PCP was never intended to explain why sub-groups of individuals behave in similar ways, but rather to help understand why individuals behave in the variety of ways that they do (which is why it is called *personal* construct psychology). The PCP models are therefore useful in focusing on the commonality and possible aetiology of construing among delinquents, but have not yet proved to be predictive nor are intended to be explanatory for the whole range of offending behaviours.

However, if one returns to the focus on the individual, the PCP perspective proposes that some people choose to offend for the same reasons as others choose not to. Each individual will behave in a way that is most consistent with their way of construing themselves, others and events, in order to achieve a more predictable and manageable world. Working with the PCP perspective enables the clinician to achieve a greater understanding of the offender's view of the world and how this relates to their offending, and therefore to set realistic goals for change.

CHAPTER 2

PCP Assessment of Offenders

Using the personal construct psychology approach to work with offenders does not necessarily mean abandoning other theoretical frameworks or approaches to assessment. This chapter describes how the PCP approach can complement existing nomothetic methods of assessing offenders, by emphasising what is unique about an individual client. Using PCP still involves all the usual gathering of information and interviewing that is essential in a comprehensive assessment, but also provides an additional framework and methods with which to understand the client's view of the world and the meaning of their offending. This chapter describes the PCP approach to the clinical interview, and introduces the techniques of the self-characterisation and repertory grid.

INTRODUCTION

The assessment of offenders and their behaviour is one of the primary functions of most clinicians working with this client group. Although different professionals have their own specific areas of focus and expertise, any assessment usually relates to one or more of the following aims:

- Reaching a formulation, or an understanding of the function of the offending behaviour, its development and maintenance, and how it relates to the client's other difficulties
- Assessment of suitability for treatment or the client's ability to change
- Assessment of risk or dangerousness, which is what differentiates work with offenders from that with other client groups.

The PCP approach to assessment and treatment is very much an *idiographic* one, in which the focus is on the client as an individual. However, as discussed in the opening chapter, when working with offenders and particularly when assessing risk, it is important to set this idiographic assessment within the context of the standard, or *nomothetic*, assessment of that client group as a whole. It is important to know how an individual client who has a history of violent or sexual offending compares to others with similar histories, in order to reach a conclusion about where they lie along the spectrum of risk of reoffending. The contribution of the PCP approach to assessment is a further understanding of what is unique about *this particular client*.

THE PCP APPROACH TO ASSESSMENT

In discussing formulation, G. Kelly (1955/1991) was concerned to avoid the labelling and 'disease model' of psychological disturbance. He saw the aim of assessment as being to formulate the client's problems in terms of their construing of the world, rather than in terms of the traditional constructions used by psychiatry. He therefore described the formulation of a client's difficulties by using the term *transitive diagnosis*, which 'suggests we are concerned with transitions in the client's life, that we are looking for bridges between the client's present and his future' (Kelly, 1955/1991, Vol. 2, p. 153). This term emphasises that there are always options open to the client and that their problem is not static. As discussed in the opening chapter, this view therefore offers a hopeful and positive approach for clinicians working with offenders, even the most recidivistic. Kelly outlined six key questions to address in assessment.

1. *Exactly what is unique about this client, when do they show it, and where does it get them?* This involves obtaining a description of the client's 'deviant behaviour patterns' (Kelly, 1955/1991, p. 155), and the gains and losses accompanying these (i.e. the client's validational experience).
2. *What does the client think about all this, and what do they think they are trying to do?* What is the client's construction of their problems, how do they think other people construe these and how do they construe their 'life role' (i.e. where they see themselves going in life?).
3. *What is the psychological view of the client's personal constructs*, i.e. how can they be understood? What different types of constructs does the client use?
4. *In addition to the client himself, what is there to work with in this case?* In other words, what is the context in which the client is seeking to adjust?
5. *Where does the client go next?* What other procedures are important, e.g. other professional constructions of the client's presenting

difficulties? Are any immediate interventions necessary to protect the client and/or others?

6. *How is the client going to get well?* In other words, planning the details of management and treatment.

Ravenette (1992) provides a recent account of the PCP approach to assessment in which he suggests that the assessment interview can be shaped by considering the four basic issues which underline personal construct psychology. To reiterate:

1. How a person behaves depends on how they make sense of themselves and their circumstances.
2. How a person sees themself is crucial to this, i.e. what is 'me' and 'not me'.
3. You cannot assume that the same words and language have the same meaning for everyone, so it is important to explore with each person what their particular use implies.
4. The concept of 'constructive alternativism' means that there is always another way of seeing things, so one of the aims of an assessment is to see if the person can envisage the possibility of change.

If the frameworks from both of the above authors are applied to the assessment of offenders, the following specific questions are raised:

- What is the client's understanding of their offending behaviour, and how does this make sense to them? In other words, how do they construe the world in general and their offending in particular, and what is the relationship between the two?
- How do they construe themselves and significant others, including their victims (where relevant)? Is offending or deviant behaviour compatible with their core role, i.e. their sense of 'what is me'?
- How does their offending and sense of self link to their childhood experiences and other difficulties in their life—past or present? In what way have those experiences shaped their construing of the world and their role in it?
- Does the client see the need to change or believe that change is possible? In other words, is there a discrepancy between the construing of their 'current self', 'offending self' and 'ideal self'? Do they see their 'ideal self' as a role which it is possible to achieve?
- What are the potential obstacles to change, i.e. ways of construing that enable the client to avoid being invalidated when they offend?

A number of aspects of the process of assessment emphasised by G. Kelly (1955/1991) will already be very familiar to clinicians working with offenders. He stressed the importance of obtaining information from a range of sources, including the behaviour itself, information from the client and significant others and observation during the interview. In common with other theoretical approaches, he emphasised the importance of the clinician obtaining a clear description of the problematic behaviour before attempting any formulation or intervention. If applicable, this could involve behavioural observation and verbatim record-keeping, paying particular attention to the pattern of deviant behaviour and the way in which it links to other significant life events.

Although G. Kelly (1955/1991) did not see developmental factors and prior experiences as being responsible for influencing subsequent behaviour, such experiences do indicate the evidence that has shaped the person's construct system. A client's past history is of value if the client themselves thinks that it is, or if evidence emerges to suggest that preverbal construing is relevant, or that the client has long-standing difficulties in making relationships (Dalton & Dunnett, 1992; Fransella, 1995). Although traditionally, personal construct therapists have not taken a comprehensive personal history from a client, this can therefore be an important part of the assessment. This is particularly the case when the clinician hypothesises that childhood and family experiences have contributed to the development of socially deviant construing, as is the case with many offenders. In addition, a person's offending is only one manifestation of their personal construct system, and therefore this needs to be understood as a whole, as well as the part that relates to their deviant behaviour.

WHAT TO ASSESS: THE STRUCTURE AND CONTENT OF CONSTRUING

As discussed earlier, George Kelly (1955/1991) did not describe psychological disorders in terms of conventional diagnostic categories, but rather in terms of the way in which a person is construing. Chapter 1 outlined the different professional constructs which he provided to enable the clinician to construe the construction processes of clients. The clinical interview and other techniques outlined below, enable the clinician to assess the contribution of both the *structure* and *content* of the client's construct system to the understanding of their offending behaviour.

Structural Disorders in Construing

The structure of construing refers to the way in which a person's constructs are linked together to form their construct system. For example, one important structural characteristic of a construct system is whether the system is tight (i.e. rigid and inflexible) or loose (i.e. few associations between constructs). Winter (1992) reviews the evidence for structural disorders of construing in different client groups, including those with deviant and offending behaviour, and the chapters in Part II describe both empirical research and case studies which illustrate the relevance of structural characteristics in the construing of offenders.

A second, related structural characteristic which can provide valuable information about an individual's construing, is the degree of cognitive complexity in their construct system. Cognitive complexity is the degree to which a person's construct system is complex or differentiated, defined by Bieri et al. (1966) as 'the capacity to construe social behaviour in a multi-dimensional way'. The tightness of an individual's construct system and its cognitive complexity are closely related, and both can be measured using data from analysis of a repertory grid (see Chapter 4). However, the clinical interview may also suggest that a person has a cognitively simple or undifferentiated construct system, if they are viewing the world in a very black and white, 'all or nothing' way. For example, an offender client may see other people as either being all good or all bad, or have a very simplistic notion of what is 'past behaviour' and what is 'future behaviour'. When all a person's constructs are tightly organised, if one proves to be invalid, this is likely to have implications for the whole construct system, including core constructs. This would be very threatening, and such a person is therefore likely to be very resistant to change, going to great lengths to try to prove their original hypothesis (i.e. display hostility in the Kellian sense).

The Content of Construing

The whole premise of PCP is that each person's way of construing is unique, and personal construct theorists would therefore reject the notion of an imposed 'norm'. However, G. Kelly (1955/1991) accepted that difficulties could arise out of the intrinsic *meaning* of a person's constructs. This aspect of PCP highlights the essential difference between this and cognitive approaches. The latter sees difficulties arising when people make *errors* in thinking, or 'cognitive distortions'. The principle of constructive alternativism means that, in PCP terms, people are not making errors in the way they construe events, but rather are making alternative constructions of reality. None the less, if individuals fail to revise those constructions in the face of invalidating evidence, Kelly (1955/1991) considered such construing to be disordered.

The approach of this book is consistent with that taken by Winter (1992), in that the actual content of a client's construing is not described as disordered. However, he notes that the content of the construct system is very pertinent to an understanding of a client's predicament and their likely response to therapy. Four main aspects of the content of construing can be assessed from the information obtained from either a clinical interview, self-characterisation or repertory grid.

The Predominant Content of the Construct System

A number of studies have shown that there is a relationship between the types of constructs used and the nature of the problems presented by clients. For example, Howells (1983) found that 'one-off' violent offenders used fewer constructs concerning obedience to the law than multiple aggressive offenders, possibly indicating that their offences were not committed in the context of a criminal career. There are two possible explanations for the relationship between construing and behaviour, both of which may be relevant in an individual. First, Sperlinger (1976) suggests that individuals elaborate their construct system (i.e. construe in the way which makes most sense) in relation to the problem they are experiencing, as this is the area which is presenting them with particular difficulties. This elaboration is then reflected in the fact that such individuals have a large number of constructs relating to the problem area, compared with others from the same culture. In addition, it may be the very features of an individual's construing which determine the individual's symptoms or problems and their persistence (Winter, 1992). This is consistent with Fransella's (1972) view of an individual's symptom representing a 'way of life', based on her work with people who stutter.

Winter (1992) notes that the correlational nature of most of the research in this area makes it difficult to compare and evaluate the above explanations (or, in PCP terms, 'the various constructions of the data' (p. 112). However, in terms of clinical assessment of individuals, it is clearly useful to note the predominant content of the construct system, as this may well relate to their offending behaviour. Among the case examples discussed in Part II, the relationship between the types of constructs used and the nature of the offending behaviour is particularly noticeable in the cases of men who have sexually offended against children outside the family (see Chapter 9). Landfield (1971) devised a classificatory system for constructs which enables the clinician to see if certain types of constructs are over- or under-represented. Although it may be too unwieldy to categorise all constructs elicited during assessment, this system can provide the clinician with a useful framework within which to operate.

Construing of the Self

One of the most important aspects of a person's construct system is how they construe their 'self'. The significance of a person's core role structure has already been discussed, and it is clearly important to assess how a client's core constructs may contribute to their offending. Another important aspect of a person's construing is the relationship between their perceived actual self and ideal self. Many offenders show a significant discrepancy between the way they construe their self compared to their ideal self, and this is generally considered to be a reflection of low self-esteem. However, others do not show such a discrepancy, and the way they construe their 'offending self' may be closer to that of their ideal. Whichever the pattern, understanding their construing will enable the clinician to gain a greater insight into the factors contributing to the development and/or maintenance of the person's offending, and indicate the direction of treatment. For example, there are many offenders who do not regard themselves as having committed an offence, but whose behaviour is seen by others as clearly deviant. Most sex offenders construe their behaviour as justified, and therefore may experience little discrepancy between their self and their ideal self. The self-characterisation technique (see later) is often particularly pertinent in eliciting core constructs.

Construing of Others

The way in which a person construes other people clearly influences their own behaviour. For example, if others who are deviant or who offend are seen as role models (i.e. are construed as similar to their 'ideal self'), then this is going further to validate their own offending. There is some evidence to suggest that young offenders are more likely to construe other people in ways which validate their own behaviour (Noble, 1971; Miller & Treacher, 1981). Equally, construing others in an overfavourable light can also cause problems, as Howells (1983) demonstrated in his study of one-off, extremely violent offenders. Assessing how the client construes other people, including family, peers and victims, is therefore important. This information can be fairly easily obtained from the clinical interview, and assessed in a more formal way using a repertory grid.

Construing of the Offending Behaviour

As seen in Chapter 1, the content of construing in offenders differs from that of non-offenders most pertinently in terms of its lack of commonality. It is clear that many offenders construe events and behaviours in ways which are markedly different from the rest of society, instead showing commonality of construing with other offenders. Assessing the personal meaning of offending to a client is therefore crucial to understanding why their behaviour makes sense to them, and why they may be resistant to change. This involves assessing whether their behaviour has positive or negative implications, and the dilemmas raised by considering change. For example, a man with a long history of violence may have gained a reputation among peers as a person 'not to be messed with'. The client themself may construe not being violent as 'letting the other person get away with it', and have to undergo major revision of their constructs and core role structure before considering change as a possibility.

THE CLINICAL INTERVIEW

Before using any of the techniques more specific to PCP, as with any assessment, it is important to carry out a comprehensive clinical interview. George Kelly (1955/1991) described PCP as a *credulous approach*, which is highlighted by the classic quote:

> ... if you do not know what is wrong with a person, ask him; he may tell you. (Kelly, 1955/1991).

However, Kelly described two different approaches to the clinical interview. One, which he termed *uncontrolled elaboration* of the problem, is not in any way directed by the clinician. The other approach is more directive and focused, and is termed *controlled elaboration*. The two approaches are useful in different circumstances. One difference between working with offenders and many other clients presenting with mental health problems is that offenders do not necessarily see their own offending behaviour as problematic. Uncontrolled elaboration involves asking the client about both their own and others' view of the problem (or reason for the assessment), listening and asking non-threatening questions, and may be particularly useful in establishing rapport with offenders who may be suspicious and hostile towards perceived authority figures.

However, it is also the case that when working within the legal framework, and with offenders who may be likely to omit relevant information, the clinician does not have the luxury of allowing this type of uncontrolled elaboration of the problem, and needs to be much more directive. Kelly suggested that other contra-indications to the uncontrolled approach are if the client is very repetitive, if their construing is very loose and unstructured (i.e. jumping from one topic to another), or if they are showing considerable guilt. In this latter case Kelly suggested that continued and undirected elaboration of the loss of role that they have experienced may eventually lead to the person becoming hostile (continually attempting to get evidence to support their way of construing) and paranoid, or suicidal. Inarticulate offenders or those with poor verbal skills may also find it easier to follow a structured interview. Although allowing the client to talk freely about their offending enables the clinician to gain greater access to their personal construct system, in the majority of assessment situations with offenders, it is important to obtain details that the person may not otherwise disclose. Taking a more directive and controlled approach to the clinical interview is therefore usually very important with offenders. There are parallels here with the use of supplied, as well as elicited, constructs in a repertory grid with offenders (see later).

Kelly (1991) suggested a number of questions to ask a client during a controlled clinical interview. Although the content and focus of the questions will undoubtedly be familiar to most clinicians, the purpose is different from that of other approaches to assessment. The following questions were designed to help the client (1) to place the problems, if possible, on a time-scale, and (2) to see them as fluid and transient rather than intransigent, and then to interpret them as responsive to (a) treatment, (b) the passing of time, and (c) varying conditions. The questions below have been updated and would need to be further reworded in order to be relevant to the individual offender, their behaviour, the setting, and the purpose of the assessment.

1. What do you see as your main difficulties?
2. When did you first notice these difficulties?
3. What else was happening in your life when these difficulties first appeared?
4. What previous treatment have you tried?
5. What changes have you noticed either with treatment or over time?
6. Under what conditions are the difficulties most noticeable?
7. Under what conditions are the difficulties least noticeable?

As mentioned earlier, the extent to which an offender sees themself as having a problem for which they need help varies considerably. It may also depend on the setting in which the assessment occurs, and whether or not this is voluntary. It may therefore be useful to amend the first question to 'What, *if anything*, do you see as your main difficulties?', which enables a greater rapport to be established and more information obtained. If the individual says that they do not see themself as having any problems, the clinician can then explore with them how they came to be in the assessment setting, and the way other people are construing their behaviour. Regardless of whether or not the client themself construes their offending as problematic, if they do not completely deny the behaviour, questions 2 and 3 are important in understanding its onset and development. As the assessment of offenders usually involves reaching conclusions and recommendations about future plans, it is also essential to know what has previously been tried in the past, how effective this was, and what changes have occurred (questions 4 and 5). The final questions relate to identifying patterns in offending, and can be asked regardless of whether or not the offender construes their behaviour as being a problem.

G. Kelly (1955/1991) described a number of ways in which the clinician can maximise their understanding of the client and the problem (or offending behaviour). First, throughout the interview it is helpful for the clinician to feed back to the client the terms they use, to clarify the meaning of these. It is important to have a shared meaning of 'tensed up' or 'blowing a stack', and useful techniques for exploring constructs in more detail are described in Chapter 4. However, it is also important to be aware that some offenders use words as a way of distancing themselves from their behaviour, such as some sex offenders who talk about their 'relationship' with their victims, in order to convince themselves that this was an equal relationship and that their victims were really consenting. In these cases, avoiding collusion means that the clinician may need to use a different language in order to help the client reconstrue their offending behaviour.

Secondly, it may be necessary to confront the client with the problem if there is something they do not mention themself. With offenders this may be other previous offences, or the effect on the victim. Thirdly, as mentioned earlier, Kelly advocated the use of a 'credulous' approach, 'taking what he sees and hears at face value' (G. Kelly, 1955/1991). This is something that may be very difficult, or even dangerous to do with offenders, who initially may be ambivalent about change and not see the harm in their behaviour. However, an alternative construction of this approach with offenders is to take an *empathic* approach, which enables the client to feel accepted and valued as a person, while still being challenged about their behaviour and construing.

Ravenette (1977, 1992) also described principles and strategies of the PCP approach to a clinical interview which are very pertinent to working with offenders. Although his work was with children and adolescents, the client groups are similar in that it may not necessarily be the client themself who is presenting as being in need of help. In such a case, the client may see the interview as meaningless and irrelevant.

Ravenette (1977) emphasised the importance of providing a clear structure to the clinical interview, which provides a framework to enable those who are verbally inhibited to talk more freely, and contains those clients who are garrulous. He also suggested that 'if we want to know someone well we should explore the areas in which he (or she) is expert' (p. 265). With offender clients this means investigating their expertise in their own offending behaviour, which may enable the clinician to better understand why the client may be resistant to change. For example, some offenders describe themselves as an 'expert' in their field of offending, and will talk at length about their skill at committing burglaries or exposing themselves to women in a way which minimises their chance of being caught. Some such individuals describe their offending as the only thing in their life at which they have ever been any good.

The clinical interview should enable the clinician to begin to form initial hypotheses about how the client makes sense of themselves, their offending behaviour and the world around them. The clinician should have a greater understanding of how the client's core role structure and patterns of construing have been shaped by their personal history, childhood experiences and family background. The aim of the interview is not overtly to 'find' constructs, but to be able to infer these from the information which has been elicited, hopefully in collaboration with the client. In order to both confirm preliminary hypotheses and further assess the structure and content of the client's construing, assessment techniques specific to PCP can be employed.

TECHNIQUES FOR ASSESSING CONSTRUING

The Self-characterisation

This assessment technique is less widely used than the repertory grid, and yet is an easy way of eliciting constructs, particularly those which relate to the person themself and their core role. The client is given the following instructions:

> I want you to write a character sketch of ... {client's name} just as if he (she) were the principal character in a play. Write it as might be written by a friend who knew him (her) very *intimately* and very *sympathetically*, perhaps better than anyone ever really could know him (her). For example, start out by saying '... is ...'
>
> (G. Kelly, 1955/1991, Vol 1, p. 242).

These instructions are aimed at facilitating an in-depth character description, which by taking the role of a third person, should not be too threatening and should encourage greater perspective taking. Kelly applied various methods of content analysis to the self-characterisation. However, in practice it is usually enough for the clinician to be alert to the main constructs which emerge, together with other features of the characterisation such as its sequence, organisation, and any repetition of themes. It is useful to note whether or not an offender client refers to their offending in the self-characterisation, and how this is construed in relation to themself. Kelly also noted that people were more likely to begin the sketch with 'safe' information or a statement about their current orientation to life, and end with more intimate themes, perhaps relating to where they see themselves going. For example, it is interesting to compare the self-characterisations of two women, both of whom had been convicted of a serious violent offence against someone they knew. Both women had been admitted to a secure hospital, where they were detained under the legal category of psychopathic disorder.

> Amanda tries her best at things but sometimes gets on the wrong track. When she has done something wrong she learnes (*sic*) from it and tries to do better next time. Amanda is polite, clean and looks after herself, and has a good sense of humour. She likes sport, particularly running, and tries to keep fit. She is more contented in herself now and is keen to get on with life again. Hobbies are: running, music, reading and most importantly her relationship with Paul, her boyfriend. She is a sociable person who is far less aggressive than in times gone bye (*sic*).

> Amanda does prefer some sort of structure in her life so that she knows where she stands. She also prefers people to be honest with her even if the criticism is not nice. Overall Amanda is a sensitive person who can get close to people if time is taken to build up a relationship.

> Amanda has experienced violence both as a receiver and as a giver but by nature is not a violent person.

> The people who Amanda is closest to at present are: her mum and sister, Paul, her gran. Amanda wants a fresh start in life but uses her past to direct her.

In Amanda's self-characterisation a recurring theme relates to the different ways in which she construes the past and the present. She shows awareness of her past difficulties, but also of her strengths, and sees herself now as focusing on the future. Core constructs appear to include those to do with being 'polite' and 'sociable', and she appears to be a person to whom close relationships are important. Interestingly, despite a history of previous violence before the current offence, Amanda does not construe herself as being a violent person 'by nature', and the aforementioned constructs are more important in defining her core role.

In contrast, the following self-characterisation written by Pat, who also had a history of violence, is generally less well organised and uses fewer psychological constructs relating to past difficulties. Her core role includes an important component to do with 'not letting people walk over her', and she generally construes herself in a positive way. There are fewer references to the need to learn or change and she appears to take less responsibility for her current status.

Pat is more sensitive than she lets on, too self-conscious at times, a fairly easy-going person not as tough as she likes to make out, loves motor bikes, loves her family and is generally very friendly to others, she mix's (*sic*) as well as she can but sometimes likes the pleasure of her own company I believe it gives her time to think about things. She does get a bit broody about some things. When she spends too long buy (*sic*) herself It takes quite a bit to realy (*sic*) upset her and you have to upset her at least 3 times before she takes offence she does make allowances for people but will not and does not like people walking over her, I know she has leadership qualities but prefers to keep quiet Does not like the spotlight on her. Apart from all that she's a good mate and should be allowed to get on with her life If I was going to give someone a million pounds it would be Pat.

The view of the clinical team was that both Amanda and Pat were not yet ready to be discharged from hospital. Pat's view of herself was therefore more discrepant with this construction than was Amanda's self-perception. The hypothesis that Pat would therefore be less likely to engage productively in therapy than Amanda, was in fact, supported.

For clinicians who want to examine or compare self-characterisations in a more quantitative way, Jackson (1992, p. 82) has developed a way of scoring different psychological characteristics that emerge from the information provided in the character sketch. Although this is based on her work with children and adolescents, it is also relevant to adults.

1. *Views of Others:* A count of the number of times the individual refers to the view taken of him or her by other people.

2. *Personal History and Future:* A count of the number of times the subject refers to their past or possible future in psychological terms.

3. *Psychological Cause and Effect:* A count of the number of times the person makes an assertion of a cause and effect kind in psychological terms. Explicit psychological cause and effect statements were scored 3. Implicit statements scored 1.

4. *Psychological Statements Score:* A count of the number of psychological statements of any kind made by the person. If they listed a series of likes and dislikes in the same sentence which were all on the same topic (sport, food and so forth) the total list was given as a score of 1.

5. *Contradictions Score:* A count of the number of pairs of themes or general assertions which were contradictory in some way. Marked contradiction between two assertions was scored 3, a mild degree of contradiction between two assertions scored 1.

6. *Insight Score:* A count of the number of statements reflecting the individual's awareness of their own shortcomings and resulting problems.

7. *Self-esteem:* Awareness of claims of competence were given up to five points and another five points for claims of moral virtue, depending on intensity and frequency of statements.

8. *Prompts:* This is a count of the number of prompts needed to complete the characterisations.

9. *Non-psychological Statements Score:* A count of the number of non-psychological statements. These are often purely behavioural statements, activities or physical descriptions.

10. *Self-characterisation Total: ('Good Psychologist' Total):* This is the total of scores 1 to 7 minus 8 and 9.

The validity of this scoring method is suggested by the findings that children who could be described as 'good psychologists' (i.e. who used a large number of psychological cause and effect statements) tended to be more insightful and take account of others' views (Jackson & Bannister, 1985), and were also more popular (Jackson, 1992). Jackson concluded that self-characterisations may be used to identify adolescents with low self-esteem and deviant ways of making sense of themselves. In the clinical setting, the technique is one which can provide a useful starting point from which to explore the client's way of construing themselves, and in Figure 2.1 is applied to the two examples, Amanda and Pat, discussed above. It can sometimes be difficult to decide whether a particular statement 'fits' a certain category. However, the overall pattern of scores can provide useful information; for example, although both Amanda and Pat made a number of statements indicating positive self-esteem, Amanda also made more 'insight' and 'personal history and future' statements than did Pat.

Laddering and Pyramiding

Laddering and pyramiding are both techniques that are used to clarify constructs which have been elicited from a client, and the procedures are described in detail elsewhere (e.g. Fransella & Dalton, 1990; Fransella, 1995). Essentially, laddering is a skill which was first described by Hinkle (1965), and aims to identify a person's more superordinate constructs (i.e. those further up the hierarchy). This is done by asking the person which pole of a given construct they would prefer to be like, and why. This procedure is then repeated to enable the person

Amanda	Pat

1. <u>Views of Others</u>

Score = 0

Score = 0

2. <u>Personal history and future</u>

Score = 7

Score = 1

– done something wrong – learns from it
– tries to do better next time
– keen to get on with life
– less aggressive than in past
– experienced violence as receiver and giver
– wants a fresh start
– uses past to direct her

– should be allowed to get on with her life

3. <u>Psychological cause and effect</u>

Score = 2

Score = 2

– when she has done something wrong she learns from it
– prefers structure so she knows where she stands

– likes own company ... gives her time to think
– gets broody when too long by herself

4. <u>Psychological statements</u>

Score = 19

Score = 17

– tries her best
– sometimes on wrong track
– learns from doing wrong
– tries better next time
– likes sport
– more contented in herself
– keen to get on with life
– list of hobbies
– sociable
– less aggressive
– prefers structure
– prefers people to be honest
– is sensitive person
– can get close to people
– experienced violence
– not by nature violent person
– list of people closest to
– wants a fresh start
– uses past to direct her

– sensitive
– too self–conscious
– fairly easy going
– not as tough as makes out
– loves motorbikes
– loves family
– mixes as well as can
– likes own company
– gives time to think
– sometimes gets broody ...
– takes quite a bit to upset her
– does make allowances
– doesn't like people walking over her
– has leadership qualities
– prefers to keep quiet
– doesn't like spotlight
– is a good mate

5. <u>Contradictions</u>

Score = 1

Score = 1

– experienced violence as a giver but not a violent person

– fairly easy-going/does not like people walking over her

Figure 2.1. The application of Jackson's (1992) scoring system to two self-characterisations (*figure is continued overleaf*)

6. Insight

Score = 4	Score = 2
– gets on wrong track	– too self-concious
– once done something wrong ...	– gets a bit broody
– less aggressive than in past	
– experienced violence	

7. Self-esteem

Score = 30	Score = 30
– polite, clean, looks after self	– easy-going
– good sense of humour	– friendly
– more contented in self	– mixes well
– sociable	– leadership qualities
	– good mate

8. Prompts required

Score = 0	Score = 0

9. Non-psychological statements

Score = 1	Score = 2
– tries to keep fit	– have to upset her three times ...
	– ... give someone a million pounds

10. Self characterisation total ('Good Psychologist')

Score = (63 – 1) = 62	Score = (53 – 2) = 51

Figure 2.1. *Continued*

to climb the 'ladder' of their construct system. Fransella (1995) notes that laddering is a skill which requires considerable practice. The clinician needs to be aware of the possibility that the client may become uneasy about exploring ways of understanding the world which they have never previously considered. Figure 2.2 illustrates the kinds of constructs which might be provided by laddering from an initial construct of 'Innocent vs Knows about the world', elicited from a client with a history of child abuse.

Pyramiding was first described by Landfield (1971), and involves the opposite procedure of identifying constructs which are more subordinate in a person's construct system, or further down the hierarchy. This is done by asking the person for more specific details about each pole of the initial construct. In the above example this would involve asking 'What kind of person is innocent/knows about the world? How do you know? What do they actually do?' This is then repeated for the subsequent construct poles which are produced (see Figure 2.3).

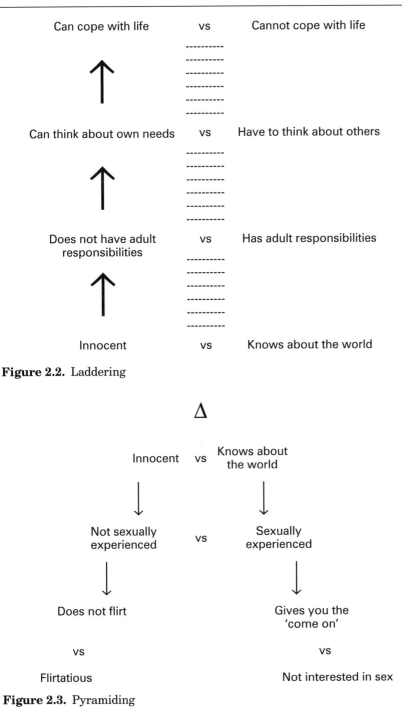

Figure 2.2. Laddering

Figure 2.3. Pyramiding

Repertory Grids

A repertory grid is a technique used to explore a person's construct system and understand how they see the world. It examines the relationship between the person's constructs and their experience, for example of themselves and other people. A plot is drawn up graphically to obtain a visual representation of an individual's view of the world in terms of important constructs, the relationships between them and the elements that are being explored (e.g. people or situations).

The use of grids can open up an exciting new dimension to the assessment of offenders. However, some clinicians avoid using the technique because they assume that grids are not useful unless they are analysed using complex mathematics or computer programs. On the other hand, others fall into the pitfall of assuming that the method is unquestionably objective and scientific, regardless of the way the grid was designed or completed. Neither assumption is correct. Landfield (1971) reminds the reader that the value of the Rep Test is no better than the astuteness of the investigator who uses it' (Landfield, 1971, p. 117), and as G. Kelly (1969a) said, '... the contribution the computer makes is to economy of the language employed, not to conceptualisation ...' (Kelly, 1969a, p. 290).

A comprehensive guide to using repertory grids with offenders is given in Chapter 4. However, the three key features of grids are outlined below.

The Elements

The elements in a grid are the items that you want to explore with the person. Commonly, and particularly in this book, the elements are people, such as different 'selves' (e.g. self now, ideal self, self when offending) and other significant people in the person's life. This type of grid is called by a number of different titles in the literature—a Person's Grid, People's Grid, or Rep Test. This latter title comes from the original standard list of elements suggested by G. Kelly (1955/1991), which consisted of 22 role titles for which the person is asked to supply names, and is known as the Role Construct Repertory Test (see Fransella & Bannister, 1977). For clinical use, however, this original list is too cumbersome and generally little used. It is therefore usual and appropriate for clinicians to devise their own list of elements, and ask the client to supply specific names. In working with offenders, a clinician might be particularly interested in including the person's victim(s), parents, offending and non-offending peers, and other role models, as well as different aspects of their 'self', such as 'self now', 'self as a child', 'self at the time of the offence' or 'self before/after prison'. There is also tremendous scope for using grids to explore how a person construes situations, events, feelings or almost any other concept in which the clinician is interested. Pictorial elements can also be used, such as photographs. Further suggestions and examples of elements to use in grids with offenders are given in Chapter 4.

The Constructs

The constructs in a grid indicate how a person thinks about and differentiates between the elements. One of the most common ways of eliciting or obtaining constructs from a person is that originally proposed by G. Kelly (1955/1991), known as the *triad method*. This involves selecting groups of three elements and asking the person, 'In what way are two out of the three people/situations alike, and therefore different from the third?' For example, if a person described their father and brother as caring, compared to their sister, this would elicit the construct 'Caring vs Not caring'. The process of eliciting constructs is described in greater detail in Chapter 4.

A Rating or other Linking Mechanism

This is the method by which each element is rated on each construct, to explore the relationship between the two. Again, Chapter 4 goes into detail about the different methods available. If the grid is then analysed mathematically (e.g. Slater, 1972) the positions of the elements relative to the constructs can be drawn up in a plot, as shown in Figure 2.4. This illustrates the grid completed by David, who had been been convicted of sexually abusing his 13-year-old daughter, and was referred for assessment by his probation officer with a view to treatment on his release from prison.

A plot of a grid provides a visual representation of the person's construct system. The axes of the plot indicate which are the most discriminating constructs, in other words, the main ways in which the person is making judgements between people (or other elements) or seeing the world. In David's case, the main way in which he discriminated between people was whether or not they were home-loving, understanding, forgiving and domineering. However, a second important way in which he differentiated between people was whether they behaved in a 'masculine' or 'feminine' way, and interestingly, he associated being 'feminine' with 'speaking your mind'. Information from the clinical interview had indicated that he generally held strong views about what were masculine and feminine characteristics, which included seeing women as much more decisive and assertive than men.

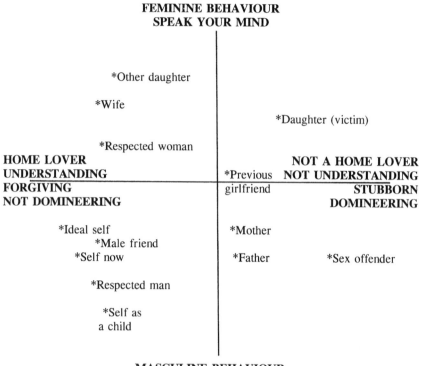

Figure 2.4. Plot of elements in construct space from David's grid

The positions of the elements in relation to the constructs indicate how each of them have been construed. The closer two elements are together, the more similar they are. For example, David construed himself in a positive way, as someone who was home-loving, understanding and forgiving, the polar opposite of the 'typical sex offender', whom he construed as domineering and stubborn. He saw himself as fairly similar to a man he respected, and there was little difference between his current and ideal self, suggesting that he did not see any need to change. Although he construed both men and women as home-lovers, he had a rather tight, or rigid, way of construing feminine and masculine behaviour in general, which meant that he found it difficult to construe any women as behaving in a masculine way and vice versa. His daughter, whom he had abused, was construed in a rather negative way, as not understanding, stubborn (i.e. not forgiving) and domineering.

Chapter 4 describes in detail the process of interpreting the information obtained from a grid. However, much information from the plot can be obtained at a glance. For example, in David's plot, the positive way in which he saw himself indicated that he considerably distanced himself from being a 'sex offender', and clearly did not see himself as in need of treatment. The way he construed his daughter as 'domineering' in contrast to himself, suggested that he may have seen her as being more responsible for the abuse than him. Similarly, construing her as 'not understanding' and 'stubborn', in contrast to his wife, who had continued to support him, again suggests that David had little empathy with his daughter, not understanding why she was angry and upset with him. Information from the clinical interview further revealed the ways in which David construed his behaviour in order for this to be consistent with his positive view of himself. Although he said that he knew his behaviour was wrong, he saw this as 'only' sexual touching, and therefore did not think that it was harmful or upsetting for his daughter. He interpreted her lack of resistance as consent, and had a rigid and tight way of construing 'real' sex offenders as men who attacked strangers at night. After much discussion in the clinical team, David was offered a place in a treatment group for sex offenders. However, not surprisingly in view of his self-concept, he decided not to take this up, saying that he did not want to attend a group with other sex offenders.

Using Grids with Offenders

Using repertory grids with offenders has a number of advantages. First, the technique does not force a response choice on the client in the same way as a questionnaire does, and the clinician can therefore 'start where the person is at', rather than impose a structure onto them. This is particularly useful when working with people who may try to tell you what they think you want to hear—grids are much less open to distorted responding. The PCP approach is also very much a collaborative one, in which the clinician works at the pace and ability of the client. If the client is unwilling or unable to elicit constructs using the triad method, then there are other ways of doing this that they will probably find easier (see Chapter 4). If they are resistant to rating particular elements or constructs, they can use the midpoint of the scale, or use the 'missing data' code if the analysis allows. Completion of a grid can therefore be a way of engaging positively with a client, as the clinician should always emphasise that there are no right or wrong answers. Finally, drawing up the plot and discussing it with a client gives them feedback about the findings of the assessment, and can be used as a basis for discussion about future work. If the client disagrees with something on the plot, the clinician can go back to the original ratings to see why that is the case. Above all, the repertory grid is a technique in which the clinician is attempting to understand the world as the offender sees it, which is an essential starting point for engagement, assessment, and discussion about future needs and rehabilitation.

SUMMARY AND CONCLUSIONS

The essential difference between the PCP approach to assessment and other theoretical approaches or frameworks, is that the PCP perspective is an idiographic one. The PCP approach to assessment aims to identify the personal meaning of offending to *this particular client*, as well as the way in which their previous history and experiences have contributed to the development of their own unique personal construct system. However, one of the differences between using the PCP perspective with offenders and with clients with other mental health problems, is that it is also important for the assessment of offenders to include a standard nomothetic assessment, which enables the client to be compared to others who have a similar history. This nomothetic assessment enables the clinician to compare this individual with others along a spectrum of potential risk or dangerousness, and to make recommendations for treatment or disposal. To this end, the use of standard 'labels' to describe individuals who have committed offences (i.e. 'violent offender', 'sex offender') serves the purpose of communication between professionals. The addition of the PCP approach then enables the clinician to assess what is *unique* about the client, and to see the world from their perspective. The problems which have led the client to attend the assessment interview can be described in terms of both the structure and content of their construing, using the professional constructs which G. Kelly (1955/1991) provided.

There are a number of aspects of a PCP-oriented assessment which contribute specifically to the three common purposes of assessing offenders; formulation, treatability and risk. First, in relation to formulation, information can be obtained from the assessment about the personal meaning of the offending behaviour to the individual. The clinical interview may indicate how the client has come to construe the world in the way which validated the development and maintenance of their offending. The repertory grid and self-characterisation may both confirm the clinician's hypotheses and provide new information to go back and explore in interview. These latter techniques also contribute to the assessment of treatability. Encouraging signs would be for the client to construe a difference between their current and ideal self, and have positive role models with whom to identify their ideal self. If their construct system is very tightly organised or cognitively simple, change is going to have major implications for their core role structure, and it is likely that the client will be more resistant. Similarly, if their offending behaviour is construed in a positive light, or non-offending implies negative consequences, change will necessarily require major revision to the construct system. Finally, with respect to future risk, the construing of other people is particularly pertinent. A repertory grid may allow a clinician to assess the way in which an offender client construes known and potential victims in a manner which is less open to distortion than direct questioning. In addition, an offender who does not perceive any difference between their current, ideal and offending self would also remain at high risk of reoffending. The clinical interview and other specific PCP assessment techniques can therefore be used to identify aspects of the individual's construing which contribute to individually oriented hypotheses about formulation, risk and suitability for treatment.

CHAPTER 3

Therapy with Offenders—The PCP Perspective

In the same way that PCP can guide the process of assessment, personal construct psychotherapy can also provide a useful framework for working therapeutically with offender clients. This chapter presents the key aspects of the PCP approach to therapy together with the specific issues raised by working therapeutically with this client group.

INTRODUCTION

Personal construct psychotherapy is the approach to psychotherapeutic treatment which is consonant with the theory of personal constructs. As discussed in the preceding chapter, a comprehensive assessment of an offender client using the PCP framework should have enabled the clinician to identify the ways in which the structure and content of their construing has contributed to the development and maintenance of their offending behaviour. The PCP approach to therapy offers the possibility of change to those clients who wish to do so, and ways of understanding the resistance to change which is shown by others.

G. Kelly (1955/1991) described therapy as 'a psychological process which changes one's outlook on some aspect of life', and described its goal as 'to alleviate complaints—complaints of a person about himself and others and complaints of others about him'. However, his view was that the purpose of therapy was not solely to reduce symptoms, but that the main aim should be to 'make one feel that he has come alive' (Kelly, 1955/1980, p. 29). Landfield & Epting (1987) develop this notion, and state that the aim of personal construct psychotherapy is 'for the person to construe his life in ways that enhance an exploratory attitude about his life. Such an attitude involves an understanding that one can make mistakes, then reinvent his life' (p. 273). The emphasis is therefore on highlighting the possibilities open to the client, helping them to see how their present construction of themselves, people around them, their behaviour and the world around them is causing difficulties in their life and exploring ways of change.

THE PCP APPROACH TO THERAPY

Although there are specific techniques available for helping clients in their reconstruing, personal construct psychotherapy does not necessarily involve the use of a prescriptive set of therapeutic tools which are incompatible with existing orientations. Dalton & Dunnett (1992) note that taking a PCP approach to assessment and treatment does not involve an either/or choice between one's existing orientation and PCP, but rather that PCP may help to make more sense of ongoing clinical practice. Different theoretical orientations and therapeutic approaches can be viewed as alternative ways of construing the client's presenting difficulties. As with assessment, PCP can therefore be seen as an *additional* framework within which to work therapeutically. This chapter therefore focuses more on the key aspects of the PCP approach to therapy than the techniques of reconstruing, since a detailed exposition of these can be found elsewhere (e.g. Fransella & Dalton, 1990).

Characteristics of the Therapist

There are a number of characteristics which are important for the personal construct-oriented psychotherapist to possess (Landfield, 1980; Epting, 1984; Winter, 1992). Clearly these are not all unique to PCP, and many are important in the establishment of any effective therapeutic relationship. However, other features are more specifically rooted in the theory of personal constructs, and together they provide a framework from which the personal construct-oriented psychotherapist operates.

1.   The therapist should be able to take the *credulous approach*, in other words, to accept that the client's way of viewing the world is 'true' and valid *to them*, even if this is hard for the clinician themself to understand. As discussed in the previous chapter, this does not mean unquestionably believing or condoning what an offender client says, which could be potentially dangerous. It does mean taking an empathic approach and listening to what the client says about their behaviour before starting to challenge it.

2. Linked to the above point is the need for the therapist to be able to *put themself in the client's position*, i.e. to subsume their construct system within their own and take their perspective. Again, this does not mean identifying with or becoming enmeshed with the client, but being able to predict what evidence is available to validate the experience of clients coming from a wide range of socio-economic and cultural backgrounds.

3. If the therapist is going to suspend their own personal system of construing or viewpoint, it is important that they replace this with a *healthy and professional construct system* which enables them to subsume the different construct systems of their clients. This means having a professional and/or theoretical framework with which to make sense of the client's constructions and generate hypotheses and formulations.

4. The therapist should allow themself to be *creative and intuitive* in order to recognise new constructs that emerge in therapy and acknowledge the advantages that different lifestyles have for the client. With offender clients this might mean acknowledging openly their ambivalence about change, and their construal of advantages in their current behaviour.

5. The therapist should try *not to be fixed* in their view about what is 'best' for the client. Although clearly the therapist cannot condone antisocial behaviours, there are other behaviours which may be considered socially deviant but are not harmful or illegal, such as cross-dressing.

6. Finally, the clinician should provide an atmosphere of *acceptance, reassurance and support*, in which the client is the expert concerning the nature and content of their own personal construct system, and the therapist has professional expertise in their knowledge of psychotherapeutic strategies.

The Process of Personal Construct Psychotherapy

As with other therapeutic approaches, personal construct psychotherapy involves a process of assessment, followed by the making and testing of hypotheses. In PCP terms, this closely follows G. Kelly's (1970) model of the *cycle of experience*, i.e. a complete unit of experience by which an individual can develop in an optimal direction (see Landfield & Epting, 1987).

The first phase in Kelly's cycle of experience is *anticipation*, in which the process of construing begins with the person making predictions about what might happen next. In personal construct psychotherapy, anticipation becomes the process of assessment, in which the clinician begins to assess the nature of the problem and explore the structure and content of the client's construct system, possibly using repertory grids. At this stage the gains of the client's behaviour must be outweighing the losses. The task for the clinician in assessing an offender, is therefore to suggest hypotheses about how the client's construct system facilitates the continuing validation of their offending behaviour.

Secondly, the *investment* (or engagement) phase is concerned with the development of the therapeutic relationship and the elaboration of the presenting problem, as outlined in the preceding chapter. Landfield & Epting (1987) suggest that during this stage it is particularly important for the therapist to provide support and reassurance, and for the client to be able to feel that there is hope for change.

In the *encounter* phase the clinician begins to put the problem (or offending behaviour) into context and formulates a tentative hypothesis about the nature of the problematic behaviour, using professional constructs from the PCP perspective and other orientations if appropriate. The emphasis shifts from the presenting difficulty to broader aspects of the client's life and other relevant problems are explored. By this phase, the relationship between the client and the therapist should have strengthened, in that the therapist has a greater understanding of the client's construct system, and the client has a greater understanding of themselves and the process of change.

The next phase (*confirmation and disconfirmation*) involves further exploration of the way in which the structure and content of the client's construct system maintain their offending, and then reconstruing aspects of the construct system. In particular, the *tightness* or *looseness* of the construct system is observed. A tight construct is 'one which leads to unvarying predictions' (G. Kelly, 1955/1991, Vol. 2, p. 7), and therefore tends to lead to black-and-white, unidimensional thinking, in which overgeneralisations are made. PCP techniques to help a client either tighten or loosen their thinking are briefly outlined later in the chapter, and it is necessary to read further to develop the necessary skills.

In the final phase of therapy (*constructive revision phase*) the hypotheses are tested. The therapist focuses on how able the client is to use the material addressed in therapy, and observes what sense they have made of the therapist's interpretations. In this context an interpretation is defined as 'an attempt to take a piece of work and place it in the context of other aspects of the client's understandings of himself and his world' (Landfield & Epting, 1987, p. 292). This is the point in therapy when the therapist and client develop new meanings and ways of construing. There are a number of signs which the therapist can use as indicators that the interpretation has been useful to the client and is assisting with change.

- The client may develop insight into things which were not previously clear
- They may begin to provide additional material which serves to illustrate the interpretation further
- The client starts to use the new construction to interpret other life events
- The client starts to experience a new mood about the way things are going, in which things are not as dreadful as before
- The client begins to report contrast in the way they see things now compared to previously
- The client starts to move on to other life issues which now appear more important than the issues previously worked on
- The client begins to offer more of their own summaries
- They are able to move from vague feelings to more specific ones without the help of the therapist.

Landfield & Epting (1987) note that this type of therapeutic movement is usually accompanied by the client becoming more assertive with the therapist and less dependent. However, it is important for the therapist to recognise that this phase can also be a very anxiety-provoking one for the client, in which their old and familiar construct system and core role structure are undergoing a process of change. Until the client develops a new role or set of constructs with which they feel comfortable, they often describe feeling as if they are in a state of 'limbo', identifying with neither their 'old self' or as yet, their 'new self'. In Kelly's terms this places the client in a state of anxiety, threat or guilt, and they will continue to need support and reassurance from the therapist throughout this time. For example, many offenders reach a point in therapy when they realise that they were construing their victims and their behaviour in ways which allowed them to continue offending without experiencing guilt. However, if they have not yet built up a viable alternative construct system, they may be vulnerable to construing themselves as 'all bad', and become self-punitive in a way which is not conducive to their psychological well-being.

Approaches to Changing Construing

Although it was noted earlier that the approach of the therapist was more important in 'defining' personal construct psychotherapy than the use of a specific set of techniques, the therapist and client may both come to agree that aspects of the client's construing are maintaining their problematic, or offending, behaviour. In this case, one of the tasks of the therapist is to help the client in the process of reconstruing their view of themselves and their world. There are a variety of different types of therapeutic reconstruction for which the therapist and client might be aiming (see Fransella & Dalton, 1990; Winter, 1992).

1. *Attempting to reverse the client's position with respect to one of the main discriminative constructs*, i.e. to construe a person or event in terms of the opposite pole to the original one. This is sometimes referred to as 'slot-rattling', and is the most superficial change that can occur in construing as there is no attempt to reformulate the construct itself. However, it can play an important part in therapy with some offenders. For example, a young man with a history of convictions for violence construed other people in terms of whether they 'Use their fists to sort out trouble vs Use their mouth to sort out trouble'. Therapy enabled him to both reconstrue his view of himself and to put this into practice, so that he came to think of himself as a person who would only ever 'use his mouth' in confrontations, rather than his fists. Although his use of this construct *per se* still led him to get into confrontations with other people, the 'slot-rattling' at least meant that others were less at risk of harm, and he himself was less likely to receive further convictions for violence.

2. *Applying another construct in their repertoire to ongoing events.* Again, this is seen as a rather superficial means of change, although it can sometimes be very useful. For example, a child sex offender who construes the normal behaviour of children as evidence that they are 'interested in sex' may be encouraged to experiment with alternative ways of construing, such as that the children are 'curious' or 'looking for affection'.

3. *Making preverbal constructs more explicit.* This involves the therapist increasing the client's awareness of constructs that are influencing their behaviour, but of which they are not explicitly conscious. For example, role play with a sex offender may enable them to realise the importance of constructs relating to 'power' in their choice of victim and method of offending. Although this could be done simply by the clinician suggesting this hypothesis to the client, the use of more active methods may be more facilitative in enabling the client themselves to develop insight.

4. *Testing constructs for their predictive validity.* This can be done through both discussion in the sessions and by setting up experiments for the client to test outside of therapy. For example, a client

with a history of aggression and heavy alcohol use may associate 'drinking alcohol' with 'being a man'. He may therefore assume that his peers would think less of him if he reduced his alcohol intake. Although there may be some reality to this, the client could be encouraged to discuss whether *all* his peers would make this association, predict who may do so (and who may not) and how one could tell, and to experiment by reducing his alcohol intake on a predetermined occasion to test out whether or not this was the case.

5. *Increasing or decreasing the range of convenience of certain constructs*, in other words either applying them more generally or decreasing their applicability. This aspect of reconstruction is often one of the most pertinent in PCP-oriented therapeutic work with offenders. Either applying a construct in a limited way or overusing certain constructs can be a significant contributor to the development and/or maintenance of deviant, problematic or offending behaviour. For example, a woman who construes all interactions with others in terms of whether she 'wins' or 'loses' is likely to have major difficulties in relating to other people, and therapy would involve encouraging her to decrease the applicability of her construct of 'Win vs Lose'. Another way of increasing the range of convenience of constructs is to apply them to predicting new or future situations. This enables the client to generalise new skills or new ways of thinking, and is important in terms of preventing relapse of offending. Constructs can also be made more impermeable (i.e. less applicable) by tightening them to very specific situations or individuals. For example, a child sex offender who construes all adult women as 'domineering' can be encouraged to tighten this construct so that it relates only to his own previous partners, rather than to all women in general.

6. *Erecting new reference axes*, in other words, formulating new constructs and changing those which are discriminative. This was seen by G. Kelly (1969a, p. 231) as 'the most ambitious undertaking of all'. He suggested that new constructs are most likely to be produced when the person construes elements which are not adequately anticipated by their existing constructs. This can be facilitated in therapeutic work (either through discussion or in a grid) by avoiding familiar or threatening elements and presenting the client with new elements, such as the therapist, or a fixed role which the client is asked to play (see later). An atmosphere of experimentation is created and the therapist should be able to give the client supporting evidence to validate their new way of construing.

Techniques for Reconstruing

G. Kelly (1955/1991) suggested a number of specific therapeutic techniques to help clients reconstrue their view of the world. Clinicians who are interested in developing specialist skills in personal construct psychotherapy are referred to Fransella & Dalton (1990) and Winter (1992), who describe the techniques outlined below in considerable detail.

1. *Elaborative techniques* primarily involve encouraging the client to imagine the possible outcomes of alternative courses of action or ways of responding, therefore elaborating the consequences of their construing. These require the therapist to be questioning and directive and involve 'identifying, exploring and perhaps resolving' inconsistencies in the client's personal construct system (Winter, 1992, p. 247).

2. *Enactment* refers to informal role-playing in which both the client and the therapist take the parts of the client and other significant people. This allows the client to experiment with alternative behaviour without this being too threatening to their core constructs or view of themselves, and also to understand the perspective of others.

3. *Loosening* serves a number of functions: to extend a construct's range of convenience, to encourage a client to recall events they might not otherwise, to assist in making preverbal constructs more accessible and verbal, and to encourage the client to 'shuffle some of his ideas into new combinations' (G. Kelly, 1955/1991, Vol. 2, p. 332). Fransella & Dalton (1990) describe specific PCP techniques for encouraging loosening of construing, although note that the therapist needs to be sure that the client can cope with the initial loss of control implicit in all loosening procedures before embarking on this approach.

4. *Tightening* represents the other end of the Creativity cycle from loosening, and is a way in which a person elaborates their view of the world by becoming more explicit about it. In order to complete the Creativity cycle, once the client's constructs have been loosened and realigned, they need to be tightened again so that the client can test out the predictive capacity of their revised way of construing. Tightening techniques in PCP therefore aim to increase the predictive capacity of constructs. This can be done by asking the client to comment on their own statements or behaviour, or about how what they have said all fits together (*judging*). Asking a client to *summarise* points by placing them in some kind of order is also a tightening process. Other tightening techniques involve the therapist asking the client to *relate* different ideas, put them in a *historical*

time frame, or to *bind* constructs to specific times in their life. The therapist can also directly make it clear to the client that they have not understood something and ask them to explain it again, or ask the client for *validating evidence* to support their construing. *Challenging* the construing of a client is also a way of encouraging tightening. The way that this is done depends on the degree of threat that the client is able to tolerate. G. Kelly (1955/1991, Vol. 2) suggested that challenges could range from the mild, e.g. 'I don't want to misunderstand you, so could you just go back over what you were saying?' (p. 357), to those which are more confrontative, pointing out the discrepancy between what they have said at different points in the session.

5. *Facilitating experimentation* involves confronting the client with a new situation in the session, or in role play. The therapist should encourage the client to make predictions about the consequences of alternative ways of behaving. G. Kelly (1955/1991) also suggested that the client should be encouraged to predict negative outcomes, as well as positive, in order to reduce the consequent anxiety if indeed this did occur. A key aspect of the therapist's skills in facilitating experimentation is the ability to work in the *'as if'* mode (Fransella & Dalton, 1990), in which the therapist encourages the client to approach an event as if their new construction of it were correct.

6. *Fixed Role Therapy* is an enactment-based procedure (i.e. based on role play), in which the client experiments with taking on the fixed role of a character sketch, which they and the therapist may work on together. This is based on their initial self-characterisation and should not be an ideal figure which would be alien to the client, but retain certain of the client's core constructs and make them feel that this character would be good to know. The use of fixed-role therapy with a young sex offender is described by Skene (1973).

THERAPEUTIC WORK WITH OFFENDERS: SPECIFIC ISSUES

Clients entering into personal construct psychotherapy must be open to change, and willing to experiment with thinking and behaving in a different way (Landfield & Epting, 1987). The approach was therefore originally developed and used with those clients who were requesting help themselves, and were keen to explore the possibilities for change. This is clearly not the case with many offender clients. Offenders usually come into contact with therapeutic services via the legal process, i.e. after they have behaved in a way which has caused *other people* concern. Even if the client has not been charged or convicted of an offence, they are still more likely to be referred for assessment or treatment at the request of others, than at their own request. It is therefore not uncommon for an offender client to have been 'ordered' by the court to undergo treatment, either in the community (e.g. as part of a probation order) or in hospital. Although such a treatment order would not be made without an assessment by the professionals providing the treatment, the individual client themself may be resentful of the lack of choice which they feel they have over their situation. There is therefore a real question of whether a client can truly engage with personal construct-oriented psychotherapy when they do not perceive themselves to have made that decision. This is consistent with the arguments of some authors that it is not the role of behavioural scientists to mediate in conflict between the individual and society, or to change individuals to conform to the norms of society (e.g. Feldman & Peay, 1982).

A further difference between offender clients and those with other difficulties is that the problematic behaviour is likely to distress or harm other people rather than, or in addition to, themselves. Although one aim of therapy may therefore be for the client to recognise the ways in which their patterns of construing are contributing to their offending, the overall aim is usually for them to reduce their risk of reoffending. This additional behavioural change is not necessarily the aim of therapy with other clients. Although for some offender clients, reconstruing aspects of their construct system may in itself be the most important aspect of therapy, others may require the addition of more directive behavioural self-control strategies, for example to modify deviant sexual fantasies, or to control their expression of anger. Other theoretical frameworks may also be useful with different individuals. For example, some clients may construe their 'past behaviour' as occurring at a time in their life when they frequently made mistakes, and so prefer to view their previous appraisals of the world within the cognitive framework of 'irrational thinking'. For other clients, their offending is only one aspect of a wide range of personality difficulties, and if they construe these as having a biological origin, medication can be helpful. Similarly, offender clients who are diagnosed as having a mental illness can benefit from both a pharmacological and a psychological approach to the construal of their difficulties (see Chapter 10). Although addressing the way in which offenders appraise events is now recognised to be an important component of effective treatment (Ross et al., 1988), for some clients it may not necessarily be sufficient to reduce the risk of further offending.

Finally, there are a number of common themes which emerge in therapeutic work with offenders more frequently than with other client groups. Whatever the therapeutic approach, the clinician may often be working with offender clients who are resistant to change, those who demonstrate Kellian hostility, and those for whom either a lack of, or a preoccupation with, guilt, is a major issue in therapy. These issues can all be usefully examined from the PCP perspective.

Working with Hostility

A difficulty often encountered when working with offender clients is that they display hostility in the Kellian sense, i.e. they are continually trying to get evidence to support a prediction that has already been shown to have failed (G. Kelly, 1969b). A hostile client may be one who is continually trying to get the therapist to reject them, in the way that they perceive themselves to have been rejected by most other people throughout their life, or they may belittle or sabotage all attempts at therapeutic help, as they construe themselves as unable to change. Such hostile clients habitually mistreat others to try and get them to counter-attack, so they can then prove that they are the 'enemy'. G. Kelly (1955/1991) suggested that with such clients, the therapist needs to be aware of the counter-hostility that they can provoke. He viewed the primary task of the personal construct psychotherapist as that of trying to elaborate the client's construct system by aggressive exploration, i.e. to accept alternative explanations when predictions do not turn out as they expected. However, Fransella & Dalton (1990) note that this is a difficult and lengthy task. If the client comes to realise the extent of their own hostile misinterpretation of the world before developing a viable alternative core role structure, they are in danger of experiencing considerable guilt (i.e. loss of core role) and likely to protect themselves by retreating back into predictably hostile patterns of construing. For clinicians who are not experienced in the use of personal construct psychotherapy, it may therefore be more useful to use the notion of hostility primarily as a way of making sense of the client's behaviour.

Working with Guilt

It is probably more pertinent when working with offender clients than with those with other mental health problems, to help the client to experience a reality-based degree of guilt, both in the traditional and the Kellian sense. G. Kelly (1955/1991) defined guilt as an awareness that one's 'self' had been dislodged from one's core role structure, and experiencing either little guilt or an excessive degree can both pose different therapeutic problems when working with offenders. A client who experiences little guilt because their offending behaviour is compatible with their core role, is likely to experience a sense of threat at the prospect of change. They will therefore resist this at all costs, remaining at a high risk of reoffending. Only if the client is able to build up a viable alternative view of themselves as a non-offender, is it then reasonable to expect them to experience guilt at the recollection of their past behaviour and the prospect of reoffending.

An equally difficult problem is posed by the offender client who has committed a harmful act or acts, and is preoccupied by an overwhelming sense of guilt in the traditional sense. Such clients may therefore become 'stuck' and unable to anticipate alternative ways of future construing. From the PCP perspective, this is likely to be experienced by individuals whose offending behaviour is not only completely incompatible with their core role structure, but also demonstrates a lack of both commonality and sociality with the rest of society. In other words, not only do most people not share the way in which they construed events, they also find it difficult to understand the offender's constructions. A preoccupation with guilt in the traditional sense is observed in some offender clients who have killed their victims, and who have to try to search for some way of making sense of their own behaviour. For example, a mother who kills her baby whilst convinced that she is protecting the child from harm, may only be able to move forward from a paralysing guilt by construing herself as 'ill' at the time. Similarly, Pollock & Kear-Colwell (1994) describe a personal construct analysis of two women who had been victims of prolonged sexual abuse as children, and had seriously stabbed their partners as adults. Both women construed themselves as 'guilty abusers', despite their histories of victimisation. Previous therapeutic attempts to focus on their roles as victims therefore dislodged them from their core roles as abusers, leading to increased guilt and self-destructive behaviour. The authors suggest that 'acknowledging the client's guilty feelings for the offence and self-perception as abusive and destructive allows therapy to progress towards a rational analysis of the individual's actions and guilt' (p. 21).

Working with Resistance to Change

Even with those offender clients who express consistent motivation for psychotherapeutic treatment, there is often some ambivalence about giving up a rewarding, but illegal, behaviour. The clinician assessing or attempting to work therapeutically with an offender client is therefore likely to meet a range of responses, from overt resistance to change through to admitted ambivalence and more covert forms of resistance. From the PCP perspective, resistance is not seen as a 'thing' to be overcome by the therapist, but rather as a 'hold up' which indicates that the therapist has not fully understood the client's construing (Fransella, 1989). Because the therapeutic relationship is seen as a partnership, the client still holds some responsibility for the lack of movement forward, but the onus is also on the therapist to gain a greater understanding of why this is the case. This could be done using the 'resistance to change' grid (Hinkle, 1965; see also Fransella & Dalton, 1990), or by examining areas of *conflict* and *inconsistency* in the client's construing. Tschudi (1977) has been influential in devising what he called the ABC Model to examine such inconsistencies and dilemmas in construing, and it can be a particularly useful technique in working with offenders, as illustrated in Figure 3.1. The procedure involves the therapist and client first defining the *actual state* (i.e. the current problem) presented by the client and also the *desired state* (i.e. what they would like to work towards in therapy). Tschudi (1977) regards these two states as opposite poles of a construct, A. The client is then asked to state what are the disadvantages of their actual state and the advantages of their desired state (Construct B). Finally, in order to elicit what is preventing movement by the client, they are asked for the advantages of their actual state, and the disadvantages of their desired state (Construct C). This elicits the *implicative dilemmas* which the client is facing; in the example below, the client is resistant to change because of the undesirable implications to them of not being physically aggressive.

Once the dilemmas faced by the client have been verbalised it is then easier to explore them in therapy. However, Fransella & Dalton (1990) note that this technique must be used carefully by the therapist at the appropriate time, for example, it may not be appropriate to ask the client for the advantages of their current difficulties in the first few sessions. If the therapist hypothesises that the client will be unable to

	Actual state		Desired state
A.1	Physically aggressive	A.2	Not physically aggressive
	Disadvantages		Advantages
B.1	Lose partner/job Risk criminal conviction	B.2	Keep partner/job No criminal conviction
	Advantages		Disadvantages
C.1	Seen as tough People can't treat you like dirt Don't let other people walk over you	C.2	Seen as weak Other people can treat you like dirt Let other people walk over you

Figure 3.1. Tschudi's (1977) ABC Model for examining dilemmas in construing

accept that there are advantages, then they should not use this technique for the time being.

Resistance to therapy can also be seen as a constructive choice, in which a PCP analysis of the persistence of apparently self-defeating behaviour may help the clinician to understand why the person continues to behave in that way (Winter, 1988, 1992). It can be useful to communicate this perspective to other people, who may be more concerned about the client's behaviour than the client themself. Winter suggests that there a number of specific features of construing that may be relevant in understanding resistance to change.

- If the therapist implies that *comprehensive changes* are required in the client's core constructs or role structure, this can lead to a sense of threat, and a subsequent wish by the client to avoid the change and stick with what is familiar.
- If the client's construct system is very *tightly organised*, then change will imply a loss of structure, which is likely to lead to greater unpredictability and increased anxiety.
- If the client's core role structure includes the notion of *themself as a failure*, then the prospect of success may appear very unpredictable and anxiety-provoking, and something therefore to resist. Some of the case examples in Chapter 8 illustrate this pattern of construing and its consequences in personality disordered offenders.

Finally, the whole structure and content of the client's construct system may mean that the payoffs for continuing to offend are construed to be greater than the risk or consequences of change. Winter (1992) suggests that in most cases, when a client is being seen at the request of others, and may themselves have no wish to change, the personal construct psychotherapist may accept the client's viewpoint as a valid alternative construction and not intervene. However, when the client is likely to harm themselves or others, as is the case when working with offenders, he notes that 'this is a perilous course' (p. 316). If the client's behaviour poses a risk to either themselves or others, most clinicians would feel 'duty-bound' to at least attempt to help the client see the benefits of change. Fransella (1985) has explored this dilemma in relation to the PCP perspective on working with clients with anorexia nervosa who do not want help. She sees persuading such a client that they *do* need help as contrary to the whole philosophy of PCP, in which individuals are responsible for themselves. If the person's way of construing serves their purpose, then clinicians have no right to say 'you should be different' (p. 129). However, Fransella (1985) accepted that there are occasions on which clinicians do say this, such as when a person has violated the norms of society. It is therefore useful to make a distinction between 'one's theoretical framework and one's personal strategy or beliefs' (p. 135), or those of society.

Finally, if an offender client is resistant to change, the clinician's response may partly be determined by the setting and the degree of control that they have over the therapeutic process. For example, if the client does not physically attend an outpatient appointment or there is no basis for detaining them in hospital against their will, there is clearly little that the therapist can do, even if their behaviour is potentially very worrying. On the other hand, if there is *some* onus on the client to meet with the therapist, either because this is a condition of treatment, or because they are detained in hospital or prison, then this at least provides an opportunity for the therapist to understand the client's perspective and the basis of their resistance to change. From this, the therapist can encourage the client to consider the possibilities for change, and the consequences of not doing so, both for themselves and others. There are similarities here with motivational interviewing techniques, which have been used with clients who have committed sexual offences (Mann, 1996), as well as more traditionally with people who have problems with addictive behaviours (Miller & Rollnick, 1991). There are therefore a variety of ways of using the PCP perspective in the assessment and treatment of offenders, depending on their readiness and resistance to change.

1. As a framework for assessment only (if the client is attending an assessment on a voluntary basis and does not want to change).
2. As a framework for discussing resistance to change with the client, and pointing out alternatives (if the client is attending assessment and/or treatment on a compulsory basis and is ambivalent about or does not want to change).
3. As an approach to assessment and treatment (if the client is attending either on a voluntary or compulsory basis and is open to the idea of change).

SUMMARY AND CONCLUSIONS

This chapter has described the key elements of personal construct psychotherapy, which is primarily an approach to treatment that reflects the philosophy and theory of personal constructs. As such, this can be adopted by therapists from different theoretical orientations, and integrated into existing therapeutic practice. George Kelly (1955/1991) also suggested a variety of specific therapeutic techniques which can be used when the therapist and client are working towards reconstructing aspects of the client's construct system, and these are briefly outlined.

The main dilemma for the therapist in using the personal construct approach to therapy with offenders is that the client themself may not be the person who is requesting help. Clearly, if the individual does not attend appointments, refuses to discuss their behaviour with the therapist or maintains consistently that they do not want to change, then there is little that any therapist can do to intervene, even if the client's behaviour is potentially dangerous. However, with most offender clients, their resistance to change is not quite so overt. In most cases, the potential harm to others caused by the client's behaviour would outweigh the personal construct clinician's reluctance to point out the benefits of change. If the client at least attends the therapeutic session and talks about their behaviour, it is possible to assess the factors which may underlie ambivalence and resistance to change, identify potential areas of conflict in construing, demonstrate understanding of the client's perspective, and ensure that they are fully aware of the possibilities for change.

The therapeutic techniques of personal construct psychotherapy will not therefore be of benefit to all offender clients; some will not wish to change, and others may benefit from a different or additional approach. However, for those offender clients who can recognise the ways in which their constructions have contributed to the development and maintenance of their offending behaviour, and who wish to change these, the approach of personal construct psychotherapy can be an invaluable framework in which to work.

CHAPTER 4

Repertory Grids and the Measurement of Change

Julia Houston and *Chris Evans

For clinicians using a personal construct psychology approach, understanding a client's construct system is a crucial part of the assessment. Although repertory grid technique is only one of a number of assessment tools, it is commonly used and has wide applicability. This chapter therefore aims to enable the reader to use the technique, by giving a step by step account of design, administration, analysis and interpretation. Readers who are not previously familiar with PCP may find it helpful to read some of the clinical chapters in Part II first, to get an idea of how grids can be used.

INTRODUCTION

One of the pertinent features of personal construct psychology is that as well as providing a theoretical model of the way in which individuals make sense of their world, techniques are also made available for the more structured assessment of personal construing. A repertory grid is one of the most useful tools for assessing personal constructs and therefore for understanding an individual's view of the world. Grids are commonly used for both clinical and research purposes, and if used appropriately, can provide a fascinating insight into the unique way in which a client construes the world. Although there may be some

* Dr Chris Evans, B.A., M.R.C.Psych., M.Inst. Group Analysis, Senior Lecturer in Psychotherapy and Consultant to the Prudence Skynner Family Therapy Clinic, Section of Psychotherapy, Department of General Psychiatry, St George's Hospital Medical School, Cranmer Terrace, London SW17 0RE

commonalities of construing among similar types of offenders, as described in Part II, the individual differences between them mean that no two clients ever complete a grid in the same way. However, because grids use numbers and can involve mathematical analysis, there is a danger of using the technique in isolation from the theory on which it is based. A repertory grid can become an indication of the *clinician's* construing, rather than that of the client. Alternatively, some clinicians may erroneously assume that repertory grids always require complex computer analysis, and be put off using the technique because they do not have access to, or are not familiar with, computers.

The rest of the chapter gives a guide to the process of completing and interpreting a grid with an offender client. This includes an indication of the valuable information that can be obtained even if analysis is not proceeded with, as well as a guide to simple manual analysis. Throughout the chapter the parameters which are necessary to ensure that the grid represents the client's construing are emphasised, keeping the technique firmly rooted in the theory of personal constructs. Several authors have written clearly about the design, analysis and interpretation of repertory grids (e.g. Beail, 1985). The following account is particularly oriented for the clinician working with offenders.

CHOOSING THE ELEMENTS

As outlined in Chapter 2, the elements in a grid are often people. People are used as elements when you are interested in exploring the client's view of themselves and their interpersonal relationships, and suggestions for elements to use with offender clients are outlined below (see Figure 4.1). Although in one sense the choice of elements is limited only by your creativity, there are a number of important principles that must be taken into account for the grid to be truly representative of the client's construing.

1. The elements must be chosen with a clear *purpose* in mind, otherwise you may end up with a great deal of redundant information. It is therefore helpful to have a hypothesis that you want to test, or at least a clear idea of the relationships you want to explore, and to select the elements accordingly. For example, consider the case of a man who had been violent towards his girlfriend's child. For a grid assessment it would be useful to include a range of children and adults as elements, including his girlfriend's children, other children that he knows, his 'self as a child', parents, partner and other adult friends. You could then test out hypotheses about his own

childhood by seeing how he construes his 'self as a child' and parents, explore whether he construes adults and children in appropriately different ways, and see if any difference emerges between his construal of his victim and other children.

2. The elements must be within the *range of convenience* of the constructs to be used, i.e. both relevant and applicable. Constructs are only relevant to a particular context and apply to some things but not to others. The elements chosen must therefore be reasonably homogeneous; for example, it would generally not be appropriate to include both people and situations.

3. The elements must be *representative* of the pool from which they are drawn, or again there is the danger that the grid will be misleading. If it is to include significant people in the person's life it is always worth asking the client whether there is or has been anyone else who is important in their life, as you may have overlooked an important relative or disliked person. It is important to include elements which will elicit both positive and negative ratings to achieve an informative grid.

Self now

Self at the time of the offence/Self as an offender

Ideal self

Self as a child

Self as seen by others

Mother

Father

Brother

Sister

Friend who also offends

Friend who does not offend

Partner/spouse

Boss

Victim(s)

A liked person

A disliked person

Figure 4.1. Suggested elements to use with offender clients

4. The *total number of elements* included should be taken into consideration, given any practical constraints on your time. The larger the grid (i.e. numbers of both elements and constructs), the more time-consuming it is to complete with the person and possibly to analyse, depending on the method chosen. Although there is no theoretical limit to the numbers of elements and constructs, clinical experience suggests that 10 by 10 grids (i.e. 10 elements and 10 constructs) can usually be completed by the person in about an hour, and often sooner, depending how quickly the person grasps the technique. However, grids smaller than 10 by 10 may fail to capture a representative picture of the person construing, so it is useful to think of this as a minimum guide.

ELICITING CONSTRUCTS

G. Kelly's (1955/1991) view was that the constructs that you aim to elicit will already be in the person's repertoire, and therefore you just need to get access to them. There are a number of standard ways of doing this.

The Triad Method

As described in Chapter 2, this was the method originally proposed by George Kelly (1955/1991). It involves selecting groups of three elements (e.g. self, mother, father) and asking the person, 'In what way are two out of the three people alike, and therefore different from the third?' This elicits one pole of the construct, and the next step is to elicit the opposite or contrast pole. Different authors have described slightly different ways of doing this. (Fransella & Bannister, 1977; Beail, 1985). The traditional way is to ask the individual how the third person or situation is different from the other two. Other ways involve asking 'What is the opposite to...? (the first construct pole), or 'How would you describe someone who is *not*...? (the first construct pole). Although some authors have concerns that the use of the word 'opposite' may mean that the individual just gives you the semantic opposite to the word, rather than what is meaningful to themselves, our clinical experience has been that this is not the case, and many clients find this latter technique easier to grasp.

Triads can either be selected at random or by the clinician in order to explore a particular contrast (e.g. mother, girlfriend, previous girlfriend). G. Kelly (1955/1991) suggested 22 triads which each had a rationale, and these are described in detail by Fransella & Bannister

(1977). However, this number of triads assumes that the clinician has used Kelly's standard list of elements, which is usually too cumbersome for everyday practice. Figure 4.2 therefore outlines triads which may be particularly useful in exploring the construct system of an offender client, including some of Kelly's original suggestions.

Self, Mother, Father

Self, Brother, Sister

Father (Mother), Offending friend, Non-offending friend

Self, Offending friend, Non-offending friend

Mother (Father), Partner, Previous partner

Partner, Friend, Victim

Other triads could be selected in order to test out specific hypotheses, such as those described in the later case example (see page 86).

Figure 4.2. Suggested triads to elicit constructs from offender clients

Whether the triads are selected in advance or at random, because each person's construct system contains a limited number of the most important constructs, eventually the same ones should be elicited by either method. In clinical practice it may be useful to select at least some of the triads in advance. However, if this method is used, it is important to ensure that each element occurs with a similar frequency in the triads, and to try to use different elements in successive triads. The process of selecting triads and eliciting constructs is further described in the case example later in the chapter.

The Dyad Method

Some people have great difficulty in using the triad method, particularly those whose thinking is very concrete. They may respond by saying, 'They're all the same' or describe each person/situation in turn. The dyad method involves presenting pairs of elements, and asking how those two are alike or different, and then eliciting the opposite pole as described above.

The Descriptive Method

Some people still have difficulty eliciting constructs using dyads, or may be resistant to engaging in the assessment. Constructs can still usefully be elicited, either by using a self-characterisation (see Chapter 2), or from their conversation. For example, Cummins (1992) describes using the conversational elicitation of constructs with clients who were victims of child sexual abuse and were reluctant to commit anything to paper. 'People' elements can also be presented to the client singly, asking them to describe what that person is like. Although this method does not employ the use of contrasts, it can be useful with individuals who otherwise may not be able to complete a grid.

Supplying Constructs

As well as using elicited constructs from any of the above methods, constructs can also be supplied by the clinician. The advantage of supplying constructs is that it enables the clinician to test hypotheses about a person's way of construing. This is particularly useful if a client has not provided any constructs which may be important in understanding their behaviour, or which fail to address the clinician's concerns. For example, if a client with a history of violence does not provide any constructs relating to aggression, you may want to supply a construct such as 'Aggressive vs Not aggressive'. Supplying constructs is also a quicker method of designing a grid with an individual, and enables comparison between grids.

The disadvantages of supplying constructs are that these constructs may not be so relevant to the person, and that it is not strictly consistent with the theory of PCP, since you are supplying your own verbal label to something which may not have the same meaning for the client. However, if you are uncertain about the relevance of supplied constructs to a client, this can be checked, either by asking them directly, 'Do you know what I mean by...?' (Salmon, 1976) or by asking the subject to rank elicited and provided constructs in order of importance (Isaacson, 1966). If the supplied constructs are known to be representative and meaningful, this can be a very useful technique, and one that can be used in conjunction with eliciting constructs. In addition, there is some evidence that meaningful results are obtained by using supplied constructs (Nystedt et al., 1976) and that these are significantly related to individuals' behaviour (Fransella & Bannister, 1967). Practically, it is important to ensure that supplied constructs are well understood by the client, and that you avoid putting words into their mouth. If both elicited and supplied constructs are used, the supplied constructs should be presented after those that have been elicited.

Constructs to Avoid

There are a number of types of constructs that should be avoided, or which need clarifying if they are elicited. A clear account of these is found in Winter (1992). However, it is important to remember that the client is eliciting what is meaningful to them. It is generally not appropriate for the clinician to try to encourage the client to clarify their constructs just so that it is easier to complete a repertory grid. In addition, if a client persists in eliciting the types of constructs outlined below, this is a source of important information about the way they construe the world, and is likely to contribute to the understanding of their offending behaviour.

Situational

These are constructs which describe a situational characteristic of the element rather than the element itself, e.g. if the client says that two people both 'live in Tooting' or 'are on probation'. These constructs are highly specific and limited in their range of convenience, i.e. application to other elements. In this case the clinician may want to ask the client if there is a more important way in which the individuals are alike (although bearing in mind that 'what is superficial for the investigator may not be superficial for the client'; Winter, 1992, p. 24).

Excessively Permeable

These are constructs which apply to all of the elements but show little scope for variation, e.g. the construct 'Men vs Women', in a grid where most of the elements were men. However, the clinician again needs to take care that they are not excluding something important to the client, and excessively permeable constructs can still be used in grids which use dichotomous scoring (see below). Some constructs may initially appear to the clinician to be excessively permeable, such as 'Young vs Old' or 'Male vs Female', but the client may use these with wide applicability. For example, a child sex offender may construe himself and his child victim as both 'young', in contrast to an adult friend.

Excessively Impermeable

These constructs are rather like situational constructs. They do describe the element, but in a way that will not be applicable to most of the others. For example 'good at ten-pin bowling', 'he's magic at regrinding valves'. Here the clinician needs to question the client further, to elicit a more permeable construct.

Vague

These are constructs which are applied so loosely as to convey very little information, such as 'OK vs Not OK'. However, it is important to be sure that you are not rejecting a construct that sounds vague to you when it is quite precise to the respondent (and *vice versa*). You can check this out by asking the client, 'Can you say a bit more about that?'.

Role-specific

Like situational constructs, these describe one role of the element rather than the element itself, such as 'both care about me' or 'both believe I'm innocent'. Some forms of role-specific construct might be very useful if they apply to the roles you want to understand and are applicable to most of the elements, e.g. 'I've been abusive towards them'. Otherwise, the clinician may clarify with the client whether the construct has greater applicability by redefining a role-specific construct to one which is more general, saying something like, 'Are both individuals also caring people generally?'.

Repeated

The problem of repeated constructs comes in two forms: literal repetition and use of virtually or actually equivalent words. The problem should only arise with elicited constructs and both forms raise a decision for the clinician or researcher using the grid. If you accept repeated constructs you may be rightly reflecting something of the restricted range of constructs that the person uses. Alternatively you may be missing out on the actual diversity that the person uses, as the elicitation procedure has, for some reason, got 'stuck' with the construct that is being repeated. Most clinicians and researchers reject literal repetitions and may reject similes as well. The choice has to be made on the basis of the intentions you have in doing the grid.

LINKING CONSTRUCTS TO ELEMENTS

Eliciting constructs from a person will reveal important information about the way they construe the world, and some clinicians may choose not to proceed further in terms of analysis. However, the way in which constructs are used in relation to the elements, will provide further valuable information about the structure of the construct system as a whole, as well as how the person differentiates between the elements. The elements and constructs are therefore written out in the format shown in Figure 4.3, and usually linked by one of three main methods.

REPERTORY GRID

NAME: _____

Date: _____

	Self	Ideal Self	Mother	Father	"	"	"	"							
	1	2	3	4	5	6	7	8	9	10	11	12	13	14	
1 Happy															Unhappy
2 Trusting															Not trusting
3 Outgoing															Inward
4 Lazy															Works hard
5 Aggressive															Not aggressive
6 "															"
7 "															"
8 "															"
9															
10															
11															
12															
13															
14															

Figure 4.3. Example of grid format

Dichotomous Scoring

With dichotomous scoring the client is asked to give each element a score of 1 or 0, depending on whether it is closer to the left or right pole of each construct. This form of scoring is probably the only form to be used if you are going to do only manual analyses of the grid data (see Appendix II). If you have access to computer analyses, most clients can provide more reliable gradings than just a 0/1 distinction and these finer discriminations will increase the utility of the grid.

Ranking

With this method the client is required to place the elements in rank order, which provides a fine degree of discrimination between them. It also enables the clinician to check that each construct really is meaningful for each element. However, ranking also has the disadvantage of forcing the person to indicate a difference where they may feel there is none, and also tends to be more time-consuming. It may not be viable with larger numbers of elements.

Rating Scale

This tends to be the most popular method, and the one which Shaw (1980) noted was used in 70% of all published studies. The client is asked to rate each element on each construct, usually using either a five- or a seven-point scale. This provides information about how often the person uses the extreme ratings, and with which elements, whilst also providing the option of an 'in between' score, which clients tend to find useful. Some grid workers additionally use the midpoint for 'non-applicable' ratings. Although this makes it possible to analyse grids even when the computer methods of analysis do not have an ability to handle missing data, nevertheless it conflates two qualitatively different responses. Some people (Chris Evans included) always use an even number of points on the rating scale, so the client cannot use the midpoint as a way of avoiding apparent commitment to a view. This also allows use of the midpoint as a 'missing' or 'unclassifiable' value, and preserves the distinction between this and other ratings.

INTERPRETING GRID INFORMATION BEFORE ANALYSIS

Even at this stage useful information can be obtained from the client's selection of elements, eliciting of constructs and use of ratings. The following points should be considered wherever possible.

- *How easy or difficult is it for the client to fit names to the roles provided?* This gives the clinician an indication of the extent of the client's social network, and information about significant others (or lack of them). Is it difficult for them to provide the name of a liked person? a disliked person? a partner? What is the gender balance of names provided?
- *Is the client happy to supply names to roles or are they guarded and suspicious?* One client assessed prior to joining a treatment group for sex offenders refused to give any names, referring to all elements by their role titles, such as 'my male friend', 'a person I dislike'. He

did not consider himself to be in need of treatment, and attended only 'to prove to Social Services that I am not at risk of reoffending'. His refusal to supply names not only reflected his unwillingness to co-operate, but also his general distrust of perceived authority figures and reluctance to acknowledge that he had a problem.

- *How does the client link the triads?* This will be discussed in greater detail in later chapters looking at specific types of offenders. The way in which the client links the triads gives useful information about how the person construes themselves and others. Which two out of the three elements do they construe as similar? For example, themself and a positive role model? a disliked person? a child?

- *What kinds of constructs are elicited?* Do similar themes recur, for example those to do with being nice/caring/loving, or is there a preoccupation with being difficult to trust/deceitful/two-faced? Landfield (1971) has attempted to classify constructs into different types. This categorisation has been used in the research literature (e.g. in the studies of Howells (1979) and Horley (1988) with sex offenders), although it may be too unwieldy for everyday clinical use.

- *Is there a preoccupation with egocentric descriptions?* These are constructs which, if overused by the client, may suggest a lack of self-confidence, e.g. 'know it all', 'cocky', 'thinks they're great'. Other types of egocentric constructs are those which are self-referent, in which the client fails to objectify their description of others, e.g. 'cares about me', 'I trust them', 'honest with me'. Landfield (1971) suggests that these self-referent responses in an adult are linked with immaturity, and may reflect a more dependent form of construing.

- *What sort of contrasts of meaning are provided?* When the client gives the opposite pole to the construct elicited, is this highly idiosyncratic (e.g. 'Caring vs Suspicious') or a reflection of their problematic behaviour (e.g. 'Puts up a good fight vs A wimp')? Does it indicate unreachable high standards (e.g. 'Difficulty in parenting vs Perfect parent' or 'all or nothing' thinking (e.g. 'Friend vs Enemy'. Are positive poles elicted before negative ones more often then would be expected on a 50:50 probability?

- *How complex are the constructs?* The relative concreteness or abstraction of a client's constructs may well be an indication of their cognitive complexity, although it is important not to assume that verbal construing is always a reflection of the discriminations which a person makes.

- *Are any constructs overused?* Landfield (1971) defines overuse as the appearance of a construct 20% of the time, which may point to core values, primary concerns or conflict areas.

- *How quickly are the ratings made?* The speed at which a client rates the elements may reflect their degree of impulsiveness. Both this and the extremity of ratings (see below) have been studied in detail by Thomas-Peter (1992) and are discussed in Chapter 10.
- *How extreme are the ratings?* Does the client vary the ratings across the scale, or do they use only the midpoints? or the extremes? Landfield (1971) suggests that both high and low polarisation indicate problems of adjustment, with the former being associated with extreme anxiety and personality disorder, and the latter with withdrawal and depersonalisation. Many offenders tend to show more use of the extremes than the midpoints, which often reflects a unidimensional view of the world in terms of either 'Good vs Bad' or 'Past life vs Present life'.

There is no need to proceed further with analysis if you do not want to—already you will have elicited rich information about the client's view of the world and the nature of their construing. However, further analysis can produce more order in that information and can reveal patterns in the client's construing that might otherwise be missed. Further analysis can be done by hand or on a computer, depending on the available resources. Most portable computers now have more than enough power for even very mathematically sophisticated grid analyses.

METHODS OF ANALYSIS

Manual Analysis

In practice, manual analysis is not frequently used. The simplest method is to rearrange rows and columns so that similar elements are positioned close to each other and patterns can be seen at a glance. This is described in further detail in Appendix II.

Computer Analysis

There are a number of different computer programs available for the analysis of repertory grids. Again, these are described in more detail in Appendix III. The main programs in use are INGRID (Slater, 1972) and FLEXIGRID (Tschudi, 1984), which are based on Principal Components Analysis. CIRCUMGRIDS (Chambers & Grice, 1986) is also easily available and some of the standard packages in the SPSS programs can also be used. For example, the correlations options facilitate comparison of constructs, and the distance computations facilitate comparison of elements. Any respectable statistics package will provide these analyses. The great advantages of computer analysis are speed and that some programs also provide plots or simplifying tabulations. The disadvantages are that it requires access to a computer and funds for the software (other than CIRCUMGRIDS which is freely available).

Most computer programs give similar information on the printout about the relationships between the constructs and the elements. Winter (1992) gives a detailed account of the output from the INGRID program, which is one of the most commonly used packages and provides measures similar to others. Information available includes:

- *Correlation between constructs.* This is a matrix of construct inter-correlations ranging from +1.0 to −1.0, enabling you to see which constructs are being correlated by the client and assuming that this reflects the psychological relationships between them.
- *Element sum of squares.* This provides an indication of how mean-ingful each element is to the client. A high score indicates that the element has been rated towards the ends of the construct poles, whereas a low score indicates that it has mostly been rated near the midpoint. High scores may indicate that the element is an important one and low scores may reflect an element that does not stimulate the same intensity of ratings. Low scores may be obtained either because the client knows that person less well, or because even though they know them well they do not see the person as particu-larly unusual in any way, or possibly because these are the only ratings that they feel safe to give that person.
- *Distances between elements.* This table indicates how similarly the elements are construed in relation to each other.
- *Loadings of elements and constructs.* These tables occur on the INGRID and FLEXIGRID printouts and are used to plot the grid (see next section).
- *Percentage of variance accounted for by each component.* This indi-cates the percentage of variance accounted for by each of the compo-nents extracted on the Principal Components Analysis, and is potentially a very useful piece of information about the client's con-struct system. The higher the percentage of variance accounted for by the first component, the more tightly organised and unidimen-sional the person's construct system appears to be. In a sample of normal subjects, Ryle & Breen (1972) found this figure to be 39% on a 16 by 16 grid, although much higher figures are commonly found for clinical subjects. The figure is often used as a measure of the cog-nitive complexity of the person's construct system, with a more cog-nitively complex system reflected in a wider spread of variance across the earlier components. However, the percentage variation on the first principal component is related to the size of the grid, which makes comparing data from different grids difficult. In general, the

higher the total possible number of principal components (i.e. the larger the grid), the lower will be the percentage variation on the first component. What is psychologically interesting is that people often show patterns in which most of the variation *is* distributed across the first few components, even in quite large grids. It is also important to note that other measures of cognitive complexity have also been derived from grid scores (Bieri et al., 1966) and from elicited constructs (Crockett, 1965). Bannister (1960) also developed a measure of the tightness of organisation in an individual's construct system, which he called the Intensity score. These measures are described in more detail in Appendix IV. However, there is much overlap between the measures devised by different researchers, and the research literature itself is inconsistent in terms of which measure of 'tightness' is used (Winter, 1992). In clinical practice, it is usually sufficient to use the percentage variation on the first component as a rough guide to the complexity or simplicity of the client's construing, as this is easily observable from the computer printout.

PLOTTING THE GRID

This is something which is really only done after a computer analysis, and is sometimes produced for you as part of the program output. Having a visual representation of the client's construct system makes it easier to understand, and is a useful focus for discussion with the client themselves. Although grids can be plotted in different ways, they all have two main features in common. First, the axes of the plot indicate which are the main discriminating constructs in the person's construct system, in other words, the main ways in which they are making judgements between the elements or seeing the world. Secondly, the positions of the elements in relation to the constructs indicates how each of them have been construed. The closer two elements are together, the more similarly they have been construed by the client. For a two-dimensional plot of a grid the loadings on each of the first two components are used to indicate the positions of both the elements and constructs. Component 1 is usually represented as the X axis, and component 2 as the Y axis. The convention that has evolved is to represent the constructs as lines from the origin to the loadings and to plot the elements as points at the loadings for the components in question.

There are a number of different ways of plotting the data. There is a rough hierarchy of precision in plotting constructs. The most precise is that in which the construct lines extend exactly to the point marked by their loadings on the components being plotted. This ensures that the length of the lines reflects the variation on the component; a construct that records little variation gets a short line not extending far from the origin and a construct that records a lot of variation gets a long line. The use of loadings rather than vectors ensures that the extension of the lines is scaled so that distances along two components are plotted to the same scale. However, this way of plotting grids is not often seen in the published literature, and may be confusing for use in clinical practice. A more common, although less precise, usage is not to plot the full lines for the constructs but only to mark where they would cut some 'frame' for the plot, either a circular or a rectangular one. Many authors simply put the construct labels on the plot at approximately the point where the extension of the loadings would cut some frame which is no longer plotted (see example shown in Figure 7.1., page 162). Some people using this approach mark both the emergent and opposite poles, which may be helpful as it puts the actual words onto the plot. However, plotting just the emergent poles is often perfectly adequate.

Finally, the simplest approach is that in which the constructs with the strongest loadings on each of the two components are written onto the component poles, losing information about how much they may have been somewhat 'off' to one side or the other of the component (see example shown in Figure 4.6., page 88). This approach can be the easiest to 'eyeball' and it links very easily with giving a sense of how the principal component analysis worked. This is the approach which often provides the clearest feedback to clients, and has been used for most of the examples in this book.

One other simplification is that many grid plots may not label the components, or may not note the percentage variation on each component. This makes it difficult to know how much of the information in the grid is captured in the plot. This information can be omitted from simple plots used for clinical purposes. However, ideally grids to be used for research or academic presentation should be labelled with the component number and percentage variation on each axis. A footnote or note in the text should indicate the numbers of elements and constructs and the rating system used in the grid.

Interpreting the Plot

The information provided by either manual or computer analysis of repertory grids can be interpreted further. Winter (1992) suggests that by following a series of steps which address specific questions, the clinician can avoid feeling overwhelmed by the wealth of computer output. The following questions are therefore useful as guidelines.

- *How much variance is accounted for by the first and second components?* This gives an indication of the client's cognitive complexity and in what way to draw up the grid graphically. Other structural characteristics of the construct system that the clinician may be interested in (e.g. its tightness or looseness) are described by Winter (1992).

● *What are the main discriminative constructs?* This information can be obtained by comparing the loadings of constructs on the components, which is printed in tabulation form on the computer printout. It is useful to note whether any of the supplied constructs are important discriminators.

● *What is the predominant content of the client's constructs?* The guidelines for interpreting grid information prior to analysis should have enabled the clinician to make initial observations about the client's construing. However, these may become even clearer after a grid is plotted.

● *How is the self construed?* What is the distance between the client's elements of 'self', 'ideal self' and 'self as offender'? In other words, how similar or different does the client construe their offending self from their current and ideal selves? What further information can be obtained about the client's self-esteem, their perceived self-isolation and their relationship with significant others?

● *How are other significant people construed?* How does the client construe their victim(s)? their parents? other authority figures or role models? the opposite sex? adults and children?

● *How do they construe their offending behaviour?* Information about this may be obtained if a construct pole relating to the client's offending has been elicited or supplied, e.g. 'Aggressive vs Not aggressive', 'Sexually attractive vs Not sexually attractive'. Does this construct correlate with other constructs which have positive or negative implications?

● *Are there any other major areas of inconsistency or departure from social consensus in relationships between constructs?* Winter (1992) outlines other ways in which the relationships between constructs can reveal logical inconsistencies. For example, is the positive pole of one construct (e.g. *'in* control of drinking') associated with the negative pole of another (e.g. *'let* others walk all over you')?

ASSESSING AN OFFENDER CLIENT USING A REPERTORY GRID: A CASE EXAMPLE

The following case example describes the process of using a repertory grid in the assessment of an offender client, including the initial design and administration of the grid, through to its analysis and interpretation.

Frank was a 33-year-old man who had been convicted of the indecent assault of a 10-year-old girl, whom he had befriended at a park and taken back to his home. He had two previous convictions also for the indecent assault of pre-pubertal girls. He had an ambivalent relationship with a woman that had been 'on and off' for several years, and described considerable anxiety in his relationships with adults in general, and women in particular. A repertory grid was used as part of the initial assessment, prior to his attending a treatment group in prison for men who had committed sexual offences against children.

Because of time limitations, I (Julia Houston) decided to keep the grid size as close as possible to 10 elements and 10 constructs. I was mainly interested in Frank's construing of adults (including himself) and children, so element roles were selected which would address this (see Figure 4.4). Pictures of a male and female child and adolescent were included as elements in order to see how Frank construed children in general, as well as his own victim. Although I was primarily interested in the specific and personal way in which Frank construed adults and children, this combination of personal and standardised elements also provided the potential to compare Frank's patterns of construing with that of other men attending the group.

Self now

Self as a child

Self as an offender

Ideal self

Victim

Partner

Male friend

Female child

Female adolescent

Male child

Male adolescent

Figure 4.4. Elements used in Frank's grid

Interestingly, Frank could not remember the name of his recent victim, when supplying names for the element roles. This suggested that the girl might have been a rather depersonalised 'object' (in the conventional sense) to Frank, an interpretation which would later be suggested to him in the group. He also had difficulty coming up with the name of a male friend, saying 'I don't associate with many people'. This suggested that, apart from his partner, he had few social relationships with adults. He eventually named a friend of his father's, whom he had occasionally met at a football match.

The triads were selected in advance, both to save time during the assessment session, and also to examine Frank's way of contrasting particular elements. The triad combinations and constructs which Frank provided are shown in Figure 4.5.

1. Self, Victim, Partner
    Self and Partner seen as alike;
    'Old-fashioned vs Modern'
    'Temperamental vs Easy going'

2. Victim, Female child, Female adolescent
    Victim and Female child seen as alike
    'Young vs Mature'

3. Victim, Friend, Self
    Unable to say which two were alike
    Described friend as 'good-natured'

4. Self as a child, Victim, Female child
    Self as a child and Victim seen as alike
    'Trusting vs Suspicious'

5. Partner, Friend, Victim
    Partner and Friend seen as alike
    'Good-natured vs Mean'

6. Female child, Female adolescent, Self
    Female child and Self seen as alike
    'Trusting vs Suspicious'
    'Easily led vs A leader'

7. Male child, Female child, Male adolescent
    Male child and Female child seen as alike
    'Innocent vs Promiscuous'

8. Female child, male adolescent, Female adolescent
    Male adolescent and Female adolescent seen as alike
    'Good-natured vs Mean'

Figure 4.5. Triads and constructs elicited from Frank

Frank had no difficulty grasping the concept of supplying constructs with most of the triads, and often provided two different emergent construct poles. This proved to be quite useful, as many of his constructs were repetitive and revolved around the theme of whether or not people were 'trusting'. Even at this stage, therefore, important information was emerging about the predominant constructs which Frank used to construe adults and children, and how this may relate to his offending. For example, in triad 4, Frank said that his victim and his 'self as a child' were alike as they were both trusting, and went on to say that 'you can tell if a young girl is trusting or not by looking at her'. The other interesting contrast was in triad 6, in which Frank described himself and a picture of a female child as alike, as they were both 'easily led'.

Four constructs were also supplied to Frank, based on constructs which both previous clinical experience and the literature suggested were meaningful to child sex offenders (Howells, 1979; Houston & Adshead, 1993). These related to whether or not people were 'understanding', 'easily controlled by others', 'domineering' and 'sexually provocative'. Frank rated the grid using a scale from 1 to 5. He did this fairly quickly and never used the midpoint of the scale, which raised hypotheses about his impulsiveness.

Frank's grid was analysed using the INGRID computer programme (Slater, 1972). The highest correlations between constructs were those between 'young' and 'innocent' (0.69), and 'domineering' and 'sexually provocative' (0.64). The scores on the 'element sum of squares' table suggested that, of all the four picture elements, the one of the female child was the most meaningful to Frank, with a similar score to that of his female victim.

Forty-nine per cent of the variance (on the 10 by 11 grid) was accounted for by the first principal component, and 16% by the second component. This indicates that 65% of the total grid variance is described in the two-dimensional loading plot. The plot illustrates the different ways in which Frank construed adults and children (see Figure 4.6). The main component is described by constructs relating to dominance, control, innocence and maturity. Frank saw his female partner as domineering, not easily controlled by others and temperamental, the polar opposite to his victim and pictures of an unknown boy and girl. Interestingly, the plot illustrated that Frank also saw the picture of the female adolescent as more similar to his adult partner than to the other children. He

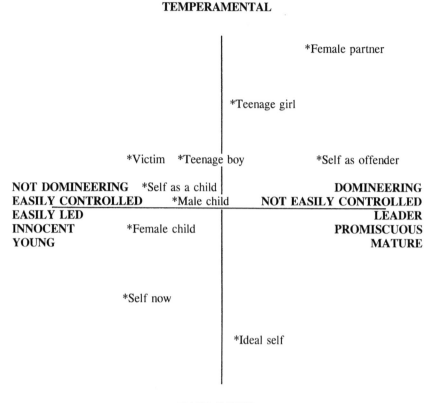

Figure 4.6. Plot of elements in construct space from Frank's grid

also closely identified himself as a child with his victim. The different ways he construed his current, ideal and offending self indicated some degree of insight into his need to change.

Frank participated well in the group, disclosing information about himself and challenging other group members. He openly acknowledged that he saw children as being less threatening than adults, particularly women, and that he therefore sought out the company of children. In common with many other men who sexually offend, he initially had difficulty in construing his offending as harmful. He disclosed that as a child, he had been both sexually and physically abused by his father, and contrasted this experience with his own offending, emphasising that he had not physically harmed any of his victims. By the end of the group, Frank was starting to broaden his construing of the notion of harm. However, he agreed with the therapists that he would benefit from further therapy, and so was referred on to a second group.

ALTERNATIVE GRID PROCEDURES

As mentioned earlier, as well as the personal grid which uses people as elements, there are a number of different kinds of grids. One slight change which can be useful for some clients with identity confusions, is to make up a grid in which the client is *all* the elements, each in a different role or situation; for example, 'me when I was at junior school', 'me in a good mood watching a video', 'me on edge, looking for a fight', etc. An extension of this is to consider the client in a number of different relationships, for example 'me as a husband', 'me as a son', 'me as a friend to John', 'me as an offender'. Where there seem to be issues about situational specificity of offending or other behaviours or feelings, a grid made up entirely of those situations may throw light on the construing of these situations, and how they differ.

Another grid technique is to take a number of problem situations (e.g. 'disagreeing with my wife', 'disagreeing with my boss', 'being given the wrong benefit at the Social Security office') and then to use various possible reactions or sources of support as constructs (e.g. 'walking away', 'being assertive', 'getting into an argument', 'hitting out'). The client then rates the likelihood or perceived usefulness of each of the different reactions. This grid technique was used by Watson et al. (1976) to explore the construing of prisoners.

The *dyad grid* is also a useful tool. Each element in a dyad grid is a relationship, for example 'me towards my mother'. It is generally best to consider the two 'directions' to each relationship as separate elements. For example, the first element might be 'me towards my mother', the second, 'my mother towards me', the next 'me towards Jean (victim)', 'Jean towards me', etc. It can also be useful in work with couples to ask the clients to do a grid from their own perspective, and then to do another grid imagining how they think their partner would complete his or her grid (Ryle & Breen, 1972). Another extension of the dyad technique is to elicit constructs and elements from each member of a couple separately, and then pool these in a grid which they both complete (see Winter, 1992). As well as exploring significant features of their individual construing, this technique also indicates the extent to which the couple are able to use each other's constructs and the degree of commonality in their construing. This may be useful when seeing a couple for a risk assessment, or when a man who has commited an incestuous offence is being considered for return to his family. Finally, *self-identity grids* have also been developed for exploring the degree of similarity which an individual perceives between themselves and others (Norris & Makhlouf-Norris, 1976). These have particularly been used with young offenders, for example to operationalise the concept of self-alienation (Lockhart, 1979; Stanley, 1985; see Chapter 5).

There is also nothing intrinsic about the grid procedure which precludes its use with people who have a learning disability. Some modifications may be required, such as using conversational approaches to elicit constructs or presenting the elements in an additional visual way. Fransella & Bannister (1977) review studies which have used modifications of grids with people with a learning disability, and Davis & Cunningham (1985) describe the use of the PCP perspective in clinical work with this client group.

THE USE OF REPERTORY GRIDS TO MEASURE CHANGE

Repertory grids have been used with offender populations both as a measure of the effectiveness of a treatment intervention *per se* (Norris, 1977, 1983; Beckett et al., 1994), and also as a measure of short- and long-term change in an individual client undergoing treatment (Shorts, 1985; Hoskyns, 1988). There are a number of advantages of using repertory grids to measure change and evaluate therapeutic outcome. Winter (1985) notes that any appropriate instrument for such a task ideally needs to combine objectivity of scoring and sensitivity to psychological change, with sufficient flexibility to devise individualised outcome criteria relevant to the particular client (or group of clients). He suggests that the grid technique meets these criteria particularly well, with a range of methods for manual and computer scoring of individual grids (as outlined earlier), and techniques also available for the comparison of pairs or groups of grids (See Appendix V). The idiographic nature of grids and their immense flexibility are further advantages for their use as a tool to measure therapeutic change. Furthermore, it is difficult for clients to complete a grid in order to secure a particular result, i.e. to fake either good or bad. The versatility of grids is seen by the wealth of research literature on their use as an outcome measure for individual, group, marital and behavioural therapies, as well as for hospital and medical treatment regimes (see Winter, 1992). However, there are limitations in the use of grids for the purpose of evaluating treatment programmes with groups of clients. Bailey & Sims (1991) note that studies which report grid measures averaged over a study population may overlook the existence of subgroups in the population. Of course, this is a risk with any uncritical use of univariate group comparisons, but the problems may be greater with grids than with more conventional measures precisely because of the grid's capacity to reveal complex individual differences. Linked with this issue, similar grids have to be administered to all the subjects, in order for standard measures of change to be compared, usually those relating to the *structure* of their construing. The essentially idiographic nature of grids means that more information about changes in the *content* of construing after treatment, can be obtained when they are designed and used to measure change in a specific individual. The use of grids to measure change in an individual's pattern of construing is therefore also more in keeping with the theory of personal constructs.

Grid Measures of Therapeutic Change

A wide range of measures have been derived from repertory grids over the years. Clinicians wanting to measure therapeutic change for research purposes are referred to Winter (1992), where these are outlined in detail, and specific computer programs which measure change are described in Appendix V. However, for the clinical purpose of examining an individual client's grid for change, the following indicators are usually sufficient, and are illustrated in greater detail in the case examples in Part II.

Changes in the Structure of an Offender's Construct System

1. *Nature of the discriminative constructs.* The formulation of new discriminative constructs is one of the most difficult therapeutic changes to achieve, since it involves changing the whole way in which the client perceives the world. When this does occur it is very satisfying for both the clinician and the client, as corresponding behaviour change is usually accompanying. Such change can be directly observed from the plot of a grid. Alternatively, depending on the computer analysis used, data may be provided about the extent to which a construct differentiates between elements, and therefore of its usefulness. For example, in the INGRID programme (Slater, 1972), this information is obtained from the score labelled 'variation about the construct mean'. A clear example of an offender client whose discriminative constructs changed following treatment, is discussed in detail in Chapter 7 (Sex Offenders).
2. *Cognitive complexity/tightness and looseness of the construct system.* These two measures are considered together, since, as discussed earlier in the chapter, there is considerable overlap between them.

If the grid is analysed by a computer program, the percentage of variation accounted for by the first component gives a rough indication of the cognitive complexity or sophistication of the client's construct system. This may be particularly relevant in therapeutic work with personality disordered offenders, who often have very cognitively simple, 'all or nothing' ways of construing the world (see Chapter 8). Tightness of construing (i.e. inflexibility) has also been a particular focus in grid studies of change and a predictor of outcome in the treatment of people with alcohol problems (Hoy, 1977; Bailey & Sims, 1991). The evidence suggests that successful treatment is associated with a general loosening of construing.

3. *Correlations between constructs.* This can either be observed directly from the plot or measured from a computer output which includes a table of this information. Changes of particular interest are those which relate to previous inconsistency or conflict, or to the client's offending behaviour.

Changes in the Content of an Offender's Construct System

Clinicians more commonly report changes in the content, rather than the structure, of a client's construct system. This is because the latter changes, as outlined above, are often more substantial and take longer to achieve. Although therefore in treatment the aim may be to achieve changes in both the structure and content of an offender client's pattern of construing, initial changes will probably consist of the way self and significant others are construed within the same overall structure.

1. *Construing of the self.* As with the structural measures, changes in the content of construing can be observed directly from the plot and discussed with the client, or more objective data taken from the table of 'distances between elements' if there is a computer print-out. However, it is important not to assume that a decrease in the distance between self and ideal necessarily represents an increase in self-esteem. As Norris (1977) described, it could also represent a lowering of the ideals previously aspired to, and should be checked out by referring back to the original ratings. Similarly, Arnold (1988) demonstrated that global self-esteem (measured by an adapted Rosenberg Self Esteem Scale) correlates with, but is not identical to, the discrepancy between actual self and ideal self on a repertory grid. However, he noted that the grid measure gives more detail about the person's self-concept than the Rosenberg measure (Rosenberg, 1965), and its use might therefore be preferable in diagnosis and evaluation.

2. *Construing of others*. Changes can be directly observed from the grid or from the table of distances between elements, for example, comparing the distance between a victim and a liked person.

3. *The formulation of new constructs*. The formulation of new constructs represents a fundamental change in a person's construct system, even if they are not discriminative. This is why repeating an elicitation procedure with the client following an intervention can be important, rather than simply repeating the 'pre-treatment' grid.

The above indicators of change are useful in the clinical setting with clients in an informal way, to examine change after an intervention. However, Winter (1985) raises a note of caution, particularly if the clinician wants to use the technique for an outcome study. For example, although studies have generally shown a high degree of stability in grid measures (Sperlinger, 1976), changes have also been demonstrated in untreated control groups (Koch, 1983). Even if the clinician/researcher predicts grid measures that are likely to accompany successful treatment and those that are not likely to change, problems may still occur. This is because the clinician's own construct system may influence how they interpret that of their client and thus reduce reliability. If a clinician wants to use a grid as an experimental outcome measure, it should be independent of the treatment procedure (i.e. only used to evaluate therapy, not to plan it) and ideally use standardised guidelines for the prediction of change (see Winter, 1985).

Finally, individualised predictors of change can also be used for *group* experimental designs. However, the researcher also has to decide whether to standardise the grid measures by using the same supplied constructs and elements for each client, or to allow the grids to be more personally meaningful by using elicited constructs. The former design allows for greater comparative analysis, but loses important information about the nature of individual clients' construing. Without using elicited constructs both before and after treatment, it is also not possible to assess whether the client has formulated new constructs, a reflection of a more fundamental change. A compromise may be to supply a few constructs which are a particular focus of the study, but allow for the eliciting of the rest (e.g. Norris, 1977, 1983; Shorts, 1985; Houston & Adshead, 1993).

THE RELIABILITY AND VALIDITY OF REPERTORY GRIDS

In relation to the repertory grid, Fransella & Bannister (1977) point out that the multiplicity of forms of grid means it does not make sense to talk about *the* reliability of *the* grid, any more than it would to talk about *the* reliability of *the* questionnaire. Furthermore, the nature of the changing construct system means that grids are not necessarily expected to show the same result over repeated presentations. None the less, for methodological rigour, it is important to know what aspects of the grid might be expected to change, and which scores show greater stability.

The general findings from the research have indicated that there is similarity in the constructs elicited from individuals over two occasions, even when different elements are used (Sperlinger, 1976). Early studies showed test–retest correlations of around 0.8 (Bonarius, 1965), but later reviews have indicated that although average reliabilities are usually quite high, there is a wide range (Fransella, 1981). Another area of investigation has been the comparison of elicited and supplied constructs. After reviewing the research, Winter (1992) concluded that, at least with individuals who are considered to have some kind of psychological difficulties, only the use of elicited constructs will provide a truly accurate picture of the characteristics of their construct system. This is, of course, consistent with Kelly's Individuality Corollary and the essence of Personal Construct Psychology. However, Warr & Coffman (1970) concluded that, by careful selection of constructs, it was possible to obtain a set of supplied constructs which had similar meaning for the individual as their own personal constructs.

Research has also focused on the stability of different structural features of construing on different occasions. In a large cross-cultural study, Feixas et al. (1992) investigated the reliability and convergence of several structural measures derived from grids, including percentage of variation accounted for by the first component, cognitive complexity, self–ideal discrepancy and self–other discrepancy. The scores showed high test–retest reliability for periods of up to one month, with the average modal reliability coefficient being 0.85. Although the percentage variation score was one of the least reliable, the average stability coefficient was still 0.67. Feixas et al. (1992) also observed a systematic tightening effect across subsequent administrations, and suggested that the very completion of a repertory grid may help to clarify the implicit predictions in a person's construct system. This effect has also been found when the person has gained experience or relevant information about the elements (Bodden & James, 1976), and after a single assessment for psychodynamic psychotherapy (Tibbles, 1992).

There are certainly individual differences in the stability of people's construing. Studies have suggested that a person's construing may be more unstable at certain times, such as when undergoing psychotherapy, when given feedback of grid results, and during childhood and adolescence (see Winter's 1992 review). With some individuals, it is therefore possible to predict the stability of their grid scores and of certain constructs. In addition, because one's construing of objects tends to be more predictable than that of people, physical constructs such as 'Tall vs Short' tend to be more stable than psychological constructs such as 'Kind vs Unkind'. In fact, it would be rather strange if there were not these differences in stability. This is consistent with Slater's (1969) suggestion of including 'control' elements and constructs in the grid, on which little or no change would be expected, and with which the 'experimental' elements and constructs can therefore be compared.

A number of studies have also examined the ability of grid measures to predict aspects of individuals' behaviour. Although most of the research has used one of the different measures of cognitive complexity, there are still conflicting findings about the relationship between this measure and an individual's communicative abilities (O'Keefe & Syfer, 1981). However, there is evidence that it is possible to predict, on the basis of a grid, the decisions and choices which a person is likely to make (e.g. Cannell, 1985). This is consistent with Kelly's (1955/1991) proposal that the choices which people make are shaped by the characteristics of their construct system. Other studies have found differences in the construing of male and female children and adults (e.g. Landfield, 1971; Neimeyer & Metzler, 1987). The ability of the grid to differentiate between subjects from different cultures also indicates 'the potential value of using the relatively culture-fair methodology of the repertory grid to assess subtle differences in social cognition that result from distinctive socialization practices in different societies' (Feixas et al., 1992, p. 37).

SUMMARY AND CONCLUSIONS

This chapter provides a step by step account of the design, administration, analysis and interpretation of repertory grids. Used properly, grids can provide an illuminating insight into the way in which an individual construes the world. The advantages of using grids to measure change in therapy include their versatility in addressing issues which are particularly pertinent to an individual client, the difficulty a client has in faking either good or bad, and the provision of a visual indicator of change which can be discussed with the client and other professionals. However, if the technique is used in isolation from the theory of personal constructs, it merely becomes a channel for the clinician to impose their own way of construing on the client. It is therefore important to choose the elements and elicit constructs in such a way as to accurately reflect the nature of the client's construing. Readers who are new to PCP and repertory grids may want to re-read this chapter several times and look at some of the case examples in Part II, to become familiar with the range of new concepts involved.

Clinical Applications of Personal Construct Psychology with Offenders

The second part of this book moves from focusing on the theory and practice of PCP with offenders in general to addressing the issues which are more specific to different client groups. Although personal construct theorists do not usually use traditional nosological categories to describe clients, these have been retained for ease of communication and because the areas of commonality in the construing of different offender groups are of interest as well as the individual differences.

Each chapter in Part II follows a similar structure. The PCP perspective on each of the different types of offenders is outlined and the research or clinical literature on patterns of construing is reviewed. Problematic behaviours can result either from disorders of the *structure* of the construct system (e.g. if the construct system is too tight or too loose) or from a socially deviant *content* (e.g. the way in which the person construes themselves, other people and their behaviour). Case examples are used to illustrate both the variety of personal meanings of offending to that client group and the implications of the PCP perspective for assessment and treatment.

The chapters in Part II highlight the way in which different aspects of construing are relevant to the understanding (and therefore the treatment) of different types of offender clients, although there is inevitably some overlap between chapters. The content of their construct system appears to be particularly important in the development and maintenance of the offending of some individuals, such as young offenders, or those who have committed sexual or habitually violent offences (see Chapters 5, 6, 7). For other individuals, such as those diagnosed with a personality disorder, the whole structure of their construct system appears to validate their offending (see Chapter 8). In addition, within any group of offender clients, it appears that it is those whose construing is cognitively simple (and therefore similar to those described as personality disordered) who may have a poorer prognosis. Finally, for other offenders there may be a complex interaction between longstanding or premorbid patterns of construing and the effects of a mental illness or intoxicated state on the process of construing (see Chapters 9, 10), and with such clients it is particularly important to identify the relevant contribution of these different factors.

CHAPTER 5

Young Offenders and Delinquency

Adolescence is a time in which normal developmental changes in construing occur, particularly in the way in which one's self is construed. However there is evidence that young offenders show different patterns of self-construing compared to those who do not offend, particularly in relation to their self-identity. The research on patterns of construing in young offenders is reviewed, and the implications of the PCP perspective for assessment and treatment are discussed. Case examples are used to illustrate the advantages of both the client-centred philosophy of PCP and the structured techniques available for the exploration of personal construing, in working with a client group that can often be difficult to engage and who may have difficulty in verbal expression and communication.

INTRODUCTION

McMurran & Hollin (1993) define a young offender as 'a person within legally prescribed age limits, not suffering from mental disorder, who commits an act capable of being followed by criminal proceedings' (p.2). This definition excludes those whose behaviour is conduct-disordered, but not necessarily illegal (such as bullying), and does not require the young person to have been caught. In practice, the distinction between a 'young' and an 'adult' offender is usually made at the age of 18 years, and the term 'delinquency' is usually used to refer to criminal activity which is perpetrated by adolescents.

Offending in adolescents peaks at around the age of 16–17 years (Wolfgang et al., 1987), accounted for by a rise in the number of offences committed by new offenders. There is also a relationship between juvenile and adult crime, with those individuals who receive convictions at an early age (10–12 years) being most likely to continue offending into adulthood. However, the large amount of undetected and unreported crime makes it difficult to assess exactly what proportion of adolescents commit offences. The research literature estimates that over 80% of adolescents commit an offence of some type, and notes that this figure would be higher if unrecorded offences were included (McMurran & Hollin, 1993). However, this figure includes both status offences (i.e. those which only apply to adolescents, such as under-age drinking) and index or notifiable offences, which are serious offences regardless of the age of the perpetrator (such as burglary, theft and assault). Farrington (1992) suggests that *most* young offenders do not commit serious index offences. This was also illustrated by West's (1982) study examining offending among 14-year-old boys, in which the rates of minor offending (e.g. criminal damage) were much higher than those for the more serious offences (e.g. using weapons in fights). Although most adolescents therefore commit a criminal act at some point, whether or not this leads to a court appearance depends on the nature and seriousness of that offence (McMurran & Hollin, 1993). Adolescents who engage in minor vandalism and petty theft are less likely to receive convictions than those engaged in car theft, serious assault and breaking and entering (West & Farrington, 1977). Even those adolescents who commit sexual offences are not always prosecuted, and issues pertaining to their own offending are not always separated from those of their own victimisation. However, with those young offenders who do make it into rehabilitation programmes, the work of Ross and colleagues (Ross & Fabiano, 1985; Ross et al., 1988; Izzo & Ross, 1990) means that the importance of addressing their thinking ability and content is now widely acknowledged.

THE PCP PERSPECTIVE ON YOUNG OFFENDING AND DELINQUENCY

Normal developmental changes in construing occur throughout childhood and adolescence. The main feature of change during childhood is an increase in the *organisation* of the construct system, with constructs becoming more complex and logical, and increasingly more psychological than physical (Salmon, 1976). During adolescence, studies have shown that the central changes in construing occur in the way in which one's *self* is construed. Self-esteem tends to be lower in mid-adolescence, compared to early and late teenage years, and at this mid-point there is also less identification of the self and ideal self with others (Strachan & Jones, 1982). In later adolescence, Carr & Townes (1975) showed that an increase in differentiation of the self from others occurs, until early adulthood when this begins to decrease.

As discussed in Chapter 1, theoretical attempts to understand deviancy from the PCP perspective have focused primarily on the role of the self-concept in the development of delinquent behaviour. Both Brennan (1992) and D. Kelly (1992) suggest that an individual behaves in a deviant way because that is consistent with their view of themself, a view which is compatible with other approaches that relate delinquency to the enhancement of self-esteem (Kaplan, 1980) and the choice of a rational social identity (Reicher & Emler, 1986). Although, there is no evidence for a consistent causal link between self-concept and delinquency in general, for some individuals it may be a very important contributor to the development and maintenance of their offending. PCP studies of young offenders have therefore put particular emphasis on understanding the nature of their self-construing, in terms of both self-concept or identity, as well as self-esteem. Stanley (1985) uses the concept of alienation to describe the ways in which the self-construing of young offenders may differ from non-offenders. Alienation is a term usually used in the field of social psychology to describe attitudes relating to the self and social environment. *Social alienation* refers to feelings of estrangement which may be experienced in relation to other people, particularly significant others. *Self alienation* is another way of conceptualising low self-esteem, and refers to feelings of separation which can occur between aspects of one's identity, particularly actual self and ideal self. Both of these concepts can be measured using element distances from a repertory grid in which the elements include actual, ideal and social self, as well as other significant individuals (Lockhart, 1979; Stanley, 1985). Studies which have explored the nature of construing in young offenders are outlined below.

PATTERNS OF CONSTRUING IN YOUNG OFFENDERS

The Structure of the Construct System

As discussed in the earlier chapters, one of the main structural features of construing which can lead to difficulties in social relating is that of *cognitive simplicity*, i.e. the tendency to construe the world in a unidimensional, 'all or nothing' way. If a person's way of construing the world is very simplistic, they are not able to anticipate subtle discriminations in social behaviour and interpersonal relationships. This is then likely to hinder these individuals in their development and maintenance of social relationships. Using repertory grids, Hayden et al. (1977) found that there was a significant relationship between the adaptive social behaviour of boys in a residential treatment centre and their degree of predictive accuracy and cognitive complexity and in construing. The more differentiated the constructs were within the construct system of an emotionally disturbed boy, the more appropriate was that boy's behaviour in social situations. The more accurate a boy was at predicting the sequence of another person's behaviour, the more appropriate their behaviour was in social situations in general. These abilities were unrelated to either overall intelligence, or the separate ability to develop abstract concepts. Having a poor ability to anticipate and discriminate between social situations may therefore contribute to the rapid oscillations in social predictions, behaviour, friendship patterns and affective state often seen in this client group.

Grids were also used by Heather (1979) to examine the structure of delinquent values, in a study based on the argument of Matza & Sykes (1961) that there *is* similarity between the values of delinquents and those who conform. The findings suggested that there was an equivalent structure in the value systems of delinquent and non-delinquent adolescents, in that both groups of individuals possessed 'conventional' and 'subterranean' values. In his conclusion, Heather (1979) therefore hypothesised that the probability of delinquent acts being committed was a function of the relative strengths of dominant and subterranean sets of values. Some delinquents whose 'subterranean' sets of values are dominant may consciously commit themselves to delinquency. However for others, Sykes & Matza's (1957) 'techniques of neutralisation' (see Chapter 1) may be relevant in understanding how such individuals construe their offending in ways which enable them to legitimise this.

Construing of the Self

Consistent with the wider research literature, repertory grid studies of young offenders have also demonstrated that they have lower *self-esteem* and poorer self-image, compared to non-offenders (Noble, 1971; Jackson, 1992). However, the main aspect of young offenders' self-construing to have been studied, is the notion of their *self-identity*, i.e. the role models and individuals with whom they identify. Repertory grid studies are consistent with the early research on the role of parental deprivation in the aetiology of delinquency (Rutter, 1969), with the implication that the parents of delinquents are often poor and inconsistent role models (Miller & Treacher, 1981). In a grid study of delinquent boys, Noble (1971) found that the young offenders both perceived themselves as less like (and wanted to be less like) their fathers, compared to the non-offenders. This supported Noble's (1971) hypothesis that there would be a lack of a suitable male identification figure for the delinquent boys. Similar results were found for a lack of perceived similarity to their best friends, who were not always those with whom delinquent acts were committed. Whereas the non-delinquents wanted to be more like fathers and best friends than television heroes, the reverse was true for the delinquents. Noble suggests that the results support the hypothesis that criminal identification may occur through positive reference to criminal roles portrayed on the media, when warm relationships inside the family do not strengthen the identification with appropriate role models.

To be more in keeping with the theory of personal constructs, the above study was replicated by Miller & Treacher (1981) using elicited rather than supplied constructs. These authors then carried out a second study using a larger sample of people as elements, to try to clarify the nature of the delinquents' 'poor social anchorage' (i.e. lack of identificatory role models within the family). The delinquents perceived the adults around them (i.e. parents, teachers) to be less adequate role models than did the controls. Although the delinquents saw themselves as being more like the adults at the time of the study, they wished to be less like them in the future. However, the reverse was true for their identification with the television heroes, indicating the salience of these fantasy figures as role models for the delinquents, compared to the real adults in their lives. In terms of comparison with their ideal self, the delinquents wanted to be more like the character of a tough policeman, who used skills as a fighter to succeed, whereas the non-delinquents wanted to be more like a scientist character, who used his intellectual skills. Miller & Treacher suggest that, as the non-delinquents are more likely to have a well differentiated personal construct system (following Hayden et al., 1977), they can use their 'scientific' predictive skills to anticipate the behaviour of the scientist, and identify with him. In contrast, the policeman ignored interpersonal skills and solved problems by 'direct action', which the delinquents may find easier to anticipate. The authors question whether the delinquents had been exposed to family and other social situations that lacked adult figures who used 'reasoning' methods for solving problems.

An absence of positive role models was also observed in two individual case studies of young offenders using the PCP perspective. Lockhart (1979) administered self-identity plots to a 15-year-old boy, Jimmy, at admission to and discharge from a residential treatment unit. He had been charged with a number of offences, including burglary and arson, and had experienced a disruptive childhood with parental conflict at home. On admission Jimmy identified his actual self most closely with two boys who were described by him as 'a delinquent' and 'a truant', and as significantly unlike his parents and a disliked teacher. His ideal self was considerably isolated on the plot, close to no other elements, and also at a distance from the element of 'delinquent'. His ideal self was therefore identified in terms of who he did *not* want to be like, rather than in terms of any positive role models. Lockhart suggests that the persistence of Jimmy's delinquent behaviour throughout his teenage years may partly have been explained by the fact that, although he indicated some desire to change his delinquent lifestyle (i.e. his ideal self was at some distance from the 'delinquent' element), he had no one on whom to model his ideal self. He spent time in counselling exploring his relationship with his father, leading to a clearer understanding of the figure on whom to model his ideal self. At discharge he construed himself as more similar to non-delinquent family members, which was seen as encouraging for prognosis. This was validated at follow-up two and a half years later, at which point he had received no further convictions.

Stanley (1985) also administered a self-identity grid to a teenage boy, David, who was admitted to a Young Offenders Unit after having assaulted a young girl and stolen underwear from a clothes line. David was unwilling to discuss his offences and was virtually mute with staff for several months. The grid indicated that David construed no other individual as similar to either his actual or ideal self. In other words, similar to the case example described above by Lockhart (1979), David 'knows what he is not, but cannot identify what he is; he knows what he does not want to be, but not what he wishes to become' (Stanley, 1985, p. 56). The main therapeutic approach taken with David during his stay on the unit involved exploring this perceived sense of social isolation, and an improvement in a range of social and communicative abilities was gradually noted. A second grid was administered just over a year later, in which a variety of other individuals were perceived as more similar to both his actual and ideal self. Although there is no further information about whether David reoffended in the future, Stanley suggested that admission to the unit, which had a high staff ratio and a peer group with whom he was in close proximity, appears to have begun to alter David's pronounced social isolation in a positive way.

There is therefore consistent evidence to suggest that the construing of many young offenders reflects a lack of positive role models, and that their self-identity is either defined in terms of deviancy, or in terms of what they do *not* want to be like. However, this clearly does not hold true in every case. For example, Miller & Treacher (1981) found that brothers of delinquents often emerged as salient role models, biographical data indicating that often the brother had often 'escaped' from the delinquent's family system, having a job or owning a car.

Finally, in a more recent study of the self-construing of adolescents, Jackson (1992) also found differences between those described as problematic (those who had been cautioned by the police or convicted of a criminal offence, or had contact with the psychiatric, social work or educational psychology service) and those who fitted none of the range of problem criteria. The 'problematic' group had both lower self-esteem and lower 'good psychologist' scores on their self-characterisations (i.e. the measure which indicates how able they were to construe themselves in psychological, as opposed to behavioural or physical, terms; see Chapter 2). Problematic individuals were less popular with their peers, and were seen by their peers as hard to understand. Jackson (1992) concluded that those adolescents who find it hard to understand themselves and others may get into a vicious circle of increasing difficulty in self-construing. A sense of self is necessary for effective social interaction with others, as this helps to make sense of and reflect on one's social experiences. An initial difficulty in making sense of one's self may make it harder to see other people's points of view. Such a person may then become isolated and unpopular, and therefore experience further difficulty in self-construing.

Construing of Others

Unlike the offending of some other client groups (e.g. sex offenders, violent offenders), that of delinquents is not usually targeted against any particular victim group. For example, with car theft, the purpose of the offence is usually that of 'borrowing' the car for a short joy-ride, rather than permanently depriving the owner (Kelly & Taylor, 1981). There has therefore been no research into the ways in which delinquents construe the victims of their offences. The hypothesis would be that, similar to other offenders, they construe other people in ways which legitimise their own behaviour. However, an important finding to emerge from studies of the construing of young offenders, is that they often have difficulty in understanding other people and predicting their behaviour. As discussed earlier, Hayden et al. (1977) suggested that this difficulty results from a unidimensional, cognitively simple construct system. Their study found that those delinquent boys who had difficulty predicting the sequence of another person's behaviour, showed more social and behavioural problems. This finding was supported by Jackson's (1992) study, in which problematic adolescents were less accurate in their predictions about others' views of them, compared to the control group. Miller & Treacher (1981) also concluded that the delinquents' preference for 'exciting' action heroes as role models indicated that they have difficulty in understanding and identifying with real adults. They interpreted the non-delinquents' preference for comedians as favourite television characters as evidence that, in contrast to the delinquents, they *were* able to construe the socially perceptive constructions of the comedians.

The Meaning of Delinquent Behaviour

The above studies have so far focused on understanding the way in which the construing of young offenders is different from that of those adolescents who do not offend. However, it is also important to explore how their pattern of construing contributes to the personal meaning of delinquency to young offenders. Kelly & Taylor (1981) describe an idiographic use of the PCP approach to understand the personal meaning of car theft for individual young offenders. Car theft is the biggest single category in recorded juvenile crime, and the authors describe a cycle of 'frustration at not being able to drive–offending–disqualification–frustration' that makes this type of deviance particularly resistant to change. They used the method of serial deviant case analysis to explore a number of factors thought to be relevant to car theft. This technique involves forming and amending hypotheses to account for all instances of the phenomenon in each of a number of cases studied. The standard repertory grid administered to each of four young offenders consisted of supplied elements of standard situations (e.g. 'Before I saw the car', 'Getting caught', 'Something that makes me feel excited/powerful/grown-up' and constructs elicited by the usual triad method.

Over the course of their case studies the authors formed the hypothesis that drivers were not a unitary group in their perception of car theft. For example, for the first boy, 19-year-old David, who had convictions for car theft dating back to the age of 15 years, driving a stolen car was strongly identified with 'winning a fight', the situation which he nominated as making him feel powerful. His offence pattern was to take a car and deliberately drive past a parked police car. He saw himself as involved in a personal battle with particular police officers, and intended to prove his power by getting away with the theft or losing the police in a car chase. Car theft for David therefore served to validate feelings of power in himself by 'emerging unscathed from a risk-taking situation'. Alternatively, for a number of other boys, car theft served the purpose of reducing their usual actual/ideal self discrepancy, as it was something that they were good at doing and made them feel powerful.

Interestingly, not all young offenders in the above study construed car theft as a positive experience. The main discriminating factor was whether or not they had ever got home safely without being caught. Those who had reached home safely at least once, construed their behaviour in positive terms, and the experience served to reduce the discrepancy between their actual and ideal self. However, both those who were illegal passengers in stolen cars and those who had never reached home safely, construed the experience negatively. No one situational element was consistently associated with driving the stolen car. Not suprisingly, it appeared that car theft met different needs for different individuals, for example gaining a feeling of power or social prestige, or finding excitement, and Kelly & Taylor (1981) conclude that the behaviour can only be fully understood within the context of each individual's self-image.

The following case examples illustrate the variety of meanings of delinquency for young offenders, and the different ways in which these relate to their self-concept.

Philip, a 17-year-old boy, was seen for a psychological assessment before appearing in court, having been charged with breaking and entering and theft from shops. He had numerous previous convictions for similar offences, dating from the age of 15 years. The unusual feature of Philip's offending was that he always left a 'calling card' in the building. Philip was the youngest of three children from a professional family, and was the only family member to have got into trouble with the police. Both his family and previous professionals had found it difficult to make sense of Philip's repeated offending. In the clinical interview, Philip described how he took pride in leaving his 'card' in places that he had broken into, as if to say 'I've done it again...I've beaten your security system'. However, although the form of his offending meant that he could always easily be identified as its instigator, Philip maintained that he did not care about getting caught. From the PCP perspective therefore, Philip was not behaving in an irrational way, but rather in a way which continued to lead to predictive certainty; he offended, got caught and convicted, usually received a probation order, and then several months later, reoffended and the whole cycle started again. It was therefore important to understand what the meaning of the theft was to Philip, and why this was more important than the consequences of getting caught. It soon became clear in the interview that although Philip currently saw himself as 'the black sheep of the family', this had not always been the case. Philip described an idyllic childhood, being close both to his parents and to his siblings, with frequent family outings and holidays. This began to change when his two older siblings left home and his parents began to have difficulties in their relationship. A repertory grid, in which the elements consisted mainly of Philip and his family at different points in his life, indicated that important constructs elicited by Philip were 'Close to family vs Not close to family', 'Treats others as an equal vs Treats others as a child', 'Independent vs Dependent' and 'Argumentative vs Not argumentative'. He construed his 'current self' as argumentative and dependent, with his 'ideal' and his 'offending self' being the opposite to this. He construed all his family members as being less close to the family than they had been previously, and his parents also as more argumentative. The grid contributed to a hypothesis about Philip's offending, which was that, following the departure of his siblings from the family home and the apparent deterioration in his parents' relationship, his offending represented an attempt by him both to exert his own independence and also to unite his parents in concern about his behaviour. Although Philip did not express concern about his offending, he was distressed at the changes in his family relationships over the past few years, and both he and his parents agreed to start family therapy.

Winter (1992) described the case of a school prefect, John, who was well thought of at school and church, until he broke into the church hall one night and burnt it down. His repertory grid indicated that he dissociated himself from his fire-setting, seeing himself as the least likely to commit arson of all the elements in the grid (see Figure 5.1). However, committing arson was associated with a range of other constructs, and implied being 'inferior', a 'loudmouth', 'muddled', 'resenting authority', and 'struggling to achieve'. Winter notes that these implications provided a basis for exploring whether John harboured unexpressed resentment towards authority, and found his school work more of a struggle than his teachers imagined. The grid did not include the elements of ideal and social self, but from what is known about John's construing, one would hypothesise that there would be a marked discrepancy between his actual self and self seen by others.

The implications of different delinquent activities were also explored in a case example described by Ravenette (1977). Joseph, a 15-year-old boy, had been in trouble with the police for breaking into houses and 'going equipped to steal'. Joseph construed delinquent activities in terms of those that were 'aggressive', 'unthinking', 'adolescent' acts (e.g. vandalism, GBH), compared to those

CATTY AND BITCHY UNANXIOUS	CLEAR THINKER SUPERIOR
	UNLIKELY TO COMMIT ARSON
UNSOCIABLE	MEMBER OF A RELIGIOUS GROUP
MISERABLE	
NOT AS I'D LIKE TO BE	RESPECTS AUTHORITY
SEXUALLY	
FRUSTRATED Girl I	Headmaster
Dislike	
	Mother Religious Group
	Leader
UNLIKE ME	Girl I Like NOT STRUGGLING
	TO ACHIEVE
DOESN'T THINK ABOUT	DOESN'T MAKE ME
WHAT THEY'RE SAYING	ANGRY

	Self
MAKES ME ANGRY Disliked	Scout Leader INTROVERTED
STRUGGLING TO Teacher	Man I Admire LIKE ME
ACHIEVE	
Person Who Would	
Commit Arson	Father SEXUALLY SATISFIED
	HAS STRAIGHT-
	FORWARD
	HUMOUR
DOESN'T RESPECT AUTHORITY	AS I'D LIKE TO BE
	GOOD AT SPORTS AND ANYTHING
	THEY DO
UNLIKELY TO BE RELIGIOUS	
GROUP MEMBER	
LIKELY TO COMMIT ARSON	WORRIER HAS FEELING
INFERIOR MUDDLED	TOWARDS OTHERS

Figure 5.1. Plot of elements in construct space from John's grid. Reproduced by permission from Winter, D. A. (1992) Personal Construct Psychology in Clinical Practice: Theory, Research and Applications. London, Routledge

which were 'crafty' and 'near professional' (e.g. housebreaking, receiving stolen goods). Joseph identified himself with activities that linked the two clusters together (i.e. truanting, taking and driving away). Ravenette suggests that this indicated that he was at a choice point in his delinquent life, between growing out of delinquency on the one hand, and a life of professional delinquency on the other.

APPLICATIONS OF PCP ASSESSMENT WITH YOUNG OFFENDERS

Although the extent to which all offenders see themselves as having a problem varies, there is a particular tendency for adolescents to be construed by adults as having a problem, and the young person themself may not construe events in the same way. Ravenette (1977, 1992), who has worked primarily using the PCP perspective with children and adolescents, notes that it is not possible to make much progress with clients unless they can be persuaded to talk about themselves, and that interview techniques should be structured to make it easy for a young person to respond. Ravenette (1977) therefore describes a number of principles for interviewing young people to facilitate their engagement in the interview. These are derived from his work with delinquent boys and assume that the boys are fairly willing and able to talk about their delinquency. These techniques are all based around the concept of 'troubles', which can be used to represent their delinquency, or the way in which *other people* are a trouble to them, or their inner feelings. The line of questioning is outlined in Figure 5.2. The young person is oriented to the task by being reminded of the way in which other people say, 'The trouble with that boy is . . . '. He or she is then invited to say what they consider, *from their own point of view*, the trouble with different people might be. It is important to check out that the person is giving their own view, and not just repeating what adults say. Ravenette emphasises that if the young person cannot give an answer or denies that they have any trouble with some of the individuals, then that is acceptable, and is in itself useful information.

In a more recent article, Ravenette (1992) described the use of the PCP approach in his work in a regional assessment centre for adolescent boys, which included a small secure unit. His role as the educational psychologist in the team was to carry out 'one-off' assessment interviews, and he describes how using a PCP framework can be useful

1.   The trouble with most ... (mothers/fathers/bosses) is ...

2.   They are like that because ...

3.   Another reason they are like that is ...

4.   It would be better if ...

5.   What difference would that make? ...

6.   What difference would that make to you? ...

Figure 5.2. The elaboration of young offenders' complaints (Ravenette, 1977)

for the young person involved. An important part of the assessment interview is how the young person sees him/herself, and Ravenette describes three techniques which he uses to elicit meaningful personal responses and structure the interview. First, he suggests asking for three answers to a question, rather than just one. This allows for the fact that there may be more than one answer to the question. This technique means that the client does not have to struggle to find the 'right' answer, and also dissuades them from giving a superficial pat response. Secondly, Ravenette asks for a contrast to what has been said, such as 'How would you describe a person who is not like that?' This allows for further exploration of the underlying construct. Thirdly, he asks for the importance or relevance of an observation in the life of the young person, and then pursues that. The basic question 'Is that important to you?' is thus followed by 'and that?' . . . 'and that?'. The 'experiments' on which these answers are based (in PCP terms) is then sought by asking 'How come?'. The purpose of these techniques is to lead to some clarification of how the young person makes sense of things, and to help the client put into words what may have been ill formulated. This can also be facilitated by suggesting hypotheses that attempt to make meaningful links between some of the interview material. Feeding back the assessment to colleagues should enable them to communicate more easily with the adolescent, as they should have a greater understanding of the young person's own perspective.

IMPLICATIONS FOR ASSESSMENT AND TREATMENT

Jackson (1992) clearly describes how the PCP assessment of young offenders complements the nomothetic assessment. She notes that those who work with young offenders will have access to comprehensive information about the client's presenting offence, their childhood history, education, social and work record. Assessment will lead to hypotheses about the motivation for their offending, and how this relates to their experiences. However, this process of assessment may not fully contribute to an understanding of the client's self-concept, their ways of making sense of the world and relating to others. Jackson (1992) suggests that the PCP approach and techniques for understanding construing can enhance the assessment of young offenders by understanding the structures and strategies that the client uses to interact with and make sense of their world. Suggested elements and constructs to use in repertory grids with young offenders are illustrated in Figures 5.3 and 5.4. Specific issues to consider are outlined below.

Self now

Self as a child

Ideal self

Self when offending

Mother

Father

Brother/Sister

Friend who also offends

Friend who does not offend

Authority figure, e.g. teacher/boss

Figure 5.3. Suggested elements to use with young offenders

How Does the Client Construe Themself?

The way in which a young offender construes themself is a crucial aspect of the assessment. As well as exploring differences between actual, offending and ideal self, it is important to note the figures with whom the young person identifies, and whom they would wish to be like. Some clients may be 'socially alienated', perceiving both their current and ideal 'selves' as isolated from other people, and having no role models at all. Others may see themselves as similar to someone with a deviant identity, or dissociate themselves from their offending by perceiving themselves as dissimilar from deviant others. If any non-deviant individuals are seen as similar to their ideal self, this can be a useful focus in treatment.

How Do They Construe Others?

It is useful to assess how both delinquent and non-delinquent peers are construed, and explore these differences in treatment. Although the *victims* of delinquents are often unknown or never seen by them, it can still be useful to explore their perceptions (i.e. by asking 'What do you think they might be like?'), as their construing may illustrate one of the ways in which the client legitimises their offending.

How Do They Construe Their Behaviour?

The personal meaning of delinquency will clearly vary between individuals, and gaining an understanding of the meaning for the particular

Understands me vs Doesn't understand me

In trouble vs Stays out of trouble

Rash (impulsive) vs Coolheaded

Loves me vs Doesn't love me

Can talk to vs Can't talk to

Can control him/herself vs Can't control him/herself

Quiet vs Argumentative

Knows themselves vs Mixed up

(Stanley, 1985)

I admire vs I don't admire

Like me vs Not like me

Violent vs Not violent

I approve of them vs I don't approve of them

Steals vs Doesn't steal

Successful in life vs Not successful in life

Like I would like to be vs Not like I would like to be

(after Heather, 1979)

Like vs Dislike

Tough vs Weak

Starts fights vs Doesn't start fights

Does good things vs Does bad things

(Miller and Treacher, 1981)

Independent vs Dependent

Close to family vs Not close to family

Respects authority vs Dislikes authority

Listens to others vs Doesn't listen to others

Figure 5.4. Suggested constructs to use in assessment

client is the essence of the PCP approach to assessment. Information from both clinical interviews and specific assessment techniques can inform the clinician about whether the delinquent behaviour is construed in such a way as to validate some aspect of the young person's sense of self (i.e. that they are powerful) or to reduce the discrepancy between their perception of current and ideal self.

Improving Social Predictive Skills

A number of studies have indicated that young offenders are poor at predicting the behaviour of others, which then leads to difficulties in social relationships and interactions. A component of treatment that emphasised perspective taking would therefore appear to be important. In PCP terms, this involves the client learning to construe the constructions of other people. This is consistent with the demonstrated importance of social cognitive skills training in the rehabilitation of offenders (Ross & Fabiano, 1985).

Demonstrating Sociality

For many young people, it may be an unusual experience for them to feel understood by an adult. The PCP approach to assessment invites the young person to think seriously about themselves and their ways of making sense of things. From this, the client may, at the least, become *aware* of the traditional ways in which they have been making sense of the world. A new awareness of habitual choices opens up the possibility of responding in a different way, and of developing alternative ways of construing. Furthermore, if the young offender client perceives the possibility of being understood by others, this may augur well for engagement in treatment and therapeutic change (Ravenette, 1977).

Making Sense of the Client to Others

One of the differences in working with young offenders rather than adults, is that other family members, particularly parents, may be actively involved in contact with the professional services. It is often parents or other professional staff who are concerned about their child's behaviour, and who want to know 'what can be done?'. It is therefore important for adults to understand how the young person is making sense of themselves and events. Ravenette (1977) suggests that when an adult communicates with a child (or young person), if the communication bears no relationship to the child's construction of themself and others, misunderstandings can arise and friction occurs in the relationship. He suggests that a personal construct approach to interviewing should, by definition, lead to the findings of those constructions by which the young person makes sense of themselves and others. The communication of this to adults who are involved with that person, and who may be either complaining about, or struggling to understand them, improves the chances that the young person's outlooks are taken into account.

The following case example illustrates the use of the PCP perspective in the assessment of an adolescent with a long history of delinquent behaviour.

Martin was aged 17 years when he was referred for a psychological assessment by his solicitor, after being charged with theft and domestic burglary. He had received previous probation orders for convictions for breaking and entering, usually reoffending towards the end of his order. There had been increasing concern about his tendency to self-harm, manifested particularly by cutting, and about his strong interest in martial arts, military activities and weapons. Martin had been fostered from the age of four years with a family who looked after a number of children on both short- and long-term placement. Previous reports suggested that he had difficulties in academic work and in making friends at school, and had attended a special boarding school from the age of 11 years.

At interview Martin presented as younger than his years, and found it difficult to talk about himself, and the behaviours which other people were worried about. His responses ranged from complete denial to more concrete statements such as 'I can't talk about it ... I want to forget about it'. He denied that he had harmed himself or that he had any difficulty in getting on with other people, and said that he had lots of friends. However, he became more animated when talking about his interests, such as the army, the police and other emergency services. He said that he often 'daydreamed', and the content of these fantasies appeared to relate either to him being a rescuer (e.g. being a fireman) or being looked after (e.g. jumping in front of traffic and the ambulance service taking him to hospital, escorted by a police car). Mark found it easier to engage with structured assessment techniques, and had no difficulty in writing out a self-characterisation (see Figure 5.5).

Martin's self-characterisation took the form of a list. Interestingly, the content also reflected the themes of his interests and fantasies, and suggested that one of his core role constructs was that he was 'helpful'. His interest in the emergency services was also clearly a defining feature of the way in which he construed himself.

The process of completing a repertory grid was also useful in providing a structured approach to the assessment. Since Martin had said very little about his parents during the interview, they were included in the grid as elements, as was a previous probation

Martin is ...

    Sporty

    Quiet

    Sometimes lazy

    helpful to people (etc.) Dog walkers—Blind people

    Busy

    likes girls more than boys

    likely to watch motorbikes go past or the police

    like watching T.V. etc. Casualty the Bill london's (*sic*) Burning

    Saracon

    Sometimes asleep

    Helpful to animals etc (I stop bulling (*sic*) from people when
    they attack animals

Figure 5.5. Martin's self-characterisation

officer and a teacher, in order to assess his construing of people in authority. Martin said that he could not supply the name of any friends for the element role of 'A friend who also offends' as all of his offending was carried out on his own. However, he supplied the name of his older brother for the role of 'A friend who does not offend', suggesting that in fact he did have difficulty in making friends. The constructs that were elicited from Martin suggested that his construct system was primarily dominated by whether or not people offended (see Figure 5.6). There was also evidence of 'conventional' values consistent with his self-characterisation. The construct 'Not concerned about people vs Concerned about people' was elicited, and was also associated with being 'Hard to talk to vs Easy to talk to'. However, these were not highly discriminative constructs on the element plot, and therefore not as important in the structure of Martin's construct system.

Martin's grid was analysed using the INGRID programme (Slater, 1972), and the plot is shown in Figure 5.7. In terms of the structural features of his construing, a large first principal component was accounted for by the constructs related to offending. A smaller second component was accounted for by the construct 'Hard to get to know vs Easy to get to know'. The most pertinent feature was probably the marked self-isolation of his perceived

Hard to talk to vs Easy to talk to

Not concerned about people vs Concerned about people

Gets into trouble vs Don't get into trouble

Stay the same vs Don't stay the same

Been in trouble with the police vs Not been in trouble with the police

Have regrets vs Don't have regrets

Want to learn vs Don't want to learn

Learn their lesson vs Don't learn their lesson

Listen to others vs Don't listen to others

Easy to get to know vs Hard to get to know

Figure 5.6. Constructs elicited from Martin

current self. The only element which he construed in a more polarised way was his 'offending self'. Some conflict about change was identified by the fact that, although both his current self and offending self were rated at some distance from his ideal, he perceived these former elements as 'not wanting to learn' as well as 'having regrets'. Apart from his father and teacher, whom he saw as 'hard to get to know', most of the other elements were rated very closely together, towards the positive sides of the construct poles. In reality one might expect this group of individuals to be very different from each other ('me as a child', 'mother', 'probation officer', 'brother', 'sister'. One hypothesis might therefore be that Martin's rather simplistic construct system provided him with little scope for construing and predicting other people's behaviour. This would then contribute to difficulties in social relationships.

Using the PCP perspective and techniques for assessment enabled a way of engaging with Martin which may have otherwise have proved difficult, given his difficulties in verbal articulation and his denial of problems. This enabled a number of hypotheses to be suggested. First, Martin's fascination for military activities and weapons related more to his fantasies of being a powerful 'rescuer' than to a wish to harm others. Conversely, his self-harm may have related to his desire to be 'looked after'. Martin's repetitive offending and ambivalence towards change suggested that the benefits of offending outweighed the costs. One hypothesis to explore further would be that the consequences of offending

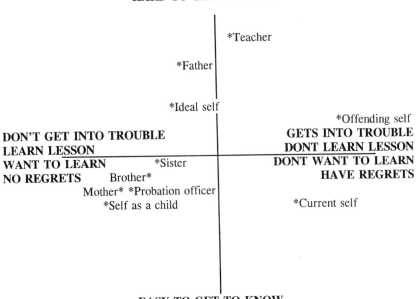

Figure 5.7. Plot of elements in construct space from Martin's grid

brought him into contact with the police and the courts, which he actually enjoyed. Since there were frequent changes in the stability of his family due to the fostering process, it may have been that his offending focused the attention of the family on him, and that the stability of a probation order made him feel more 'looked after' than he did at home. Martin was referred to an Intermediate Treatment Centre and his parents agreed to participate in some family work. The ultimate aim was for Martin to perceive that the benefits of not offending outweighed those of offending, although the potential threat that this would pose to his view of himself meant that this would not be an easy task.

SUMMARY AND CONCLUSIONS

PCP models of offending emphasise the role of the person's self-concept in the development and maintenance of their offending, and are particularly applicable to delinquency. While a deviant self-concept is not sufficient to *cause* delinquency, this may be an important contributory factor in specific individuals. Most of the studies of construing in young offenders have therefore focused on the way in which their 'self' is perceived. Empirical research and case studies have concluded that there are differences between the self-concepts of delinquents and non-delinquents, as well as in self-esteem. Delinquents are more likely to have a 'deviant' self-identity, or alternatively no positive self-identity, manifested by a sense of 'self-alienation'. There is a greater tendency for young offenders to have a lack of positive role models, and therefore also to experience a sense of 'social alienation'.

There are also structural differences between the construing of delinquents and of those who do not offend. Although research has demonstrated that the underlying structure of values in delinquents and non-delinquents is similar, the former group are more likely to have a construct system which is dominated by 'subterranean' values, as opposed to 'conventional' values. Consistent with the findings from other client groups (e.g. see Chapter 6), within a group of 'problematic' adolescents, those with cognitively simplistic construct systems and those who are poor at predicting the behaviour of others, show the most social and behavioural problems.

From the clinical perspective, using the PCP approach has a number of advantages with this client group. It is usually the case that the young person themself is not the one who is presenting their behaviour as problematic, and they may be reluctant to engage with the clinician. From the PCP perspective, the offending of a delinquent makes sense to them, and attempting to understand the client's view and the personal meaning of that behaviour enables the clinician to both establish a greater rapport and to gain a greater understanding of what is unique about that individual. The use of structured techniques for the exploration of construing is particularly useful in working with young offenders who have difficulties with verbal expression and communication.

Finally, there is a large body of research which suggests that as well as individual factors, family and socio-cultural characteristics of young offenders are different from those of young people who do not offend (Farrington, 1992). Unfortunately, there is little research into the way in which family processes influence the development of construing. As a way forward, Miller & Treacher (1981) suggest that Moos' family environment scale (Moos & Moos, 1976) could be used to generate researchable hypotheses into the ways in which family variables such as conflict, cohesion and organisation are related to the development of interpersonal construing.

CHAPTER 6

Violence and Aggression

A problem with violence or aggression is one of the most common reasons why offenders are referred to clinicians, either because of the offending behaviour itself, or due to an ongoing management problem. After briefly considering definitional issues, this chapter goes on to explore the PCP perspective on violent and aggressive behaviour. As with the other clinical chapters in Part II, the research on patterns of construing in offenders who have been violent is reviewed. Differences in the structure and content of construing between offenders who have a history of multiple violence and those who have committed a single act of extreme violence are highlighted. The implications of the PCP perspective are discussed in relation to the assessment and treatment of an offender with a history of violence. Since most violent offenders referred to mental health facilities are likely to be identified as 'personality disordered' and many may also abuse alcohol, it is useful to read this chapter in conjunction with Chapters 8 and 9.

INTRODUCTION

Although personal construct theory *per se* has not had a major impact on the theoretical understanding of violence and aggression, the perspectives of the perpetrator and victim, as well as society in general, are important both in the definition of aggression and in whether or not an act of violence or aggression is construed as a criminal offence.

Blackburn (1993) notes the lack of consensual definitions of aggression and violence, which relates in part to this dependence on the values and attributions of the observer. For example, he describes *aggression* as 'the intentional infliction of harm, including psychological discomfort as well as injury, ... *which is unjustified from the observer's perspective*' (p. 211, my italics). This description takes into account that '*what is construed as harmful depends on values and social context*' (p. 211, my italics). Blackburn (1993) defines *violence* as 'the forceful infliction of physical injury' and *criminal violence* as 'the illegitimate use of force', which includes criminal homicide, assault, robbery, rape and other sexual assaults (p. 210). However, certain of those behaviours, such as killing and assault, are seen as legitimised at different times by society, such as in war, when there is sometimes a fine line between the point at which 'justifiable' aggression becomes a war crime. Similarly, what is construed as a criminal offence may vary between sub-cultures. In some delinquent sub-cultures, aggression is seen as an acceptable means of communication, and even those who are the victims of violence would not consider reporting the perpetrator to the police. Blackburn (1993) therefore notes that violent crime 'constitutes only a small part of the phenomenon of human aggression, which, despite its negative connotations, is neither statistically abnormal, nor, for the most part, illegal' (p. 210). This assertion is confirmed by the figures for recorded crime. The last British Crime Survey found that fewer than 9% of males and 4% of females before the courts in England and Wales were found guilty of crimes against the person (Mayhew et al., 1989). However, information from other sources, such as Social Services and women's refuges, indicates that the extent of aggression in society is not reflected in the criminal statistics.

The role of anger is significant in both the definition and the theoretical understanding of violence and aggression. Here again, the perspective of the individual is important. There is a difference between *angry aggression* (which is accompanied by anger, and in which the aggression may serve to reduce an unpleasant emotional state, such as anger or anxiety) and *instrumental aggression*, in which anger may not necessarily be present, and the aggression is a means to an end, such as during a robbery. The way in which an event is interpreted is also acknowledged by social cognitive theorists to be important in the mediation of anger. Within this theoretical framework, a number of authors suggest that anger results from the way in which a person cognitively appraises the personal meaning of an event. Different theorists put the emphasis on different aspects of the appraisal. Beck's (1976) cognitive theory considers the emotional state of anger to follow the appraisal of an 'unwarranted violation' of one's self-concept, values, personal relationships or possessions. Attribution theorists also emphasise the importance of the judgements the person makes about the event, in relation to what they think *ought* to be the case (Ferguson & Rule, 1983). Novaco (1978) sees anger as resulting from the way in which people or situations are appraised, and notes that 'aversive events function as provocations because of the way they are construed' (p. 141). Both Beck (1976) and Novaco (1978) suggest that individuals whose anger is dysfunctional have underlying biases in both the content and the process of their 'cognitive schemata', and there is some empirical support for this. Research on cognitive processes has demonstrated that aggressive boys are both less accurate in interpreting the ambiguous responses of peers and have a bias to perceive hostile intent (Dodge, 1986). Slaby & Guerra (1988) also examined the content of cognition in violent delinquents, and found that they endorsed more positive and neutralising beliefs about the consequences of aggression, for example that aggression enhanced self-esteem and caused minimal suffering to the victim.

Finally, the heterogeneity of violent offenders is typified by the contrast between those who have a history of habitual violence, and those who have committed one single act of extreme violence. Since both situational factors and the person's temporary state clearly contribute to violent incidents, having committed one single act of violence does not necessarily indicate that the individual has a violent disposition (Blackburn, 1993). Individuals who have committed an isolated act of extreme violence *may* be what Megargee (1966) described as 'overcontrolled'. People with this personality type are excessively inhibited about the expression of anger and hostility, and may become increasingly frustrated over time until a 'last straw' results in explosive and extreme violence. In contrast to some habitually violent offenders, such clients may be less likely to display overt aggression in their ongoing treatment, although may have difficulty in coping with provocation.

THE PCP PERSPECTIVE ON VIOLENT AND AGGRESSIVE BEHAVIOUR

Although it may appear from the above definitions that there are commonalities between the cognitive and personal construct psychology perspectives on the understanding of anger, violence and aggression, there are also important differences. Kelly did not distinguish between cognitions and emotions, seeing this division as 'a jargon descendant of the ancient dualities of reason versus passion, mind versus body, thinking versus feeling, which has led to dualist psychologies' (Bannister & Fransella, 1986, p. 21). As discussed in the opening chapter, G. Kelly (1955/1991) construes 'emotion' in terms of a person's experience of, or resistance to, the process of change in their construct system. Although the terms 'aggression' and 'hostility' are both used by Kelly, they therefore have different meanings in PCP to our traditional definitions.

George Kelly defined aggression and hostility only in relation to what was going on within the individual's construing, without assuming any specific negative intention on their part. As seen in Chapter 1,

aggression in PCP terms does not necessarily have negative consequences and can be a very positive and creative process. However,
Kelly's use of the term 'hostility' bears a greater resemblance to what
we usually understand by this term, and is more commonly observed in
the construing of offender clients. To reiterate from Chapter 1, he
defined hostility as 'the continued effort to extort validational evidence
in favour of a type of social prediction which has already been recognised as a failure'. In other words, the term describes how people may
behave if their constructs become untenable and they have no other way
of viewing the situation. If they acknowledge that their constructs are
ill-founded, this may threaten their whole construct system and consequent sense of self. If they have no alternative way of viewing the situation, this leads to a sense of chaos. In this position, Kelly suggests that
people are likely to become hostile, i.e. to look for and create evidence
that supports their predictions. In other words, when people are being
hostile, they are often trying to force others to behave in a way which
supports their view of the world. Kelly's concept of hostility can be compared to the significance of the 'self-fulfilling prophecy' in interpersonal
theories of personality disorder (e.g. Kiesler, 1983; Safran, 1990; see
also Chapter 8), which apply to any maladaptive behaviour (e.g. excessive submission), not only that which is 'hostile'. Carson (1979) suggests
that there is a causal link between the beliefs that people have about
how others are likely to react, their own subsequent behaviour, and con-
firmatory reactions from others. This model has been used to examine
the origins of consistency in aggression in individuals, in terms of the
way that such expectancies can override other objective aspects of a
situation.

McCoy (1981) has provided new PCP conceptualisations of emotions
which George Kelly did not define. These include anger, which she
defined as 'awareness of invalidation of constructs, leading to hostility'.
For example, she argues that a person is likely to feel angry if their
normal view of the world (which includes constructs relating to their
own self-worth and self-respect) is invalidated, for example by being
unfairly treated by an employer. Although hostility may *not* always
follow from the awareness that one's constructs have been invalidated,
both this definition and those of Kelly (1955/1991), emphasise the
importance of how the *way* in which a person construes themselves,
others and situations, contributes to whether or not they will behave in
a conventionally aggressive, hostile or violent manner. There are therefore links between the PCP perspective on violence and aggression and
that of cognitive theorists, who emphasise the role of scripts, or cognitive schema, in the determination of aggression (e.g. Huesmann & Eron,
1984).

Finally, as with other types of offenders, it is likely that many clients with a history of habitual violence are actually behaving in a way which makes sense to them and is validating to their core constructs (Needs, 1988). The use of violence and aggression can also be part of a shared way of construing the world within a peer group, demonstrating commonality between individuals. With such clients, it is particularly important for the clinician to be able to understand this way of construing (i.e. demonstrate sociality). For example, this may help to make sense of why many violent offenders in treatment continue to minimise the significance of *verbal*, as opposed to *physical*, aggression. For many clients, engaging in treatment to control their violence involves a major reconstruction of their core role structure. However, the use of verbal aggression often remains part of their cultural way of viewing the world, shared by their peers, which would be too threatening to change.

PATTERNS OF CONSTRUING IN VIOLENT OFFENDERS

The main PCP study with this client population is still that by Howells (1983), who studied the construing of mentally abnormal offenders in an English Special Hospital. The majority of patients on the male admission ward on which the author was working had been recently convicted of violent offences against the person. All the patients were detained under the Mental Health Act (1959), and were therefore seen to be suffering from mental disorder; approximately half were detained under the 'mental illness' category and half under the 'psychopathic disorder' category. Twenty-nine patients had no convictions prior to the current violent offence ('one-off' offenders) while 77 had a wide range of previous convictions, including violent, sexual and acquisitive offences ('multiple offenders'). The victims of the one-off offenders had primarily been their families or close acquaintances, and more of them had died compared to those who were victims of the multiple offenders. The violence perpetrated by the one-off offenders was also rated by independent judges as significantly more extreme than that by the multiple offenders.

In interviewing the patients the focus was to achieve some understanding of the subjective context of the person's violent behaviour, to assess how he had construed reality both before and at the time of the violent incident, how he had perceived himself, his circumstances, significant others in his life, and particularly his victim. Howells (1983) also administered Role Construct repertory grids (see Chapter 2) to all the male patients admitted to the hospital and compared these to the grids of male prisoners convicted of non-aggressive offences. The subjects were required to name 18 people to fit Kelly's standard role-title list, including parents, family and authority figures, and aspects of self (actual self, ideal self and social self, i.e. 'myself as others see me'). Fifteen constructs were elicited. Howells (1983) set his study in the context of Megargee's (1966) theory of overcontrol, and therefore sampled representatives of three comparison groups: one-off extremely assaultative aggressors (overcontrolled), multiple moderately assaultative aggressors (undercontrolled) and non-aggressive controls. Differences between the groups were found in both the structure and content of their construing.

Structure of the Construct System

Characteristic structural features of construing have not been consistently demonstrated in habitually violent offenders. Early research found an association between cognitive simplicity and violence in both prisoners (Chetwynd, 1977) and psychiatric patients (Topcu, 1976), suggesting that individuals with simplistic and tightly organised construing may have a more restricted range of options with which to deal with interpersonal conflict. However, although there was no significant difference in the degree of cognitive complexity between the three groups studied by Howells (1983), structural differences *were* found in the construing of one-off violent offenders. He found that one-off offenders tended to rate elements on the positive pole of their constructs more than both multiple- and non-aggressive offenders, suggesting that these men made fewer *extrapunitive* judgements about other people. Similarly, the one-off offenders were more likely to elicit the positive poles of constructs first. In other words, one-off offenders with a history of a single act of extreme violence appeared to have difficulty construing others in a less than ideal way.

An earlier case study of the construing of a woman who committed a single act of arson, also noted her tendency to deny feelings of hostility (Landfield, 1971). The woman poured petrol in the bedroom where her three children were sleeping, and although aspects of her behaviour suggested ambivalence about her intentions (i.e. leaving the entry way clear), her youngest child died. Her construct system, as illustrated by her repertory grid, was extremely tightly structured and filled with themes of religion and morality, in which religiousness represented all that was good. One particularly important construct was 'Good, religious vs Too quiet, doesn't like children', which together with her other constructs, suggested that she must always like her children in order to be good, smart, kind, unselfish and fun. Landfield (1971) suggested that when the woman experienced momentary feelings of dislike for her children and was unable to play her usual 'good' role, this posed an extreme threat. She therefore either had to resort to suppression of her feelings or impulsively act out her 'badness'.

Construing of the Self

For both one-off and habitually violent offenders, the *content* of their self-construing is also relevant in understanding the meaning of their behaviour. As with most offenders, the two main areas of interest are self-esteem and self-perception. An unstable, fluctuating self-esteem appears to be more strongly related to anger arousal than low self-esteem *per se* (Kernis et al., 1989), and interestingly, the multiple aggressors in Howells' (1983) study showed no difference in self-esteem (measured by their Actual–Ideal self difference) to the non-aggressive prisoners. However, the one-off violent offenders saw themselves significantly more negatively than both the multiple aggressors and the non-aggressive controls. This group also obtained higher scores on measures of intropunitive thinking and lower scores on measures of extrapunitive thinking. This is consistent with the work of Megargee (1966) on over-controlled violent offenders.

Until recently, apart from Howells' (1978) case study of a poisoner (see Chapter 10), there were no detailed case studies exploring specific features of the self-perceptions of violent offenders. However, two case examples described in the PCP literature highlight the way in which the men construe themselves as being violent. Landfield (1971) described the case of a man with a history of severe violent outbursts and alcoholism, who had made a previous attempt to strangle a cell-mate. His constructs mainly consisted of whether or not people were likeable, happy, kind and intelligent, and the positive poles of these constructs were all related to not being violent. However, although he did not construe violence itself in a positive way, most of the people on the grid *were* rated as being violent, including himself, seven of his acquaintances, and his father and brother. He was unable to rate himself on the dimensions of 'likeableness' and 'intelligence', and saw himself as his 'most unsuccessful' role person in the elements. Landfield suggested that these attributes were sensitive areas for him, and possibly his heavy drinking helped to numb his negative feelings about himself. The man became vulnerable to violence when he could not block out his negative feelings and overreacted to the behaviour or slights of others in uncontrolled ways.

Needs (1988) also described the construct system of a prisoner with a history of violence, who was hostile in both the conventional and the Kellian sense. From his point of view, the only alternative to being 'wild' was being 'soft', and to give up being 'wild' would result in 'being taken advantage of'. Given the prison setting and the man's history of previous antagonistic behaviour, Needs suggested that there was an element of truth in this. The man had spent much of his life tightly defining core constructs of himself as 'tough', forthright and the victim of a devious and uncaring world, and Needs (1988) suggested that for him to give up his sustaining 'hostility' would be extremely threatening to his sense of self.

Finally, clinical experience suggests that many clients with a history of very serious violence also have a sense of perceived self-isolation, which contributes to difficulties in developing and maintaining non-violent friendships with others. A number of such clients construe themselves as 'different', 'rejected' and 'alienated', fuelling urges to seek revenge in violence. Dalton & Dunnett (1992) suggest that adults who find it hard to get close to others have often experienced this difficulty as children, and may have developed a pattern of developing overdependent relationships which cannot meet all their needs.

Construing of Others

There is consistent empirical evidence to support a social learning perspective on the origins of persistent aggression, in which the family provides a learning environment for violence to be modelled, rehearsed and reinforced (Busch et al., 1990). Although personal construct psychology construes the development of deviance from a different theoretical perspective (see Chapter 1), the way in which clients perceive family members is of great importance in understanding the origins of their current construing and violent behaviour. As illustrated in both the case study described by Landfield (1971) above (in which the client's father and brother were both construed as violent), and the later case examples in this chapter, for many habitually violent offenders, members of their family may provide important role models. For example, a violent father may be construed very positively, and/or be only the figure with whom the client identifies.

When violence is directed towards an individual, or group of individuals, it is also useful for the clinician to understand how the offender construes their victim(s). In comparison with some other offenders (e.g. sex offenders and those with psychopathic personality disorder, see Chapters 7 and 8), there appears to be little commonality in the ways in which violent offenders construe their victims. Howells' (1983) study indicated considerable variation in the ways in which victims were perceived, which emphasises the importance of analysing grids individually and examining a client's personal ways of construing. He described two case examples which illustrate this, one in which the victim was clearly viewed in a hostile way, and the other in which they were seen in a positive and even idealised way. Positive evaluations of victims were more frequent in the one-off group of extremely violent offenders, all of whose victims had died. However, Howells notes that it is also possible that idealised evaluations of victims (and biased construct systems in general) are reactions to the offence, rather than a reflection of attitudes which existed prior to the offence.

The way in which a client construes others may also shed light on why their violence is (or was) directed towards a specific individual. Landfield (1971) described the case of a man in his early forties who attempted to strangle his girlfriend when he found her in bed with another woman. When admitted to hospital he was still prone to temper outbursts. The man was previously a successful motor racing driver, who gradually became less successful, and even reckless, as a driver. He also found out that he was infertile, and had begun stealing. Eliciting constructs demonstrated his preoccupation with his failed ambition as a racing driver and also as a father, for example 'Race promotion ability vs No ability for race promotion', 'Raise a family vs Cannot raise a family'. He rated his mother very negatively, and Landfield suggested that the origins of his violence towards women may have begun with his relationship with her. His violence appeared to have become more frequent as he became less successful, starting with dangerous behaviour on the track towards other men, and generalising towards women when he also began to see himself as a failure in relation to them.

The Meaning of Violence and Aggression

In one of the few empirical repertory grid studies of offenders, Watson et al. (1976) demonstrated the importance of interpersonal events as triggers for violence in male prisoners. Each prisoner was asked to rank their likelihood of responding in different ways (e.g. punching out, smashing up, feeling depressed, getting drunk) to different stressful situations (e.g. getting the sack, being laughed at, having rows). Perhaps not suprisingly, there was a tendency for interpersonal events (e.g. being laughed at, rudeness and witnessing fights) to be seen as leading to violence whereas social situations (e.g. lack of money, job, housing) were associated with other reactions, such as thieving and feeling depressed. However, men with histories of past violence were not any more likely to anticipate responding to situations in a violent way than prisoners with other convictions. The authors acknowledge that violent offenders are a heterogeneous group, and it is therefore more meaningful to examine the factors which are relevant to understanding the circumstances under which an *individual* is violent, rather than 'placing him at a point X on a unitary violence scale' (Watson et al., 1976).

The empirical research and case studies reviewed earlier also illustrate the way in which violence has a very different personal meaning for one-off and habitually violent offenders. Howells (1983) particularly focuses on the meaning of violence for the 'overcontrolled' or one-off offender. The conclusions from his study indicated that one-off extremely violent offenders tend to have unstable, biased construct systems in which negative evaluations of others (i.e. the negative poles of constructs) are 'submerged' or not easily available. Such a person would live in a world in which they only perceived evidence of other people's good qualities, until their way of construing was undermined by the evidence around them. When faced with severe interpersonal difficulties, their idealised view of other people (including their victim) would be difficult to maintain, and the person is faced with a situation of threat (i.e. 'the awareness of imminent comprehensive change in one's core constructs', G. Kelly, 1955, 1991). Howells (1983) suggests that under these circumstances, violence may occur at one of either two points. First, it may occur in the actual situation of threat preceding the final breakdown of the person's construct system, when a particular person (i.e. the victim) may become the source of the threat, and needs to be 'obliterated'. Alternatively, violence may occur in the confused state following the invalidation of established ways of construing. As the person becomes aware that their positive constructions of others have been invalidated, they may suddenly shift (or 'slot-rattle'—see Chapter 3) their construing to the opposite pole, construing other people in very negative ways, which 'legitimises' some form of violence on a temporary basis.

The structural features of the construing of one-off violent offenders are therefore of particular importance in understanding the factors preceding their violence, and the personal meaning of this behaviour. In contrast, in men who have a history of habitual violence, it is the *content* of their construct system which appears to be more pertinent. In such individuals, the use of aggression may have become an integral part of their self-validation and their way of construing the world. This pattern of construing is likely to have been shaped by their childhood experiences, particularly if the client had a violent father as a role model. If the person has been a victim of violence as a child, this experience may become their primary means of predicting future events. A client who is habitually violent may therefore be behaving in a way which is meaningful to them, in that the behaviour validates their whole sense of self. In other words, to be violent or aggressive (in the conventional sense) is both consistent with and reinforcing for their view of themself. Such individuals may construe their victims in such a way as to legitimise their behaviour, or construe the violence itself as legitimate. They may construe their victim as an equal participant, i.e. saying 'he/she wound me up', or 'they were going for me so I needed to get in first'. They may perceive themselves as merely responding to provocation, and the violence is therefore construed as a necessary response in order to maintain their reputation or self-esteem. For individuals who are also heavy drinkers, pre-existing constructs (e.g. 'Provocative vs Not provocative' may be made more permeable (i.e. applicable) by the dilating and loosening effects of alcohol (see Chapter 9).

The case examples below illustrate the personal meaning of violence to three different clients with convictions for violent offences. They illustrate different ways in which the individuals construe themselves, significant others and their behaviour, and how the structure and content of their construing relates to the understanding of their behaviour, the complexity of their problems and their ability to change.

Robert, a man in his late twenties, had been charged with firearms offences and ABH against his girlfriend, in the context of a long-standing dispute about access to his son. He had a number of previous convictions for other violent offences, and had a specific history of physical violence towards partners. Because he also suffered from a variety of neurotic problems, including chronic anxiety and obsessional ruminations, Robert was admitted to hospital for assessment before sentencing. On the ward he was frequently verbally aggressive to both staff and patients. His repertory grid indicated that his whole way of viewing the world was one of suspicion and mistrust, with other people construed in terms of whether they were 'Honest vs Cheat and liar', 'Two-faced vs Trustworthy', 'Let people down vs Don't let people down' and 'Aggressive vs Not aggressive'. His current self and self as a child were the two most negatively rated elements on the grid, with a huge discrepancy between the ratings of his current and ideal self. His girlfriend was construed towards the negative poles of the above constructs, as was his own father, who was himself a violent man. His suspicious view of the world was important in understanding his history of violence. He often assumed that others were deliberately trying to provoke him and therefore construed his violence as justified, given the provocation. Although Robert knew that he needed to change, he was ambivalent about doing so, and also had difficulty construing himself as 'a patient', maintaining that he did not need to be in hospital. His increasing lack of co-operation with all aspects of treatment meant that a therapeutic disposal could not be recommended to the court, and he received a custodial sentence.

Brian, a 45-year-old man, also had a long history of violence, culminating in a conviction for the manslaughter of a man in a pub fight. He was transferred to a maximum security hospital after developing psychotic symptoms in prison, which quickly resolved with medication. Brian's whole sub-culture was one in which alcohol, violence and criminality were a way of life, and therefore validating of his view of himself. For the first few years in hospital he was extremely resistant to the idea of change. However, on gradually realising that he was not going to move out of maximum security if he did not engage in treatment, he slowly became less resistant, and the anticipation of change became less of a threat. He engaged in individual psychological treatment, exploring his past offending and alcohol abuse. A repertory grid indicated that he had come to construe his past self as someone who let problems build up, drank heavily, did not care about the consequences of his behaviour and frequently got into arguments. His previous friends and his victim were also seen in this way, in direct contrast to his current and ideal self, staff members and new friends. His black-and-white thinking, in terms of 'the past' representing all that was bad and 'the present' representing all that was good, was reflected in the structure of his construct system, in which 80% of the variance on his (12 × 14) grid was accounted for by the first component. Brian construed his previous violence very negatively, as the way his 'past self' had responded to situations, and was now determined to remain in control of his temper. In many ways, therefore, Brian made good progress. However, this was limited to the way he construed physical aggression. Because of the seriousness of this in the past, Brian found it difficult to acknowledge how intimidating he could be when he got into a *verbal* altercation with someone, which to him seemed minor in comparison. Like Robert above, he also tended to construe verbal aggression as a legitimate response to someone else's behaviour towards him. The process of completing the grid highlighted the difference in the way Brian construed his progress, compared to the construing of the clinical team. The view of staff working with Brian was that he still needed to learn to control his verbal aggression, as this may escalate into physical violence in some situations, whereas Brian did not perceive any further need to change. There was no difference in the way Brian construed his current 'new' self and his ideal self, which slowed down the speed of his rehabilitation.

In contrast to the above two cases, Graham had no history of violence before seriously assaulting a woman at work with whom he had become infatuated. Over a period of several months, Graham showered the woman with presents and letters. He made repeated telephone calls to her, convinced that she really did want a relationship with him, despite her refusal. He was behaving in a classically hostile way in the Kellian sense, i.e. making a continued effort to try to confirm his predictions, even though they had already been shown to be a failure. In interviews after his offence it was clear that Graham had viewed the woman in an unrealistically positive light, and was unable to construe any negative aspects to her personality. The violence towards her was precipitated by seeing her with another man, which he experienced as rejection and construed as 'letting me down', thereby justifying his violence towards her. After his offence, Graham was diagnosed as suffering from a delusional disorder, and over time, came to realise that he had misconstrued his victim's social politeness as evidence of sexual interest. However, he continued to show a tendency to develop strong attachments to both female staff and patients. Interestingly, his repertory grid indicated that he had great difficulty in discriminating between different women, and continued to construe them in an idealised way.

IMPLICATIONS FOR ASSESSMENT AND TREATMENT

The nomothetic assessment of offenders with a history of violence usually focuses on the assessment of risk and/or treatability, and the clinical interview includes the gathering of information about the client's personal and family history, education and work, relationships, drug and alcohol abuse, and history and pattern of offending. The PCP approach is useful for the additional idiographic assessment of the personal meaning of violence to that particular individual. For example, Needs (1988) suggests that grid-based investigations in the prison setting can assist with exploring both the degree of justification that an individual uses for their anger, and how they see the alternatives.

Suggested elements to use in repertory grid assessments with clients who are violent are shown in Figure 6.1. However, unlike the other clinical chapters in Part II, constructs have not emerged from either the literature or clinical practice which show commonality across this client group, and which may therefore be useful to supply. This is likely to reflect the variety of personal meanings that violence represents for such clients, and the need to focus on eliciting constructs from

Self now

Self as a child

Ideal self

Self seen by others

Mother

Father

Brother(s)

Sister(s)

Partner/previous partner

Male friend(s)

Someone I respect who is not aggressive

Boss

Victim(s)

(A child I have been aggressive towards)

(A child I have not been aggressive towards)

Figure 6.1. Suggested elements to use in assessment

individual clients. However, it can be useful to supply constructs to test out specific hypotheses about a client's construing if they do not provide these themselves, such as the construct 'Aggressive vs Not aggressive'. Figure 6.2 suggests other constructs which may be relevant for different individuals who have a problem with violence.

Clearly the type of treatment most appropriate for an individual offender with a history of violence will vary, according to the nature and pattern of their behaviour. Blackburn (1993) reviews the evidence for different treatment interventions with aggressive offenders, and notes that despite a lack of firm evidence that psychological treatments produce long-term changes in aggressive dispositions, several cognitive and behavioural methods are encouraging (e.g. Goldstein et al., 1989). The clinician who is also taking the PCP perspective will consider the following questions and issues in their assessment and treatment of individual clients.

How Does the Client See Themself?

A key aspect of the PCP assessment of any client is to understand the way in which they construe themselves. As seen throughout the chapter, offenders charged or convicted of violence are likely to vary

Aggressive vs Not aggressive

Violent vs Not violent

Strong vs Weak

Hard vs Soft

Trustworthy vs Not trustworthy

Heavy drinker vs Social drinker

Talks about problems vs Bottles up problems

Expresses feelings vs Hides feelings

Masculine vs Not masculine

Figure 6.2. Suggested constructs to use in assessment

widely in their self-perception. Those who have committed a single but extremely violent act may see this as completely out of character, i.e. inconsistent with their core role structure. They are therefore more likely to experience guilt (an awareness of dislodgement of self from one's core role structure). Offenders who have committed multiple acts of violence over time are more likely to construe this behaviour as consistent with their self-identity, but each individual will do this in a different way. Such individuals may construe their behaviour in such a way as to minimise its seriousness and legitimise their actions (see below). They may construe violence as a normal way of responding, and therefore see themselves as no different from their family or peers. For such an individual, behaving in a violent way would therefore be both part of their core role structure and validating, and the client would be less likely to experience guilt.

How Do They See Other People?

Violent offenders are likely to see their victims in different ways, depending on how they construe themselves and their behaviour. It has been shown that one-off violent offenders (who may be considered to be 'overcontrolled') tend to idealise their victims (Howells, 1983), whereas those who are habitually violent may be more likely to construe their victims in a hostile or neutral way. The construal of other people, including potential future victims, can be a crucial part of an assessment of future risk. It is also important to explore how clients construe their peer group and role models. Assessment should include an exploration of the client's 'cultural norm' in relation to violence, and how their ideal self compares with other violent or non-violent individuals.

Although this chapter has focused on offenders who are violent towards adults, the issues are equally relevant to those clients who have been, or may be at risk of being, violent towards children. In a similar way to sex offenders (see Chapter 7), most offenders who have been physically abusive towards a child construe both the child and their own behaviour in such a way as to reduce the liklihood of experiencing guilt. In assessment it is therefore important to establish the way in which the client construes their own victim in relation to children in general.

How Do They See Their Behaviour?

Offenders with a history of multiple violence vary in the degree to which they construe their behaviour as 'wrong', which is relevant to their motivation to change. The way in which a client construes their behaviour gives an indication of where to start in treatment, if treatment is indicated at all. For example, it is important to know whether the client construes violence in a positive way, and if so, how they legitimise this and what alternatives they see to being violent.

Demonstrating Sociality

The ability to construe the constructions of one's clients is crucial for the clinician working from a PCP perspective with all offenders. However, it can be particularly useful to demonstrate that understanding to the client who has a problem with habitual violence. Again, it is important to emphasise that this is not the same as condoning their behaviour, and the clinician must be careful not to collude with the client's justifications for their violence. However, it may assist a clinician in establishing rapport with a client who has a history of violence, if they can reflect back their understanding of the client's perspective. This may involve acknowledging the dilemmas facing the client in anticipating change, such as the loss of their 'reputation' among peers. The clinician can then go on to point out how other people may see the situation, and the consequences to the client of continuing to construe violence as legitimate.

Constructing Alternatives

The aims of therapy with a violent offender will differ according to the nature and pattern of their violence, and other difficulties that they have. However, one of the most common aims for clients who habitually construe violence as their first line of response is to construct alternative ways of dealing with a situation. Tschudi's ABC model (see Chapter 3) may be a useful tool for exploring this.

Accessing Submerged Poles

With offenders who have committed a one-off act of extreme violence, an important aspect of therapy is the attempt to break down excessive inhibitions about hostility (Howells, 1983). The clinician would need gently to bring the submerged poles of the client's constructs to their attention, by encouraging the client to explore their feelings and reactions if they had a more hostile view of the world. Howells (1983) notes that such attempts would almost invariably meet initial reluctance and denial (e.g. the client maintaining that they never get angry or that there is no one they dislike), and that the clinician needs to be skilful to avoid the client feeling too threatened.

Encouraging Sociality/Victim Empathy

Individual offenders vary in their ability to empathise with those who have been the victims of their violence. Those whose constructions about the use of violence show commonality with peers or family, appear to find this particularly difficult. With all clients who have a problem with violence, it can be helpful to encourage them to put themselves in the other person's position. However, in practice, those whose violence has been directed towards someone they know and care about often find this easier to do. For other offenders who continue to construe violence as justified in some situations with some individuals, it may be more fruitful initially to concentrate on increasing their awareness of and caring about the consequences of violence for themselves.

Encouraging Experimentation

Another aim of treatment with clients who have a history of violence is to enable them to come up with strategies for responding in a different way. Paradoxically, assertion skills can be useful, as many clients behave in an aggressive way after bottling up feelings about a person or situation that they felt unable to express. However, the client will need support from the therapist to try out new skills in a safe way, either within the session by using role play (Kelly's fixed role therapy), or by monitoring and reporting back experiments between sessions.

Understanding Resistance to Change

It is fairly common for offenders who have had problems with habitual violence to reach a point in therapy where they both want to and are able to control their physical aggression. However, such individuals may still get into frequent verbal confrontations with other people (e.g. staff), who then question whether their progress is real. It is often difficult to progress further in treatment and encourage the client to address their verbal aggression. To them, this may be a normal form of communication, which is part of their sub-cultural way of construing the world. With such individuals the clinician needs to encourage the client to see things from others' points of view, and work towards accepting that the norms of interaction in the pub should be different from a hospital, court or probation office. However, in some settings, such as prison, there may be some reality to their perception of the accepted 'norm', as discussed earlier by Needs (1988). The clinician may also need to accept that the client will not necessarily share their own perspective about what needs to change. For example, it is fairly common for men who have committed acts of domestic violence to engage in treatment in order to save their relationship, although they still see violence as legitimate in other situations. Their motivation for change therefore considerably lessens if their relationship ends.

The Treatment Setting

There are no research studies that have compared the effectiveness of out-patient versus in-patient treatment of violent offenders; clearly, in many cases the treatment setting is determined by legal, rather than therapeutic considerations. However, it is important for the clinician to be aware of the influence of the treatment setting on the ability of the client to develop and maintain new ways of construing. For some individuals who have a history of violence, out-patient treatment may be more effective than in-patient care, as this does not require them to take on the role of being a 'psychiatric patient'. This role may pose a threat to their core role structure and make it difficult for such clients to engage in treatment. With out-patient treatment, changes in their self-construing can happen more gradually, in what is often the more tolerant environment of their own community. However, the degree to which there is commonality between the construing of the client and that of others in their sub-culture, will also have an influence on their ability to change their core role without too much threat. For many individuals, change can only be maintained through a change of lifestyle.

Experiencing Hostility as a Therapist

As discussed earlier, there is a fine line to be drawn between empathising with clients, construing their constructions and condoning or colluding with their behaviour. However, because many clients with a history of violence have had little previous experience of being listened to and taken seriously, they may behave in a hostile way towards the therapist, both in the Kellian and conventional sense. Having a framework with which to understand this process is essential, enabling the clinician to continue constructively with the therapeutic relationship.

The following case example describes the implications of taking a PCP perspective in the assessment and treatment of a man who had a long history of violent behaviour. In this case, establishing the way in which the client construed physical aggression itself enabled this issue to be a major focus for treatment.

Gerry, a 33-year-old man, requested help to control his aggression following his release from prison, after serving a sentence for GBH. He had a long history of an explosive loss of temper, usually accompanied by heavy drinking, and had also been violent to his wife on a number of occasions. She had now ended their relationship, and part of his motivation for treatment was to attempt a reconciliation. Gerry found it extremely difficult to open up and talk about himself and his feelings. His family background was one in which the men and women took very stereotypical gender roles. Gerry was one of three brothers, and their father brought them all up with a fixed idea of what it meant to 'be a man'. There was an expectation that Gerry did not admit to weaknesses or show any vulnerabilities. His father took all three sons to the pub with him in their early teens, and had a reputation for being able to drink large quantities of alcohol without appearing drunk. Gerry therefore grew up with a very rigid way of construing how to deal with stress. He had a view of himself as someone who had to 'pretend to be hard', which meant that he was unable to talk to anyone, including his wife, about problems, and he used alcohol as a means of dealing with anxiety. When Gerry was stressed and anxious he tended to misinterpret cues from other people and was suspicious and oversensitive in his social interactions. At these times he was likely to become both verbally and physically aggressive, and then to go out and provoke further violent confrontations with others.

A repertory grid was administered as part of the initial assessment. Gerry's other family members were all included in the list of elements, to explore how he construed himself in relation to his parents and brothers. Gerry had talked positively about a previous girlfriend with whom he had had a long-term relationship, and therefore she was also included in the grid. As no constructs directly relating to aggression or violence were elicited from Gerry, the construct 'Aggressive vs Not aggressive' was supplied. His predicament was clearly illustrated by the plot of his grid (see Figure 6.3). His main way of construing others was whether or not they were aggressive, liked a drink, and pretended to be hard. Although Gerry wanted to change, the alternative to being 'hard' was to be 'weak' and 'soft'. The importance of his relationship with his wife was illustrated by the second component, which was accounted for by the construct 'Good husband (or partner) vs Waster'. Apart from himself, Gerry's ratings of other people on the grid tended to be polarised, either as being aggressive and liking a drink (such as his father, brothers and male friend) or as the complete opposite to this (such as his mother, wife, previous girlfriend, boss and ideal self).

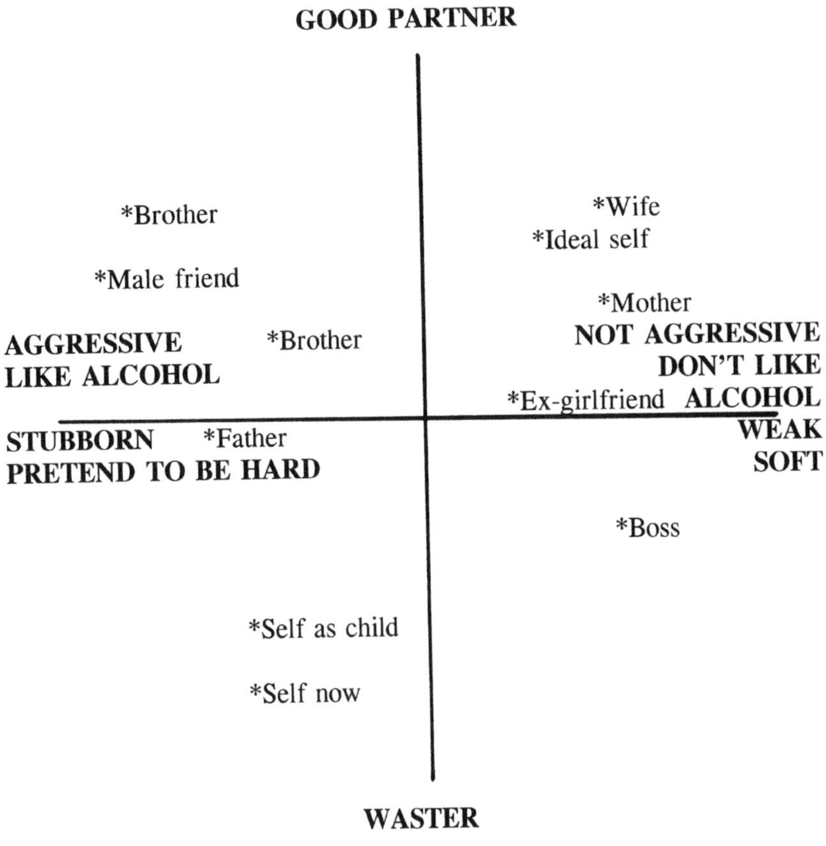

GOOD PARTNER

*Brother

*Male friend

AGGRESSIVE   *Brother
LIKE ALCOHOL

STUBBORN   *Father
PRETEND TO BE HARD

*Wife
*Ideal self

*Mother
NOT AGGRESSIVE
DON'T LIKE
*Ex-girlfriend **ALCOHOL**
WEAK
SOFT

*Boss

*Self as child

*Self now

WASTER

Figure 6.3. Plot of elements in construct space from Gerry's pre-treatment grid

The discrepancy between Gerry's current and ideal self was reflected in his keenness for treatment. He was a reliable attender and worked between sessions, thinking about issues that had been discussed, completing tasks and carrying out 'experiments', in which he tested out new ways of behaving. The process of completing the repertory grid was, in itself, therapeutic. It enabled Gerry to realise for himself the dilemmas he faced in giving up alcohol and violence, which he had previously been unable to articulate. It also highlighted the way in which he saw himself as different from the other male members of his family. One of the primary aspects of treatment involved loosening his association between non-aggression and negative personal characteristics, by exploring the negative consequences to his own aggression. He was eventually able to reconstrue interpersonal events which had previously made him feel bad about himself, and were potential triggers to his violence, such as assuming that other people were talking about him. He became able to identify situations in which he would be at risk of both drinking and being violent, and tried out alternative ways of reacting. Treatment also enabled him to explore the developmental origins of his construct system, and the implications of his father being his role model.

At the end of treatment, Gerry completed a second repertory grid (see Figure 6.4). There was a significant change in the nature of his discriminative constructs, which reflected a new way of thinking about the world. The constructs 'Pretend to be hard vs Soft' and 'Stubborn vs Weak' were no longer elicited, and consequently non-aggression and not drinking did not have negative associations. In fact Gerry now construed those people who were aggressive and heavy drinkers (including his previous self) as 'wound up' and 'aimless'. Interestingly, the nature of the way Gerry construed alcohol changed. The previous construct elicited was 'Like a drink vs Don't like a drink', which was a rather black-and-white way of construing, that did not allow for the discrimination between social drinking and having an alcohol problem. The construct elicited at the end of treatment was that of 'Occasional drinker vs Heavy drinker', which was a much more realistic way of construing people's drinking patterns. Although there was still a discrepancy between his current and ideal self, Gerry construed himself much more positively than when he had first come out of prison. At the time of ending treatment, Gerry and his wife were attempting a reconciliation. Although this was his prime motivation to change, he maintained that his whole way of perceiving himself and the world had changed, and therefore he

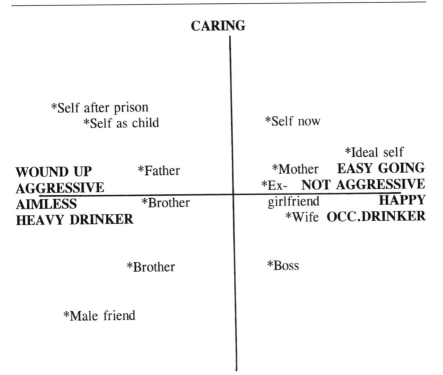

Figure 6.4. Plot of elements in construct space from Gerry's post-treatment grid

would not revert back to his previous patterns of behaviour, even if the relationship did not work out.

SUMMARY AND CONCLUSIONS

The role of personal appraisal and interpretation is acknowledged by cognitive theorists to be an important contributor to the mediation of anger and aggression. This chapter explores the PCP perspective on violence and aggression, and emphasises the way in which, for many clients with a history of habitual violence, their behaviour is validating to their sense of self. Apart from Howells' (1983) empirical study, most of the information in the literature about patterns of construing in clients with a history of violence is from individual case studies. However, there is consistent evidence to suggest that there is a difference in the structure and content of construing between those who commit one-off extremely violent offences and those whose violence has been multiple and habitual. For one-off offenders, it is the *structural* features of their construing which may be more relevant in understanding the meaning of their violence, in that there is a tendency for these individuals to submerge the negative poles of their constructs. They are therefore likely to construe other people in an unrealistically positive and idealised way, which leaves them facing a sense of threat when their expectations are not met. In contrast, for habitually violent offenders, it appears to be the *content* of their construct systems which is most relevant in understanding the way in which violence is meaningful to them. The ways in which they construe themselves, significant others, and potential victims are all important in understanding how clients with a history of habitual violence may legitimise this behaviour and how this may be validating to their sense of self.

Although there may therefore be some commonalities in construing between different violent offenders, the personal meaning of aggression is unique to each individual. The idiographic approach to assessment and treatment taken by the PCP perspective, may assist the clinician with some of the clinical conundrums posed by this client group, such as their tendency to minimise the significance of verbal aggression.

CHAPTER 7

Sex Offenders

Of all the different types of offending, it is sexual offences which usually arouse the strongest negative emotions in the general public, and often also in clinicians. Some clinicians choose not to work with sex offenders, and others do so only reluctantly. This reluctance derives from the particularly personal nature and harmful consequences of this type of offending, in which there is always a victim. Child sex offenders particularly lack commonality with the rest of society, and it is also more difficult for clinicians to demonstrate sociality with this client group. The PCP perspective has been used to explore the meaning of sexual offending to sex offenders and studies have particularly focused on the way in which sex offenders construe children and adults in order to avoid guilt.

INTRODUCTION

An overview of the current theoretical models of sexual offending and characteristics of sex offenders is beyond the scope of this chapter and is given elsewhere (Marshall & Barbaree, 1990b). However, a brief pointer to the key issues notes that theoretical work with rapists has emphasised the importance of non-sexual, as well as sexual motivations, and has classified rapists into different types (Knight & Prentky, 1990). Child abusers have typically been characterised as either *fixated/preferential* (i.e. those primarily sexually aroused by children) or *regressed/situational* (i.e. those aroused by adults, but who seek out children under particular circumstances) (Howells, 1981; Quinsey, 1986). Knight & Prentky (1990) provide a more sophisticated typology of child abusers, and the multi-factorial nature of child abuse in general is described by Finkelhor (1986). This model emphasises the contribution of (1) sexual arousal by a child, (2) emotional congruence with children, (3) 'blockage' of sexual relationships with adults, and (4) disinhibitions against sexual contact with a child.

The treatment of sex offenders is a rapidly developing area. This has been driven partly by the increase in incidence and prevalence of (largely) men convicted of sexual offences. For example, the number of sex offenders in prison in the UK rose from 1500 in 1979 to just over 3000 in 1990 (Clarke, 1993). With this increase has also come a growing recognition of the specialist treatment needs of this client population. In the UK, psychologists in maximum security hospitals have traditionally provided treatment for mentally disordered sex offenders, and those based in NHS Forensic Psychiatry Services have offered individual out-patient treatment (Houston et al., 1994). However, the 1990s also saw the development of the Sex Offender Treatment Programme within the prison service in England and Wales, which targets sex offenders serving four years or more (Thornton & Hogue, 1993), as well as the development and expansion of group treatment programmes run by probation services (Barker & Morgan, 1993). Multi-professional and multi-agency working is increasingly the norm, particularly following the recommendations of the Reed Committee review of services for mentally disordered offenders, which identified sex offenders as a group with specialist needs (Reed, 1993).

Underlying the developing *provision* of services for sex offenders, there have also been changes in the *nature* of therapeutic work with this client group. Comprehensive reviews of the treatment of sex offenders in the United States suggest particularly encouraging results from cognitive-behavioural interventions, at least with child sex offenders and exhibitionists (Marshall & Barbaree, 1990b), and many treatment programmes now take this orientation. There are two aspects of this approach which pose a potential challenge to a clinician working from the PCP perspective. First, the cognitive-behavioural assessment and treatment of child sex offenders occurs within a value framework which is not present in work with most non-sexual offenders. The underlying philosophy is that children cannot by nature give fully informed consent to sexual activities with adults, and that sexual abuse is harmful (Salter, 1988; Morrison, 1994). In contrast, personal construct theory perceives construing in which X *always* implies Y (i.e. sexual abuse is always harmful), as pre-emptive or rigid. However, the evidence indicating long-term harmful effects of child sexual abuse is well established (e.g. Briere & Runtz, 1993), and would not be disputed by personal construct theorists. Rather, personal construct theory would view the harmful consequences of abuse as being different for each individual, according to both the way the person interprets the abusive experience(s), and their subsequent anticipation of future events. The PCP perspective therefore allows for the greater recognition of individual differences in the experiences of people who have been sexually abused.

The second potential challenge for the clinician wanting to understand sexual offending from the PCP perspective, relates to how the
clinician themself makes sense of the offender's constructions. Most sex
offenders avoid the guilt which would otherwise arise from their behaviour by construing their victims and their offending in ways which minimise their own responsibility. For example, most clients initially
construe their victims as consenting to the abuse, or as behaving in a
way which invited assault. They may not therefore construe their own
behaviour as harmful or as sexual. From the cognitive-behavioural
approach, the ways in which sex offenders construe their victims and
their behaviour in order to justify their offending are construed as 'cognitive distortions' or 'thinking errors'. Challenging these ways of thinking is seen as an integral and essential part of treatment (Murphy,
1990). In contrast, personal construct theory does not view people's
ways of construing as inherently flawed, but rather as alternative constructions of reality. However, G. Kelly (1955/1991) also wrote that 'any
personal construction which is used repeatedly in spite of constant
invalidation' can be seen as disordered. From *within* their construct
system, an offender's constructs may not be internally invalidated.
However, the external legal and social consequences of sexual offending
means that construing children as 'able to give informed consent to sex'
is invalidated, and can therefore appropriately be construed as disordered in PCP terms.

THE PCP PERSPECTIVE ON SEXUAL OFFENDING

Before reviewing the PCP models of sexual offending, it is relevant to
reconsider some of the difficulties and differences in working with this
client group compared to other types of offenders. One of the main differences can usefully be understood in terms of the PCP concept of *commonality*, i.e. that people share similarities in construing when they
interpret experiences in similar ways. Of all offenders, it is particularly
those who commit sexual offences against children who most clearly
lack commonality with the rest of society. In other words, most people
do not interpret the ordinary behaviour of children as sexualised, as do
many of those individuals who go on to have sexual contact with children. Society in general condemns child abuse, and the clear legal consequences enable the clinician to emphasise the importance to the client
of them construing children in alternative ways. However, the issue is
not so clear cut with offenders who commit sexual offences against
adults. Some of the ways in which sex offenders construe women are
shared by many men in society in general. For example, before carrying

out a sexual assault, some clients describe interpreting the way a woman dresses in order to decide whether or not to commit the assault. One man who had a long history of sexually assaulting adult women construed women who wore tight clothing and short skirts as 'less likely to mind' being sexually assaulted, and those who dressed conventionally as 'more likely to mind'. The difficulty for the clinician is that many 'normal' men in society also make interpretations about women's sexual behaviour and attitudes from the way in which they are dressed. This greater degree of commonality between those who sexually offend against adult women and the rest of society, can make it harder for these clients (and some professionals) to see a need for change. The process of working with sex offenders therefore forces the clinician to examine their own ways of construing sexual behaviour. This can be an uncomfortable process, particularly if they *do* find areas of commonality.

A further difference between working with sex offenders and with other clients, is that it is often more difficult for clinicians to demonstrate *sociality*, i.e. the ability to construe the construction processes of others. In other words, most clinicians can understand the construal processes of a teenager who steals a car to impress his friends, a man who becomes violent when he feels threatened, or even a person who sets a fire to exact revenge. Although we may not *share* their perception of the world (i.e. lack commonality), we can understand how *they* construe events (i.e. demonstrate sociality), and how this therefore influences their behaviour. However, with many child sex offenders in particular, not only do clinicians not share their view of the world, it is also hard to understand it from their perspective. When a client talks about children 'giving me the come on', most clinicians have to work hard to understand this way of construing and develop an empathic therapeutic relationship. This difficulty in achieving sociality with sex offenders means that they are often construed by the media and general public in extreme and polarised ways, as 'evil' or 'perverts'. Construing such individuals in extreme ways allows people to distance themselves from the behaviour of the sex offender, and see this as something which is outside the range of normal human behaviour.

Another PCP concept which is particularly applicable to some sex offenders is that of *fragmentation*. The Fragmentation Corollary states that a person's construct system is 'fragmented' when their construing of some areas of their experience may seem inconsistent with their construing of others. This may account for the way in which some clients construe themselves very positively (e.g. as caring and successful), at the same time as construing their sexual offending in ways which legitimise this. Such fragmentation allows individuals to be untroubled by their behaviour. The different 'fragments' of their construct system are linked by superordinate constructs; for example for an incestuous offender, this might be something like 'Me at work vs Me at home'.

One of the strengths of personal construct theory is that it is applicable to all human behaviour, not just to that which is disordered or deviant. Two authors in particular have looked at what the PCP perspective contributes to the understanding of the sexual abuse of children. Needs (1992) focuses particularly on the notion of self-validation, i.e. the way in which *how* a person's view of themselves is supported or validated, determines their subsequent behaviour. A person's behaviour is their way of both clarifying their current understanding of a situation and trying out new hypotheses. Their understanding of themselves is crucial in order to develop social relationships, and this understanding is maintained when validated or supported by others. When it is not supported this may lead either to change or to attempts to buttress the view against attack. Subsequent emotions and behaviour are therefore influenced by the level of support experienced. Using this as a starting point, Needs (1992) develops what he calls 'a process-oriented view of adult sexual involvement with children'.

As outlined previously, one way of characterising child abusers has been to describe them as either fixated (preferential) or situational (regressed) (Howells, 1981). The fixated child abuser is exclusively sexually attracted to children, and prefers their company socially. Needs (1992) describes the way in which fixated child abusers, who usually have great difficulties in developing satisfactory adult relationships, validate their sense of self from an intense involvement with children. For the preferential or fixated child abuser, adult relationships may be invalidating and relationships with children validating. Their whole lifestyle and way of relating in the world may revolve around interactions with children, which are much more rewarding than attempts at adult relationships. In contrast, situational child abusers are usually sexually attracted to adults, and typically abuse children when a build-up of stressors, which often include difficulties in adult relationships, undermine their sense of adequacy. With situational child abusers, sexual activities with children are more often intermittent, typically preceded by a build-up of invalidating events. The stress of external events may lead to feelings of inadequacy and self-doubt, and sexual offending against a vulnerable child may be an experiment (in Kelly's terms) to create a powerful image of themselves. Affirming their sense of self may involve using the child as a substitute sexual partner or a surrogate revenge object. If the offender has themselves been abused, Needs suggests that the child may function as a 'proxy-image' of themselves, in which the subjectivity of the child is 'penetrated' to gain insight into their own past reactions to abuse, or into the mind of the perpetrator.

Needs (1992) acknowledges that the above suggestion about possible processes in child sex offenders is incomplete, and requires further definition and detail. In addition, the distinction between the fixated and situational offender is now considered rather simplistic. However, this PCP approach highlights the need to acknowledge the way in which a person's sexual offending may validate or support their whole sense of self. This is also relevant to consider with sex offenders whose victims are adult women or who commit non-contact offences, such as exhibitionism. As with some other types of offenders such as delinquents, for some individuals their sexual offending may represent the most rewarding aspect of their lives, in terms of the feelings of excitement and power that this generates. For others, their behaviour may be part of their self-identity (albeit a negative one), and the anticipation of change generates considerable anxiety.

A more controversial application of the PCP approach to child abuse has been described by Chin-Keung (1988, 1992). He relates some of Kelly's ideas to his experience of working with paedophiles, and uses the PCP perspective to discuss the ethics and politics of paedophilia. Chin-Keung (1988) interprets the constructions of paedophiles in G. Kelly's (1955/1991) terms of 'constructive alternativism', or alternative ways of viewing reality. Chin-Keung (1988, 1992) questions the basic assumption of many clinicians working with child sex offenders about the nature of informed consent, and construes Finkelhor's (1979) argument that children cannot by nature consent to sexual activity with adults as 'pre-emptive construing', i.e. that which is rigid and restricting. Chin-Keung suggests that whether or not children do give consent can only be tackled through empirical investigation of their construing. He therefore argues that the constructions paedophiles use to make sense of (or justify) their behaviour are not inherently wrong, as this view would be dogmatic, pre-emptive and outside the theory of personal constructs. While saying that he does not make an apology for paedophiles, Chin-Keung (1992) writes 'Perhaps one should not, if one follows the spirit of Kelly's work, take for granted that paedophilia is necessarily abnormal or evil, that it is a mental illness or a crime in need of treatment or punishment' (p. 99).

There are a number of limitations with Chin-Keung's arguments. Although the constructions made by paedophiles may not be viewed from the PCP perspective as being inherently wrong, however such individuals construe, their behaviour is unacceptable both socially and legally. In addition, the ultimate consequences of construing children as equal participants in sexual activities with adults invalidates this way of construing (i.e. the person receives a prison sentence and loses their job; family relationships break down) and can therefore be viewed as disordered. Chin-Keung (1988) himself acknowledges this when he writes 'why would one choose an orientation that could bring endless troubles?' (p. 275). Finally, some children may *appear* to give consent to the abuse, (e.g. if they have already been victims of previous abuse), but it is precisely because they are only partially informed and partially aware of alternatives, that that has to be construed by adults and taken into account. The fact that there are also laws to reinforce this, indicates that many adults do fail to construe the differences between the capacities of adults and children to give fully informed consent.

As discussed earlier, working with sex offenders therefore poses a particular challenge to the personal construct clinician. Understanding how the client construes their behaviour is important for effective treatment, and is also consistent with an empathic approach to clinical work with sex offenders, rather than a punitive one. However, there is a fine balance to be maintained between achieving such understanding for therapeutic purposes and the danger of collusion. As emphasised in the opening chapter, understanding the construing of offenders does not require the clinician to agree with or condone this.

PATTERNS OF CONSTRUING IN SEX OFFENDERS

Most of the published research on the construing of sex offenders takes the form of individual case descriptions and studies using repertory grids. In contrast to some other types of offenders (e.g. personality disordered offenders, see Chapter 8), there do not appear to be any particular common features in the structural aspects of the construing of sex offenders. The fact that most published research has focused on the content of sex offenders' construing, probably reflects the interpersonal nature of sexual offending, and the ways in which their victims and behaviour are construed in order to avoid guilt.

Construing of the Self

Consistent with the evidence that many sex offenders have a general difficulty in establishing intimacy with adults (Seidman et al., 1994), grid studies with child sex offenders suggest that such individuals often show a lack of identification with other adults, and have few appropriate role models. Needs (1988) observed these characteristics in one paedophile's grid and self-characterisation. The man's self-identity plot (Norris & Makhlouf-Norris, 1976) showed that the only individuals with whom he identified his ideal and actual self, were children. Houston & Adshead (1993) also looked at the degree of 'cognitive separation' that child sex offenders made between themselves, children and other adults, when presented with triads including themselves, their victim and another adult. For example, some men construed themselves as more similar to their child victims than to their adult partners or friends. We suggested that this may relate to Finkelhor's (1986) notion of 'emotional congruence', in which children appear to have a particular emotional significance for many child sex offenders. This isolation of self from other adults is sometimes further highlighted when clients struggle to supply the names of people they know to fit element roles for a grid. For example, Landfield & Epting (1987) described how an exhibitionist could not think of any acquaintances to fit two of his role elements, used his three brothers for a further three roles, and only identified women when specifically asked.

In addition, perhaps not suprisingly, many sex offenders tend not to see themselves as such, which is one way in which many clients avoid the guilt of behaving in a way which is incompatible with their core role. However, the distancing can take a number of forms, involving how they construe their victims and their behaviour (see later) as well as how they construe themselves. In the author's clinical experience with child sex offenders, many clients entering treatment initially construe themselves at the time of their offence in a positive light, demonstrating fragmentation of their construing as discussed earlier in the chapter. For example, one man who had abused two friends of his grandaughter over several years, often took all three girls on outings and bought them many presents. Focusing on these latter activities, he initially construed his 'self when offending' as 'loving' and 'generous' and at the opposite contrast pole to a 'typical sex offender'.

Shorts (1985) also describes this distancing from the stereotype in his case study of a rapist in a maximum security hospital, who completed repertory grids at pre- and post-treatment. At the start of treatment the man did not see himself as similar to rapists in general, but this changed over time and with treatment. He also came to recognise that other people, particularly his mother, also saw him as similar to rapists in general. Shorts (1985) questions whether the constructions of other people therefore influenced his view of himself. The man initially saw himself as someone who did not attract the opposite sex and disliked married life. He also perceived himself to be different from other adults, and the nearest adult with whom he identified was his mother. Four years later, his current and ideal self were rated as more similar, which Shorts suggested reflected an increase in his self-esteem. However, his ideal self had become closely associated with a disliking for married life and shyness with the opposite sex, with both of these 'self' elements being isolated from most females.

It is also interesting to examine the self-concept of sex offenders who have been abused themselves. My own clinical experience suggests that there are a variety of ways in which the self-concepts of such offenders differ, construing themselves at different points along the 'Victim vs Abuser' construct. For example, some men completely deny their own experiences as a victim, but also have difficulty in perceiving themselves an an abuser. This appears to occur when the individual construes their own abuse as pleasurable (or at least not harmful) and so has difficulty in perceiving their own behaviour as being abusive (see case example on page 166). In contrast, other individuals construe themselves primarily as 'victims', and use this self-concept to deny responsibility for their own offending. With a client who construed their offending in terms of 'it's not my fault ... it happened to me', one aim of treatment would be for them to make a distinction between the way they construe their 'self as a child' (e.g. in which their victim experiences are acknowledged) and their 'self as an offender' (e.g. in which their abusive behaviour is acknowledged).

The Construing of Others

Many sex offenders have difficulties in developing and maintaining long-term relationships with adults (Fisher & Howells, 1993), and the way in which this client group construes adults and children is likely to be just one of a number of contributing factors. The two main repertory grid studies with child sex offenders have both focused on how they construe other people, in particular the differences between their construal of women and children (Howells, 1979; Horley, 1988). Individual case studies have also used grids to understand the way in which men who have committed different types of sexual offences construed their victims in order to validate their behaviour and avoid guilt.

In an investigation of the meanings of children for paedophiles, Howells (1979) compared their construing of children and adults to that of non-sexual offenders. He administered two standard repertory grids, in which the elements were either all male or all female, for which the men had to supply the names of an actual person in their life. All the paedophiles had offended against female pre-pubertal children, and their victims were included as elements. In terms of the groups as a whole, both types of offenders construed men and women differently. Using Landfield's (1971) Coding System (which categorises constructs into groups), men were described more in terms of status and organisational constructs, and women more in terms of sexual and appearance-related constructs. However, the sex offenders also tended to see both their child victims and children in general as less dominant than adults. There was also a tendency for body shape to be more relevant to the paedophiles.

Horley (1988) partially replicated the above study. Again, sex offenders and non-sex offenders construed men and women differently, using more sexual and appearance constructs in relation to women. However, this study found no difference in the significance of constructs relating to dominance and submission between the groups, and the sex offenders in his study did not regard children as passive and submissive. Horley acknowledged that his study differed both in terms of the gender of the subjects' victims, and the nature of the control group (hospital- rather than prison-based). It may therefore have been that the variability of the subject groups masked genuine differences between the sex offenders and the non-sex offenders.

Notwithstanding the interesting questions raised by Horley's study, *individual* case examples of child sex offenders who have abused both boys and girls, continue to suggest that they frequently construe other people in terms of dominance and control. Houston & Adshead (1993) found that at least one of the following supplied constructs was an important discriminator in the construct systems of five out of six child sex offenders (who had offended against boys and girls): 'Dominant vs Not dominant', 'Easily controlled by other vs Not easily controlled by others', 'Sexually provocative vs Not sexually provocative'. These were three out of five constructs supplied to the men, with ten being elicited using the triad method. Although this may have been a chance finding, most changes in ratings of their victims also occurred on these constructs. However, contrary to the findings of previous authors, the men in this study initially tended to construe their *victims* as dominant and not easily controlled by others, and themselves as being the opposite, suggesting that they saw themselves as being 'led along' by their victims. This may be partly accounted for by the different pool of elements in the grids, as the previous studies did not include any 'self' elements with which to contrast children and adults. In addition, our study included both intra- and extra-familial child sex offenders, who may show very different patterns of construing, as discussed below.

Further work carried out by myself and colleagues has examined the ways in which child sex offenders construe pictures of children unknown to them. Clients attending both prison and community treatment groups completed repertory grids at pre- and post-treatment, which included pictures of male and female children and teenagers in the elements. There was a noticeable difference in the ease with which individual offenders could elicit constructs from the 'picture' elements, and in the type of constructs that were elicited. Although to some extent a person who does not see themself as a child sex offender may be more guarded about how they construe children, the difference between how clients construed pictures of unknown children did appear to reflect differences in aspects of their offending. For example, Bob, a married man in his forties, had been convicted of indecent assault against his 14-year-old stepdaughter. He had no previous convictions, and maintained that he was not generally aroused by children. He initially had great difficulty in perceiving his behaviour as abusive, construing it within the context of 'an equal relationship'. He found it hard to elicit constructs using pictures of children as elements, saying that he did not know the individuals and could not therefore see any way in which two might be alike. The constructs which he did elicit were very similar, describing general personal attributes (e.g. 'Outgoing vs Shy', 'Cheerful vs Not cheerful'. His ratings of the pictures of children were towards the middle of the scale on most of the constructs. In contrast, Edward, a man with a long history of befriending and abusing both boys and girls, acknowledged that he was sexually aroused by children, but did not perceive his behaviour as harmful. He had no difficulty with the process of eliciting constructs, and construed the pictures of children in terms of whether they were 'Knowing vs Innocent', and 'Trusting vs Not trusting'. Edward also had no difficulty rating the pictures of children on all the constructs, often using the extreme poles, and making comments like, 'she *obviously* looks . . .', 'he looks *very* . . .'.

The differences in the way intra- and extra-familial child sex offenders construe children clearly require further research. However, the suggestion that differences may exist is consistent with the finding that, as a group, incestuous fathers show levels of deviant sexual arousal to children which are closer to those of non-sex offenders than to extra-familial child abusers (i.e. about 18–19%, Marshall et al., 1986). In other words, it makes sense for differences between individuals in terms of their sexual arousal to children, to be reflected in the nature of their construing of children generally. Consequently, it follows that there are also likely to be differences in the way intra- and extra-familial offenders construe their own specific child victim(s). For example, in the case of Bob, described above, he construed his stepdaughter as more similar to himself and other adults than to pictures of other teenagers, seeing her in some ways as a 'mini-adult'. Throughout the process of completing the grid, Bob also emphasised the similarities between himself and his stepdaughter, compared to his wife. He construed his victim as 'mature', and 'knows what she wants in life', but also as more domineering and less easily controlled by others than himself. In contrast, Edward's construal of his teenage girl victim was similar to his construal of children in general. Both she and other children and teenagers were construed as 'knowing' and 'trusting', less dominant and more easily controlled by others than himself. Similarly, in the case example described by Howells (1979) of a paedophile who abused pre-pubertal girls, the two important dimensions on his repertory grid were constructs associated with innocence and inferiority. The victims of his offences were clearly seen as innocent, inferior and leadable, whereas his wife, mother and older sister all made *him* feel inferior.

Offenders towards adult women have also been shown to construe women and rape victims in ways which they use to validate their behaviour. In Shorts' (1985) case study of a rapist, the man construed others in terms of whether or not they were dishonest, deserved sympathy and put pressure on people, and whether or not they had a liking for married life and possessed heterosexual social skills. There was initially a large discrepancy between how he construed women in general compared to rape victims. Women were perceived slightly more negatively and rape victims were the most extremely rated element in terms of disliking married life and not attracting the opposite sex. Four years later, although he construed women and rape victims as similar in terms of their relations with the opposite sex, women were construed even more negatively, also being seen as 'fooling people'. Although information from questionnaires suggested that the man had progressed in some areas, the grid clearly highlighted outstanding issues of concern. Similarly, Needs (1988) also described the construing of a repeated rapist, in which women were either seen as weak and selfish, or strong and ruthless and selfish, with a minority (including his mother) being idealised.

The above studies and case examples therefore suggest that (i) the way in which sex offenders construe children and/or adults may set the scene for their offending, and (ii) the way in which they construe their specific victims enables individuals to perceive their behaviour as validated and therefore avoid guilt. The PCP concept of *hostility* (i.e. the continued use of constructs which have already been shown to be a predictive failure) is particularly relevant in understanding this latter feature of their construing. Although to some extent hostile construing is present in many offenders, the tendency to distort the data to fit their hypotheses (Kelly, 1969) is a characteristic feature of the majority of people who sexually offend. In other words, rather than amending their hypotheses about children or women when their predictions are not supported, many sex offenders persist in interpreting events in a way which confirms their original view.

The Meaning of Sexual Offending

A number of consistent themes emerge from the above studies about the way in which sex offenders construe themselves and others. These go some way towards understanding the meaning of sexual offending to this client group. Two main aspects of construing are relevant: their construal of other people in general and their construal of their own victims and behaviour in particular. What repertory grid studies contribute is an understanding of the ways in which *how* an offender construes themselves, adults, women and children, validates their sense of self. Perception of children as unthreatening, or adult women as demanding and hostile, sets the scene for their offending. However, this is not the whole story, and large numbers of men who enjoy the company of children or have difficulties in relationships with adults do not become sex offenders. As well being sexually aroused by their behaviour, men who go on to offend construe their offending in a way which enables them to avoid guilt and see it as consistent with their view of themselves.

Chin-Keung (1988) interviewed 25 paedophiles in prison and used the PCP perspective to try and understand the meaning to them of their behaviour. He tape-recorded interviews with the paedophiles, who gave their own account of their offending. In an attempt to understand how they construe their behaviour, Chin-Keung described four main types of construing. First, five men were exclusively attracted to children and saw their paedophilia as 'inborn'. This group were aware that their behaviour was not socially acceptable and experienced some anxiety and ambivalence about it. A second group of four individuals construed paedophilia as part of normal human sexuality for everybody, seeing their behaviour as harmless to children. Six men construed a continuity between their childhood sexual activities and adult sexuality, with habitual childhood sexual activities with other children playing a significant role in the development of their current sexuality. Chin-Keung does not comment on whether any of these men were the victims of abuse from adults. The final group of 10 men construed their behaviour as a consequence of difficulties in adult relationships, finding children more approachable than adult women.

Chin-Keung (1988) went on to examine the constructs the men used to maintain their behaviour. Nearly all construed the child as consenting and perceived themselves to be in a reciprocal relationship. Several saw normality as subjective, with society's attitude towards paedophilia reflecting current thought rather than a universal truth. Over half of the men distinguished children from adults in terms of constructs relating to physical beauty and attractive personality, seeing sexual contact with children in itself as more satisfying than with adults.

Being in prison, the paedophiles interviewed by Chin-Keung (1988) may have represented a particularly fixated, entrenched and high-risk group. The author does not give any information about their personal and offence histories. Construing the victim as consenting is extremely common, but interviewing first offenders or other types of sex offenders highlights more common ways of construing their behaviour. Many sex offenders distance themselves from being such an offender by construing their behaviour as non-sexual, maintaining that they were not sexually aroused or that there was no sexual intent. Others acknowledge the sexual nature of their behaviour, but construe 'sexual offending' very tightly, applying this only to 'strangers who abduct children' or 'rapists with a knife'. The majority do not see their behaviour as harmful. However, there is a difference between how offenders themselves construe their behaviour, and the way in which clinicians construe this. Most cognitive-behavioural clinicians working with sex offenders would term the above constructions 'cognitive distortions', or 'thinking errors'. A clinician using a PCP framework might not take such a pejorative view, but can still construe such perceptions as disordered, and in need of reconstruction if the person is to reduce the risk of further reoffending.

The following case examples describe the personal construing of three men with a history of sexual offending. In each case, the nature of their construing illustrates the particular meaning of their behaviour to that individual, as well as the different ways in which they avoided guilt.

Malcolm referred himself for treatment after being investigated by Social Services for the abuse of a friend's daughter. Although he was not prosecuted due to lack of evidence, the allegation brought out into the open his sexual attraction to young girls. He and his wife had no children. During the initial interview Malcolm disclosed that while working overseas as a private music teacher, he had abused numerous girls. Although some parents had suddenly withdrawn their children, he had never been directly confronted about his behaviour. It was clear that Malcolm did not construe his offending as a significant problem. He described himself as an excellent teacher, and said that he was using his skills to 'educate' young girls about sex, clearly construing all his victims as consenting. However, in a later interview it became clear that Malcolm had a very high opinion of himself, and the notion of being 'attractive to women' was a key aspect of his core role structure. He appraised every encounter with the opposite sex, regardless of their age, in terms of whether the woman or girl was 'sexually mischievous' or whether he had 'no prospect'. It therefore appeared that for Malcolm, one purpose of his offending was to validate his view of himself. One further hypothesis was that this linked to the couple's inability to conceive, and that Malcolm construed his offending as evidence of his own sexual potency. The fact that he had never been challenged about his behaviour further supported his view that his victims had always consented. Given the long-standing nature of Malcolm's offending and his voluntary attendance, the assessing clinicians were doubtful about his ability to persevere with treatment. However, with the apparent motivation of saving his relationship with his wife, Malcolm engaged in both individual and group treatment. He took an 'intellectual' interest in the process of therapy, and certainly made some superficial changes in his construing of himself and females, no longer perceiving all women as 'sex objects', nor himself as 'irresistible'. Malcolm was introduced to behavioural techniques to modify sexual fantasies about young girls, and he and his wife also started joint counselling to explore issues relating to being childless. Whether these interventions, combined with Malcolm's 'slot-rattling', was sufficient to reduce his risk of reoffending in the future still remains to be seen.

Steven, a man in his late twenties, was referred for continuing treatment following his release from prison, where he had participated in a group treatment programme. Steven had been convicted of the indecent assault of a young woman, which had been the culmination of many months of fantasy and planning. Steven had a long history of difficulties in establishing heterosexual relationships, and was extremely anxious in ordinary social interactions with women. He began to construe the sexual assault of a woman as 'the solution' to his problems, as in his fantasy, his victim enjoyed the assault. He convinced himself that he would not be caught, and that his 'new self' (i.e. after assaulting the woman) would be more confident. After completing the treatment group in prison, Steven 'slot-rattled' some of his construing, to view women as 'not enjoying being assaulted', and perceiving himself as 'likely to be caught' if he reoffended. To some extent therefore, Steven had made progress in treatment. However, some aspects of his construing continued to raise concerns about his risk of reoffending. A repertory grid suggested that he continued to construe women as being completely different from men. He saw all the women in the grid (which included his victim, an 'ideal partner', 'women in general' and a picture of a woman unknown to him) as being more sociable and outgoing than men. When exploring this in interview, Steven revealed that he felt envious at the apparent ease with which he thought women were able to make relationships, and that his 'offending self' construed women as being responsible for his own lack of success in relationships. He perceived only a slight difference between his 'offending self' and his 'current self', with the latter being more able to 'show feelings'. One recurring issue in therapy was Steven's marked ambivalence about continuing with the sessions once his parole licence had expired. He could clearly elaborate this fragmentation in his construct system, which was linked by the superordinate construct of 'Head decisions vs Heart decisions'. For Steven, continuing with treatment would have been a 'head decision', as he saw this as 'the right thing to do', enabling him to continue exploring his difficulties in relating to women and monitoring his risk of reoffending. However, he eventually made the 'heart decision' of not continuing with treatment, which is what he really wanted. He saw this decision as enabling him to put the offence behind him and get on with his life, although he acknowledged that this was not what his therapist would have recommended (i.e. demonstrating sociality).

Ambivalence and anxiety about adult heterosexual relationships were also clearly reflected in the construing of Harry, a businessman in his middle forties who had a history of cross-dressing and indecent exposure while wearing women's underwear. This had led to the breakdown of his marriage, and he had had a number of subsequent unsuccessful relationships with women. He was unsure about whether or not he wanted to stop the transvestism and settle down with a new partner. On completing a repertory grid, he construed his current self, ideal self and ideal partner as all being independent and rejecting of the traditional sex role, in contrast to his ex-wife and previous partners. At the same time he recognised that he was tense, easily irritated and a perfectionist, as opposed to his ideal self and ideal partner who would be easygoing, even-tempered and accepting of faults. In interview, Harry disclosed that he hoped women would enjoy seeing him expose, and that this would lead to a sexual encounter with a woman who accepted his transvestism. Therapy involved exploring the reality of this construal. The process of completing the grid helped Harry to clarify the nature of his ambivalence about future relationships, and eventually to reach the decision that he was content with his single lifestyle that enabled him to continue his cross-dressing in private. Consequently, he remained in control of less frequent and intense urges to expose.

THE PCP APPROACH TO ASSESSMENT AND TREATMENT

The nomothetic assessment of sex offenders involves obtaining detailed information about the client's offending behaviour, as well as a comprehensive personal, family and psychosexual history. Current cognitive-behavioural treatment approaches emphasise the importance of addressing the sex offender's processes of appraisal, and there are a number of components to such approaches. These include helping the offender to understand their 'cycle of offending' (Wolf, 1988), challenging distorted cognitions, promoting victim empathy, modifying deviant fantasies, addressing social and assertiveness skills and relapse prevention (e.g. see Perkins, 1987; Salter, 1988; Beckett, 1994).

The PCP perspective is complementary to the above approach, providing a framework with which to conceptualise each individual offender's construing and behaviour. For example, Landfield & Epting (1987) describe a number of case examples in which the constructs and grid ratings of sex offenders are discussed in detail, illustrating how a grid assessment can suggest hypotheses about their behaviour. As with previous chapters, suggested elements and constructs to use in assessment are outlined in Figures 7.1 and 7.2.

How Does the Client See Themself?

An important aspect of the PCP assessment of all offenders is the way in which the client views themself, the difference between their current and ideal self (if any), and how they saw themself at the time of their offence. Individual sex offenders will differ in terms of how positively or negatively they construe both their current and 'offending' selves. Although some individuals may perceive both 'selves' in a negative way, others perceive their 'offending self' less negatively, as their construct system is more fragmented. It is useful to assess whether or not the client construes themself at the time of their offence as domineering and controlling, compared to their victim, and note the use of other constructs which indicate whether or not they perceive themselves to have caused harm. This may suggest patterns of construing to explore further in treatment (see below).

As with most offenders, if there is also a difference in the client's construal of their 'current self' and 'ideal self', they may be more likely to engage in treatment. The case example on page 158 describes the case of a sex offender who did not initially perceive a real need to change, but eventually made good progress in group treatment where he was challenged by peers. It is therefore likely that a sex offender who initially does not anticipate a need for change, will require longer and more intensive treatment, if any change is to occur at all.

Self now

Self when offending

Self as a child

Ideal self

Victim(s)

Partner

Female friend

Male friend

For offenders with child victims:

Own child(ren)

A child I have not abused (or who has not made allegations of abuse)

Male child (picture)

Female child (picture)

Male adolescent (picture)

Female adolescent (picture)

For offenders with adult victims:

A woman I like

A woman I dislike

Women in general

Figure 7.1. Suggested elements to use in assessment

For child sex offenders, a repertory grid assessment would also indicate how the client construed themselves in comparison with their child
victim(s), i.e. whether they saw either their current or ideal self as
similar to the child. The client's construal of themselves as a child can
also provide valuable information about their own experiences of victimisation. A self-characterisation can be particularly useful with sex
offenders, as the way in which they refer to their offending (if at all) can
indicate the extent to which this aspect of themselves is either fragmented (i.e. subsumed within a separate sub-system of constructs) or
part of their core role.

Trusting vs Don't believe you

Innocent vs An easy mark

Makes me feel inferior vs I could lead them

Older vs Younger

Domineering vs Not domineering

Demanding vs Not demanding

Tell me what to do vs Don't tell me what to do

Small body vs big built

(Howells, 1979)

Safe vs Dangerous

Puts pressure on vs Doesn't put pressure on

Honest vs Dishonest

Deserves sympathy vs Doesn't deserve sympathy

Fools people vs Considerate

Attracts opposite sex vs Doesn't attract opposite sex

Likes married life vs Doesn't like married life

(Shorts, 1985)

Selfish vs Unselfish

Sincere vs Insincere

Fair vs Unfair

Weak vs Strong

Inadequate vs Not inadequate

(Needs, 1988)

Easily controlled by others vs Not easily controlled by others

Sexually attractive vs Not sexually attractive

Sexually provocative vs Not sexually provocative

Domineering vs Not domineering

Understanding vs Not understanding

(Houston & Adshead, 1993);

Responsible vs Irresponsible

Frightening vs Not frightening

Sociable vs Isolated

Calm vs Angry

Available vs Unavailable

Judgemental vs Not judgemental

Forgiving vs Unforgiving

High opinion of self vs Low opinion of self

(Beckett et al., 1994)

Figure 7.2. Suggested constructs to use in assessment

How Do They See Other People?

This is a crucial part of the assessment of sex offenders, and should focus particularly on their victim(s) and the group to which they belong, i.e. boys, girls, women. This part of the assessment indicates how an individual construes both other people in general, and their own victim(s) in particular. Repertory grids can be used to assess the degree of empathy towards victims and levels of hostility towards adults. It is interesting to note whether the sex offender client can think of specific individuals to fit the roles of adult partner and friend in a grid assessment, and whether, for example, a rapist can identify adult women friends. The assessment should aim to identify the specific ways in which the sex offender construes other people and their victim(s) in order to avoid guilt (e.g. that children can consent to sex or that women do not mind men exposing to them).

How Do They See Their Behaviour?

Most individuals who commit sexual offences also construe their behaviour in such a way as to validate their hypotheses about their victims. For example, many clients construe their sexual offending as not harmful, or as not coercive. The specific way in which an individual client construes their sexual offending can be elicited from clinical interview or a repertory grid. The clinician can test out their own hypotheses about the construing of their client by supplying certain constructs in a grid (see Figure 7.2), if these have not already been elicited.

Constructing Alternatives

Reconstructing a sex offender client's view of themselves, their victims, other people and their behaviour, is a central part of treatment. It can be particularly effective for this to occur in group settings, where the client is subject to peer pressure. Clients who are likely to remain at high risk of reoffending following treatment are those who choose to continue construing other people in a way which validates their behaviour.

Promoting Victim Empathy

As noted previously, many sex offenders construe the notion of harm very tightly and within a limited range of convenience, applying the construct 'Harmful vs Not harmful' only to physical and observable harm. They therefore convince themselves that their offending was not harmful to their victims. Other clients construe their victim's lack of resistance as implying consent. A component of treatment should aim to increase the offender's understanding of why their victim behaved in the way they did, and increase their awareness of the short- and long-term effects of their sexual offending on their victims. In PCP terms, this involves increasing the ability of the offender to construe the constructions of their victims.

Promoting Adult Relationships

Information from the assessment of a client indicates whether a difficulty in establishing and maintaining satisfactory adult relationships may be a contributory factor in the understanding of that person's offending, together with what is realistic as a treatment goal. For example, it is not realistic to expect a client who is primarily aroused by young boys to develop a sexual relationship with an adult woman. However, it may be possible for them to develop a consenting relationship with a young man over the age of 18. Information from a grid can also support therapeutic work directed towards a client's attitudes to women. Many sex offenders see women as domineering and threatening, and on exploration this view is often based on their experience with only one or two relationships. Such clients can be encouraged to loosen their construing of women by the clinician consistently pointing out the way in which they are generalising from specific examples.

Issues for the Clinician

One clinical problem that often arises when working with sex offenders, is how to move forward with clients who are adamant about the reality of their construing, and are unable to see alternatives. For example, one man convicted of sexually assaulting a 12-year-old girl construed himself very much as the victim. He maintained that the girl had made sexual advances towards him, clearly interpreting her behaviour towards him in a sexual way. Even though the clinician construed alternatives, e.g. that the girl was looking for affection and interest from the man, rather than sex, the client would not consider these, needing to hold on to his own construction to preserve the positive view of himself held by both him and his family. In this situation it would be easy either to get into repeated confrontation with the client about the events, which is likely to lead him to hold on to his view even more strongly (i.e. by inducing threat, fear, anxiety and guilt, G. Kelly, 1991), or to accept the client's version of events, which means that there is little need for him to participate in treatment. A more constructive approach with a sex offender client whose construing is as rigid as this, and who therefore it is easy to feel very 'stuck' with, is to acknowledge both *their perspective* of events but also the *consequences* of this perception. The clinician can say something like:

> CLINICIAN: So the way you see things is that when Karen touched your arm and looked up at you, she was giving you the message that she was interested in sex, and you feel strongly that you did not misinterpret her actions. So what sense do you make of her witness statement describing how distressed she was?
>
> CLIENT: She was lying, she started it.
>
> CLINICIAN: Well, the reason that you are in prison now is that as an adult, it was your responsibility to resist any such advances. What do you think you need to do differently in the future if you are in the same situation again?
>
> CLIENT: I won't get into that situation again.
>
> CLINICIAN: But how can you be sure? What would you do in the future if you thought that a young girl was giving you the message that she was interested in sex?
>
> CLIENT: Well, I'd make sure I wasn't alone with a girl in a situation where it could happen anyway. I'd just walk away.

The PCP approach therefore enables the clinician to get into a dialogue with a sex offender about reducing risk of reoffending, even when they do not perceive themselves to have committed an offence.

The following case example illustrates the use of the PCP perspective in the assessment and treatment of a man with a long history of the sexual abuse of both boys and girls, and whose way of construing his own experiences as a child played a key part in his ability to progress in treatment.

> Charles, a 48-year-old man, was serving a long sentence for a number of serious sexual offences against a group of boys and girls between the ages of 8 and 14 years whom he had befriended. He requested help at the start of his sentence, and participated in two 6-month treatment groups. Information obtained from a clinical interview with Charles indicated that he had a long-standing sexual interest in children of both sexes. He had previously been married and had admitted abusing his stepdaughter, although at the time there had not been enough evidence for him to be charged. He did not see himself as having any other difficulties in his life. He had worked successfully with a small company since

leaving school, and described himself as sociable and popular. During the initial interview Charles said that he knew that his offending was wrong, but that because the children continued to visit him after he had abused them, he assumed they were willing participants. He described his 'relationship' with his main male victim in equal terms, and did not think that his offending had had any harmful effects. His main reason for wanting to attend the treatment group was to understand more about why he had offended.

In completing a pre-group repertory grid with Charles, it was important not only to compare aspects of his construing with that of other sex offenders, but also to explore what was unique and personal to him. As well as including four pictures of children as elements to explore his construing of children in general, the elements therefore also included four different aspects of his 'self' (self now, self as an offender, ideal self, self as a child), his ex-wife and two of his victims. Because Charles had abused so many children over the years, it was quite difficult to decide who to include in the element roles of 'victim', and it would have been too unwieldy to include all of these in the grid. However, when talking to Charles it was clear that he had been particularly attracted to one young boy, Mark, who had a difficult home life. Charles saw himself as being 'fatherly' towards Mark, by buying him things his parents could not afford. As Charles had abused both boys and girls, it seemed important to also include a female victim among the elements, so he was asked which of his female victims he had known best. Interestingly, Charles found this much harder, saying that he did not really know any of them very well. This suggested that, although he was sexually aroused by both boys and girls, sexual contact with boys was more validating to his sense of self.

Charles expressed great interest in the process of completing the grid. He had no difficulty eliciting constructs using the triad method, and his constructs are shown in Figure 7.3. These mostly reflect aspects of sociability. The five constructs used by Houston & Adshead (1993) (see Figure 7.2) were also supplied to explore hypotheses about the ways in which Charles construed children.

A further construct was elicited which was not included in the grid as it was too role-specific. In other words, when presented with the triad 'Self, Victim, Ex-wife', and asked the standard question 'In what way are two of these three people alike and therefore different from the third?', Charles replied that his

Kind vs Unchristian

Like a good time vs Killjoy

Good looking vs Ugly

Friendly vs Unfriendly

Quiet vs Boisterous

Loving vs Grasping

Happy vs Unhappy

Figure 7.3. Constructs provided by Charles at pre-treatment

victim, Mark, and his ex-wife were similar because 'I have had sex with both of them . . . I have loved both of them'. This way of construing gave a useful insight into both Charles' egocentricity, and the way in which he perceived his abuse of Mark as no different to his relationship with his wife.

The plot of Charles' pre-treatment repertory grid (12 × 12) is shown in Figure 7.4. The INGRID analysis (Slater, 1972) indicated that Charles' construct system could be described by three fairly discrete components. The first component, or main way in which Charles discriminated between himself and others, mainly consisted of elicited constructs relating to being happy and sociable. Interestingly, the second component was made up of two of the supplied constructs, indicating that whether or not people on the grid were domineering and sexually provocative was a meaningful way in which Charles discriminated between them. A third component consisted of constructs related to being kind and loving.

Information from Charles' grid added to that obtained from the interview to suggest a number of ways in which his construct system facilitated the continuing validation of his offending. He saw little difference between his current and ideal self, and saw himself as being similar to his male victim. He construed all three elements very positively, as friendly, happy, kind and loving, and not domineering or sexually provocative. Charles did not therefore see himself as having a deviant self-identity, nor that he had a real need to change. Furthermore, his female victim and ex-wife were perceived to be more towards the domineering and sexually provocative poles of the constructs, as were both male and female children and adolescents shown to him in pictures. He construed

```
                    NOT DOMINEERING
                 NOT SEXUALLY PROVOCATIVE
                            |                        LOVING
                            |                          KIND
                            |                 UNDERSTANDING
*Self as a child            |

                            |     *Ideal self
                            |     *Self now         FRIENDLY
QUIET                       |     *Male victim         HAPPY
EASILY CONTROLLED           |              GOOD LOOKING
DECISIONS INFLUENCED        |         MAKES OWN DECISIONS
UGLY _____    |_____ NOT EASILY CONTROLLED
UNHAPPY                     |               BOISTEROUS
UNFRIENDLY                  |
    *Self as offender       |     *Teenage girl
                            |     *Female child
                            |     *Male child

                            | *Female victim
NOT UNDERSTANDING   *Ex-wife|
GRASPING                    |
UNCHRISTIAN    *Teenage     |
                 boy        |

                     DOMINEERING
                 SEXUALLY PROVOCATIVE
```

Figure 7.4. Plot of elements in construct space from Charles' pre-treatment grid

both his victims and the children in the pictures as making their own decisions, in contrast to himself as an offender. One hypothesis was therefore that he avoided seeing himself as 'deviant' by construing both children in general and his own victims as domineering, sexually provocative and responsible for their own decisions.

From the PCP perspective, treatment aims were therefore for Charles to reconstrue his view of himself, children in general and his victims in particular. The group required Charles to elaborate his history of sexual offending and examine his patterns of construing, and included exercises, role play and video material to increase his ability to construe the constructions of his victims. Charles participated well in the group, and began to acknowledge that he was buying all the children presents that he knew they wanted. However, at the end of the first group, there was little real change in Charles' grid. The constructs 'Domineering vs Not domineering' and 'Sexually provocative vs Not sexually provocative' were still important discriminators in the way he thought about people, particularly his female victim and the pictures of adolescents. Some 'slot-rattling' was indicated by the fact that he no longer rated the pictures of the male and female children as domineering and sexually provocative, and there was an increase in the distance between his current and ideal self. The group leaders were keen for Charles to continue treatment in a second group, and he agreed to this. During this group Charles made considerable progress, facilitated by his disclosure that he himself had been abused as a child by a teacher at his boarding school. He complied with the abuse in order to receive special favours from the teacher, thereby developing an alternative construction about why a child might return to visit an abusing adult. Charles had not previously construed as harmful, the actions of the teacher whose behaviour mirrored much of his own offending. However, by putting himself in the position of his own victims (i.e. developing sociality of construing), he gradually came to realise why they (and he as a child) had not physically resisted, and that the abuse had left long-term harmful effects on himself and his victims. Within the group Charles began to test out his new hypotheses about the behaviour of children by challenging other group members about their own patterns of construing, and describing the contrast with his previous perspective.

At the end of the second group, Charles completed a third grid. This time the whole nature of his elicited constructs had changed, to reflect the impact of his abuse on others (see Figure 7.5). Although many of his elicited constructs were still egocentric, they

Been abused vs Normal childhood

I took (would take) advantage of them vs I was (would be) kind and generous to them

Vulnerable vs Secure

I deceived (would deceive) them vs I was (would be honest) with them

Innocent vs Experienced

Full of life vs Decrepit

Figure 7.5. Constructs provided by Charles at post-treatment

reflected an important change in the nature of his construing. The plot of Charles' grid showed that after treatment, the most important way in which he discriminated between other people was in terms of whether or not he had been honest with them and taken advantage of them (see Figure 7.6). Whether or not children were sexually provocative was no longer a meaningful construct. Charles did not see himself as similar to his male victim and recognised that both his 'current' and 'offending self' were *not* easily controlled by others, in contrast to both of his victims and the children in the pictures. He no longer rated his ex-wife so negatively, and acknowledged that he had taken advantage of and been deceitful with both her and his victims. His construing acknowledged that his 'offending self' was not as dissimilar to his current self as

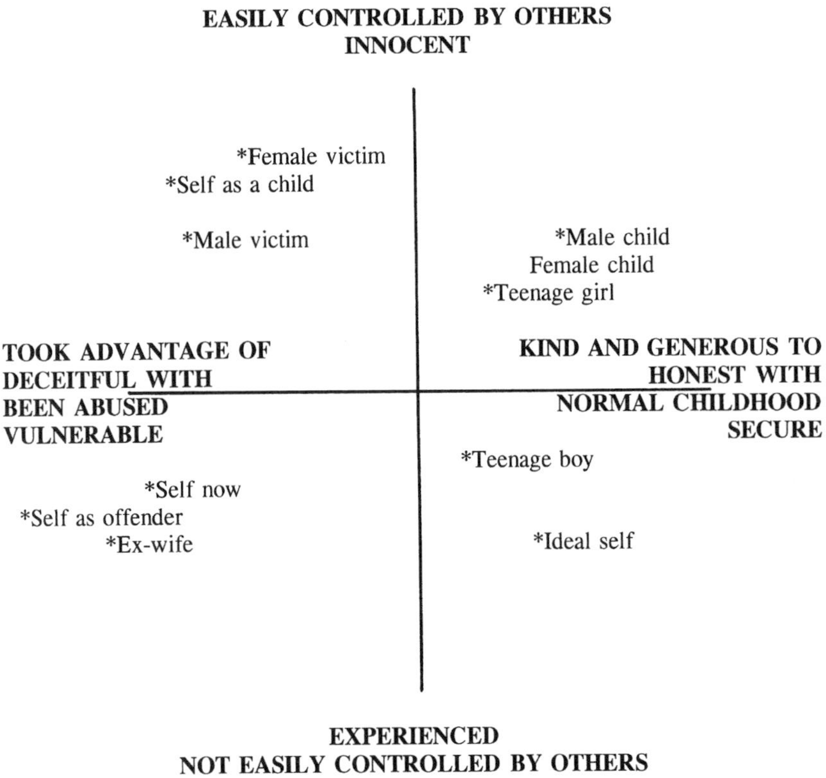

EASILY CONTROLLED BY OTHERS
INNOCENT

*Female victim
*Self as a child

*Male victim
                                    *Male child
                                    Female child
                                    *Teenage girl

TOOK ADVANTAGE OF   KIND AND GENEROUS TO
DECEITFUL WITH   HONEST WITH
BEEN ABUSED   NORMAL CHILDHOOD
VULNERABLE   SECURE
                                    *Teenage boy

*Self now
*Self as offender
*Ex-wife   *Ideal self

EXPERIENCED
NOT EASILY CONTROLLED BY OTHERS

Figure 7.6. Plot of elements in construct space from Charles' post-treatment grid

he wanted to think. Charles was keen to continue with treatment and successfully applied for transfer to a prison with a therapeutic community.

SUMMARY AND CONCLUSIONS

Most clinicians agree that there is a difference between working with sex offenders and working with other client groups, which partly arises from feelings about the nature of the offences committed. From the PCP perspective there is a particular difficulty for the clinician in demonstrating sociality with this client group. There is also a lack of commonality between child sex offenders and the rest of society, in relation to the ways in which they construe children.

There is little evidence to suggest the consistent presence of structural disorders in the construing of sex offenders *per se*. However, it is likely that those individuals who commit sexual offences in addition to having a wide range of other difficulties may show features of construing associated with personality disorder (see Chapter 8). Of all offenders, the behaviour of those who commit sexual offences is often most clearly a reflection of the *content* of their construing, particularly in terms of their construing of adults and children. The ways in which sex offenders construe themselves, other people, their victims and their behaviour are important in understanding their offending at a number of different levels. First, for some child sex offenders, the ways in which they construe children and adults mean that sexual contact with children may generally be a more validating and therefore rewarding experience than adult relationships. Such individuals may be particularly likely to construe children as less domineering and more easily controlled than adults. Other child sex offenders may construe their victim as a 'substitute partner'. Individuals who sexually offend against adult women, or who expose, are likely to construe women in ways which validate their offending, such as making interpretations about women's sexual behaviour and attitudes from the way they are dressed. Clients also differ in the extent to which their construct system may be fragmented to accommodate incompatibilities in their construing.

In addition to pre-existing ways of construing children or adults which may facilitate their offending, sex offenders also construe their specific victims and behaviour in ways which enable them to avoid or push away guilt. The consequences of these ways of construing for specific victims, the general public and the potential offender, mean that they are appropriately construed as disordered by the clinician.

Although, as with all types of offenders, there may be some commonalities in the ways in which men who have committed sexual offences interpret events, the PCP approach to assessment and treatment emphasises the importance of the ways in which the particular individual client construes the world. When working with clients in whom the consequences of their behaviour puts others in society at risk, it is important to set an individually oriented approach within the context of nomothetic assessment and treatment approaches which have produced encouraging results. None the less, particularly with the recent developments in group treatment, the PCP perspective can remind the clinician of the differences between individuals, and offer an approach which helps to steer the difficult course between aggressive confrontation and collusion.

CHAPTER 8

Personality Disordered Offenders

This chapter begins by considering definitions of personality disorder and psychopathy. The personal construct perspective is particularly useful in understanding the thinking processes of these offenders, why they persist with deviant behaviour and why they often have difficulty learning from experience. Both the content and the structure of the construing of personality disordered offenders are important in understanding the nature of their offending. Since many offenders with a diagnosis of personality disorder have committed violent or sexual offences, and/or have a problem with alcohol or drug dependence, this chapter can be seen as complementary to those other chapters in Part II.

INTRODUCTION

Clinicians working with offenders often come across certain clients who seem to cause more difficulty than most. Their offending is only one aspect of a wide range of difficulties, which seem to interlink and affect all aspects of their life. They may have additional difficulties in interpersonal relationships, problems with drug or alcohol abuse, very low self-esteem and problems with anxiety, depression, obsessional behaviour, or self-harm. Such clients may test the boundaries of the professional relationship, try to get to know the clinician on a more personal level, or maintain a hostile, distant aloofness, constantly challenging the clinician and making a normal interview very difficult. These individuals can be very frustrating to work with, apparently failing to learn from experience and behaving in self-destructive ways which lead to a persistent pattern of deviant behaviour. This can pose a challenge to the clinician's professional esteem, and lead them to feel very deskilled in their therapeutic work with this client group. These recognisable clients are often diagnosed as personality disordered, a label that can either be a help or a hindrance depending on the prevailing view about the treatability of such individuals.

The classificatory system DSM-IV defines personality traits as 'enduring patterns of perceiving, relating to, and thinking about the environment and one's self . . . exhibited in a wide range of important social and personal contexts' (DSM-IV, American Psychiatric Association, 1994). All individuals have personality traits, and they only constitute a *disorder* when they are 'inflexible and maladaptive and cause either significant impairment in social or occupational functioning or subjective distress' (p. 630). Personality disorders are therefore enduring rather than temporary, present by the time of adolescence and continuing through adulthood. In terms of this definition, a person can have a 'normal' obsessive or paranoid personality, which is only seen as a disorder if the above criteria are fulfilled.

Diagnostic criteria for 301.7 Antisocial Personality Disorder

A. There is a pervasive pattern of disregard for and violation of the rights of others occurring since age 15 years, as indicated by three (or more) of the following:

   (1) failure to conform to social norms with respect to lawful behaviors as indicated by repeatedly performing acts that are grounds for arrest
   (2) deceitfulness, as indicated by repeated lying, use of aliases, or conning others for personal profit or pleasure
   (3) impulsivity or failure to plan ahead
   (4) irritability and aggressiveness, as indicated by repeated physical fights or assaults
   (5) reckless disregard for safety of self or others
   (6) consistent irresponsibility, as indicated by repeated failure to sustain consistent work behavior or honor financial obligations
   (7) lack of remorse, as indicated by being indifferent to or rationalizing having hurt, mistreated, or stolen from another

B. The individual is at least age 18 years.

C. There is evidence of Conduct Disorder with onset before age 15 years.

D. The occurrence of antisocial behavior is not exclusively during the course of Schizophrenia or a Manic Episode.

Figure 8.1. Diagnostic criteria for 301.7 Antisocial Personality Disorder. Reproduced with permission from the *Diagnostic and Statistical Manual of Mental Disorders*, Fourth Edition. Copyright © 1994, American Psychiatric Association

Diagnostic criteria for 301.83 Borderline Personality Disorder

A pervasive pattern of instability of interpersonal relationships, self-image, and affects, and marked impulsivity beginning by early adulthood and present in a variety of contexts, as indicated by five (or more) of the following:

(1) frantic efforts to avoid real or imagined abandonment. **Note:** Do not include suicidal or self-multilating behavior covered in Criterion 5.
(2) a pattern of unstable and intense interpersonal relationships characterized by alternating between extremes of idealization and devaluation
(3) identity disturbance: markedly and persistently unstable self-image or sense of self
(4) impulsivity in at least two areas that are potentially self-damaging (e.g., spending, sex, substance abuse, reckless driving, binge eating). **Note:** Do not include suicidal or self-mutilating behavior covered in Criterion 5.
(5) recurrent suicidal behavior, gestures, or threats, or self-mutilating behavior
(6) affective instability due to a marked reactivity of mood (e.g., intense episodic dysphoria, irritability, or anxiety usually lasting a few hours and only rarely more than a few days)
(7) chronic feelings of emptiness
(8) inappropriate, intense anger or difficulty controlling anger (e.g., frequent displays of temper, constant anger, recurrent physical fights)
(9) transient, stress-related paranoid ideation or severe dissociative symptoms

Figure 8.2. Diagnostic criteria for 301.83 Borderline Personality Disorder. Reproduced with permission from the *Diagnostic and Statistical Manual of Mental Disorders*, Fourth Edition. Copyright © 1994, American Psychiatric Association

There are three clusters of personality disorders in DSM-IV. Cluster A contains those in which the individuals appear odd or eccentric, such as the paranoid or schizoid personality disorders. In Cluster B, individuals show dramatic, emotional or erratic features, such as the antisocial or borderline personality disorders. Cluster C contains those who appear anxious or fearful, for example obsessive-compulsive or passive-aggressive personality disorder. However, in offender populations it has been demonstrated that the different personality disorders are not mutually exclusive categories (Blackburn et al., 1990; Dolan, 1995), and problems with diagnostic reliability still remain. The usefulness of such diagnoses for the clinician lies in having a framework with which to conceptualise the client's difficulties and therefore to set realistic goals. Most of the clients described in the studies and case examples in this chapter have been diagnosed as having an antisocial or borderline personality disorder, and the DSM-IV criteria for these are shown in Figures 8.1 and 8.2. However, it is important to note that other types of personality disorder are also common in offender populations, such as schizoid and dependent disorders. There is also much scope for using the PCP perspective to understand the offending of these individuals, as well as those diagnosed with narcissistic disorders, who show some overlap with psychopathy.

The area is also fraught with inconsistencies of terminology. In particular, the terms 'antisocial personality disorder', 'sociopath' and 'psychopath' are all commonly used to describe individuals with persistent socially deviant behaviour. Although the *clinical* definition of the term 'psychopath' is usually used to refer to individuals who show the features of antisocial personality disorder, Blackburn (1993) emphasises that 'psychopathy' is actually a personality construct. Cleckley (1976) defined psychopathic personality using 16 criteria, including superficial charm and lack of remorse, and Hare (1980, 1991) later developed a more objective checklist of personality features characteristic of psychopathy (See Figure 8.3).

1. Glibness/superficial charm
2. Previous diagnosis as psychopath (or similar)
3. Egocentricity/grandiose sense of self-worth
4. Proneness to boredom/low frustration tolerance
5. Pathological lying and deception
6. Conning/lack of sincerity
7. Lack of remorse or guilt
8. Lack of affect and emotional depth
9. Callous/lack of empathy
10. Parasitic life-style
11. Short-tempered/poor behavioral controls
12. Promiscuous sexual relations
13. Early behavior problems
14. Lack of realistic, long-term plans
15. Impulsivity
16. Irresponsible behavior as parent
17. Frequent marital relationships
18. Juvenile delinquency
19. Poor probation or parole risk
20. Failure to accept responsibility for own actions
21. Many types of offense
22. Drug or alcohol abuse not direct cause of antisocial behavior

Figure 8.3. Checklist items for the assessment of psychopathy. Reprinted from *Personality and Individual Differences*, **1**, R. D. Hare, A research scale for the assessment of psychopathy in criminal populations, 111–119, Copyright © 1979, with kind permission from Elsevier Science Ltd, The Boulevard, Langford Lane, Kidlington OX5 1GB, UK

As well as the clinical definition of psychopathy, there is also a wider *legal* definition. The Mental Health Act for England and Wales (1983) defines 'psychopathic disorder' as 'a persistent disability of mind (whether or not including significant impairment of intelligence) which results in abnormally aggressive behaviour or seriously irresponsible conduct'. In practice, this means that many of the individuals detained under this category in hospital can be suffering from a range of personality disorders as diagnosed by clinical criteria, or may not completely fulfil strict criteria for any one of the clinical personality disorders.

The inconsistencies of terminology and heterogeneity of clinical populations defined as personality disordered are only two of the factors that contribute to the lack of methodologically sound studies of the effectiveness of treatment with this client group (see reviews by Dolan & Coid, 1995; Blackburn, 1993). Although there is often a certain amount of pessimism among clinicians about the treatability of people with personality disorders, this cannot therefore be substantiated empirically. Indeed, Blackburn (1993) notes that there is evidence that some offenders with personality disorders do appear to change with psychological treatment, with cognitive-behavioural approaches being among those which have suggested encouraging results (Beck & Freeman, 1990; Layden et al., 1993).

THE PCP PERSPECTIVE ON PERSONALITY DISORDERED OFFENDERS

Personality disordered offenders form a heterogeneous group who commit a range of different offences, including violent and sexual offending. Although it initially may appear somewhat arbitrary and repetitive to consider personality disordered offenders separately, and there is inevitably some overlap in the applicability of chapters to individual clients, not all offenders who commit violent or sexual offences, or who abuse substances, have additional personality disorders. As outlined in the introduction, there are additional characteristics of personality disordered offenders, over and above the type of their offending *per se*, which make this client group worthy of separate consideration. Some of those characteristics which are clearly conceptualised in personal construct terms, are the notions of guilt (or lack of), hostility and impulsivity.

G. Kelly (1955/1991) defined guilt as 'the awareness of dislodgement of the self from one's core role structure'. People suffer from guilt if they do things which are incompatible with their view of themselves. The way in which personality disordered offenders view themselves is therefore crucial in determining whether or not they are likely to feel guilty (in the conventional sense) about their offending. This links clearly to the PCP perspective on the development and maintenance of a deviant self-identity, discussed in the opening chapter. People behave in ways which enable them to avoid uncertainty, and if an individual already has a deviant self-identity, continuing to offend is the behaviour which ensures the greatest predictablity in their world. Dalton & Dunnett (1992) also note that if a person has a core role structure in which they have no particular fixed ideas about the kind of person they are, or what beliefs are important to them, or one in which 'anything goes', then guilt is unlikely to be a problem. The authors suggest that this might be a description (in PCP terms) of the psychopathic personality, where whatever a person does is acceptable to them, as long as they construe it as being in their interests. A further way in which an individual can avoid guilt is to construe events in a hostile way (in the Kellian sense), i.e. to distort the available data to fit their own hypotheses.

A further observation about antisocial and borderline personality disordered offenders in particular is their impulsivity. The PCP conception of impulsivity relates to one of G. Kelly's hypotheses about the process of change. As seen in the opening chapter, the CPC cycle (circumspection–pre-emption–control) describes the process which precedes choice and action in any situation. In the first stage (circumspection) the individual considers all the possible options open, secondly they choose an appropriate construct or dimension of experience (pre-emption), and thirdly they reach a decision point along the chosen dimension (control). For example, consider an individual in a situation where they feel that someone has just insulted them. Most people would consider their options (e.g. ignoring, assertive response, aggressive response, etc.), choose which is most appropriate in the given circumstances, and then decide how to implement that response (e.g. verbally, physically, immediately, later). In practice this process happens fairly quickly, but it is shaped by that person's previous experience and usual way of responding to similar situations. Impulsiveness can be seen to represent a shortening of the circumspection stage and a related restriction of options, e.g. a person would not consider any other options apart from physical aggression.

Clinicians taking a PCP perspective therefore construe offenders who are diagnosed as personality disordered as behaving in ways which are entirely consistent with their own particular construct system. If their construct system is in itself unstable, then the individual may be observed to behave in apparently contradictory ways on different occasions. However, to the individual, their behaviour makes sense. There are therefore interesting links between the PCP perspective and the recent developments in cognitive treatment approaches which emphasise the role of dysfunctional cognitive schema in the development and maintenance of personality disorders (Safran, 1990; Layden et al., 1993). Such approaches originate from the interpersonal theories of personality disorder which conceptualise personality disorders as dysfunctional interpersonal styles supported by biased schemata (Carson, 1979; Kiesler, 1983). These schema then function as self-fulfilling prophecies through their effects on other people.

PATTERNS OF CONSTRUING IN PERSONALITY DISORDERED OFFENDERS

The different ways in which the construing of this client group contributes to their offending behaviour have been the focus of a number of research studies. Compared with the research on patterns of construing in other types of offenders, there have been a greater number of empirical studies of the construing of personality disordered offenders, and fewer single case studies. However, with one exception (Klass, 1980), the research has all been carried out on patients detained under the legal category of psychopathic disorder, which is a clinically heterogeneous group. In this chapter, the terms used in specific studies are maintained, and where issues are relevant only to one specific type of personality disorder, that is specified.

The Structure of the Construct System

There has been greater interest in the structural features of the construing of those diagnosed with a personality disorder than of other types of offenders. The research indicates that personality disordered offenders often have construct systems which are structured in unusual ways, compared with those of both non-offenders and other offenders.

Widom (1976) used repertory grids to explore the personal construct systems of primary and secondary psychopaths detained in an English maximum security hospital, and compared them to those of a group of controls (male nurses). Psychopaths were selected on the basis of several criteria, following the early work of Cleckley (1976) and Hare (1976). Thirty elements of different interpersonal situations were presented, including antisocial behaviour, 'good but dull' situations (e.g. Giving blood), and those involving risk, alcohol, drugs and criminal responsibility. Half the situations were those in which the person was playing an active part in the situation (e.g. Getting caught for a crime you committed) and half were those in which the person was on the receiving end themselves (e.g. Getting caught for a crime you didn't commit). Ten constructs were elicited and eight supplied (see Figure 8.6). The grids were then administered twice, with the participants being asked to say how both they as an individual and people in general would view those situations.

Widom (1976) used a number of measures to examine the structure of the construct systems. There was no difference in the overall *intensity* scores of the psychopaths and controls (i.e. the interrelationship between their constructs, indicating how tightly organised the construct system is), or in the type of constructs elicited. However, the most significant difference between primary psychopaths compared with secondary psychopaths and controls lay in the *lopsidedness* of their construct systems, i.e. that most elements were only assigned to one pole of the constructs. In this case, the lopsidedness of construing indicated a tendency by the primary psychopaths to construe situations as dull rather than exciting. Lopsidedness or maldistribution is pathological in the sense that, carried to its extreme, it could result in the person's complete inability to make useful conceptual discriminations, and this characteristic has also been associated with difficulties in predicting the responses of other people (Hayden et al., 1977; Winter, 1988). As seen in Chapter 6, lopsided construing has also been observed in extremely violent offenders who have committed 'one-off' offences (Howells, 1983). However, it is not clear from the study whether there were proportionally greater numbers of patients legally categorised as personality disordered in the 'one-off' group of violent offenders, and as such, whether lopsided construing is a characteristic feature of that client group *per se*, or of individuals who commit a single, extremely violent offence.

Characteristic structural features of construing in personality disordered offenders have also been demonstrated by Thomas-Peter (1992). His clinical observations were that personality disordered offenders (i.e. those detained in a maximum security hospital under the legal category of psychopathic disorder) made a remarkable number of very extreme judgements, using the ends of constructs rather then mid-range or neutral points, and they also made their judgements very quickly. A computerised repertory grid task about social judgements confirmed these observations. However, whereas the control group made moderate and neutral judgements more slowly, the personality disordered group did not do this, all types of judgements being made equally quickly. Since reaction time is considered to be an analogue of cognitive processing, Thomas-Peter (1992) suggested that the impairment shown by the personality disordered offenders was therefore in making *moderate judgements*.

Both speed and extremity of judgements are associated with how personally meaningful that judgement is (Adams-Webber, 1979). Thomas-Peter (1992) therefore suggested that making an 'impulsive' judgement may reveal the significance of the judgement to the subject. It may be that for personality disordered offenders, judgements of different personal meaning and significance provoke a similar style of shortened circumspection phase of the CPC cycle normally associated with extreme judgements. A cognitive 'habit' may develop from having quickly made many personally significant judgements. Alternatively, unusual construct systems may be dominated by superordinate (i.e. abstract and more generally applicable) constructs, so that the speed of moderate judgements reflects the extremity of those particular constructs. This latter suggestion seems to be supported by clinical experience, particularly with borderline personality disordered offenders, whose construct systems are often focused around constructs associated with those which are superordinate, such as 'Good vs Bad'. This is illustrated in the later case examples.

Finally, although Widom's (1976) empirical study failed to demonstrate that the construing of psychopaths was any more tightly organised than that of non-psychopaths, other authors have suggested that there is a relationship between *cognitive simplicity* and personality disorder (e.g. Orford, 1974, see Chapter 9). This is also supported by individual case studies. As described in Chapter 1, cognitive complexity is 'the capacity to construe social behaviour in a multidimensional way' (Bieri et al., 1966, p. 185), and indicates the complexity of a person's thinking processes. People who show cognitively simple, or black-and-white, thinking often therefore construe themselves and others in similar 'all or nothing' terms. Cognitive simplicity was clearly illustrated in a case study described by Howells (1978), who used the repertory grid to explore the perceptions of a psychopath in a maximum security hospital who had attempted to poison members of his family. The man had a long-standing fascination with poisons and had reported fantasies of poisoning people he knew, maintaining that he had no remorse for his behaviour. Most of his constructs were highly intercorrelated and 80.36% of the total variance was accounted for by the first component of the principal components analysis, described mainly by the constructs 'Accepts authority vs Abnormal' and 'Goes his own way vs Goes society's way' (see Figure 8.4).

Construing of the Self

Further research on the construing of offenders diagnosed with personality disorders has focused on the *content* of construct system. A number

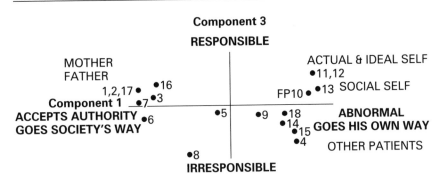

Figure 8.4. Plot of elements on components. Reproduced from *Medicine, Science and the Law* (1978) **18**, 182, by permission of the British Academy of Forensic Science

of studies have highlighted the way in which some people with antisocial personality disorders do not construe any difference between their current (i.e. offending) and ideal self, and therefore do not experience guilt in the traditional sense. Maintaining consistency between current and ideal self in the face of continued offending, can either be achieved by construing harm as self-congruent and having a deviant self-identity (e.g. Klass, 1980; Howells, 1978) or by not construing the offending behaviour as harmful (Fransella & Adams, 1966).

The way in which sociopaths perceive themselves when harming others was the main focus of the research by Klass (1980). This is the only empirical study of an out-patient population of this client group, who were recruited from a methadone maintenance clinic. The sociopath sample was selected if they met a minimum criterion of five antisocial behaviour symptoms over and above their drug abuse. Klass compared both 'persons' and 'situations' repertory grids of sociopathic and non-sociopathic methadone users to those of students. As she predicted, the sociopaths had a greater tendency to see *harming others* as consistent with their view of themselves than the non-sociopathic group, and were also significantly more likely to view *harmful acts* as typical of themselves than the students. In addition, the greater the difference between a person's view of themself and their view of harming others, the more negative reaction they expected from others to their antisocial behaviour. This is consistent with social learning theory (Bandura, 1977), which predicts a parallel between perceived self-congruence of transgression and level of actual antisocial activity. The findings are also consonant with Kelly's view (1991) of the importance of self-concept in negative self-reactions, i.e. that experiences of guilt are mediated by discrepancies between self-concept and one's actions.

Howells' (1978) repertory grid study of a poisoner provides a further example of the link between self-congruence and antisocial activity. As seen in Figure 8.4, the man construed his actual, ideal and social self, together with the name of a famous poisoner (the person he named to fit the role of 'A person I consider successful') all as socially abnormal. He saw no difference between his actual and ideal self. The construct 'Responsible vs Irresponsible' differentiated his actual, ideal, social selves and the famous poisoner from other patients who were also seen as socially abnormal. Therefore, although he saw himself as socially abnormal, he also saw himself as responsible. He elaborated this in interview, saying that although other patients or criminals may be abnormal or socially unacceptable, he viewed them as 'not responsible' because they did not plan and execute their crimes with full knowledge of what they were doing and then accept the consequences. Only himself and the famous poisoner were abnormal and responsible, as their crimes were rational and calculated and they fully accepted the consequences of these. Furthermore, the famous poisoner was the element rated closest to his self and ideal, with his parents and brother seen as the total opposite, thus modelling himself on people who were maximally different from family members.

In contrast, Fransella & Adams (1966) used repertory grids to study a 39-year-old man who had committed several acts of arson, but who did *not* see himself as the type of person to commit this kind of offence. In interview he described how tense and aggressive feelings would be temporarily relieved by the calmness that followed fire setting. His personality was described as characterised by extreme conscientiousness and dislike of change, considerable drive and strongly held opinions regarding sexual and business morality. No symptoms of a mental illness are reported. Although there is no further information about the man's personality difficulties or other mental disorder, the fact that he was referred to psychiatric hospital from prison suggests that he may have been suffering from a personality disorder.

A number of different grids were administered to the man to test hypotheses about his behaviour. The main construct with which the man construed the world was 'As I'd like to be in character vs Not as I'd like to be in character'. The most significant finding was that although he perceived no difference between his current and ideal self, he did not see himself as the sort of person who was likely to commit arson. He construed his current and ideal self, fire-related feelings and feelings of power and hostility at the 'good' pole (i.e. how he would like to be), and people who were immoral, sinful and who commit arson all being deserving of punishment at the 'bad' pole (i.e. not how he would like to be). Over time, the negative relationship between the self and arson constructs increased to the point where his view of himself was almost the direct opposite of the sort of person who commits arson. In his view therefore, when he was setting fires he was not 'committing arson', and Fransella & Adams (1966) used further grids to test out hypotheses about why he did set fires. These suggested that he saw himself as someone who enjoyed power, who was a 'punisher of wrongdoers', and believed people got the punishment they deserved. These constructs were closely associated with the way he felt when setting fires. Fransella & Adams therefore suggested that the man may see himself as carrying out a crusade against people who deserve punishment by setting fires, an act which he would not see as wrong or criminal, since he viewed himself as delivering justice. It would also have been interesting to know from the case study how the man kept the symbolism of his fire setting separate from the reality. Assuming that he did not *intend* to endanger life, one could hypothesise that he might have construed his own fire setting as 'not life-threatening', or have claimed that he 'only set small fires'.

In contrast to all of the above cases, Pollock & Kear-Colwell (1994) describe the self-construing of two female offenders diagnosed with borderline personality disorder, who *did* construe themselves as both 'guilty' and as 'perpetrators'. Both women had been seriously violent towards their boyfriends, and also had a history of significant sexual abuse. The study attempted to examine the relationship between sexual victimisation and violent offences using G. Kelly's (1955/1991) concept of core role constructs, and Ryle's (1990) notion of reciprocal role procedures (i.e. that an offender's self-perceptions as an 'abuser' or a 'victim' are complementary procedures of the same role). Repertory grids supported the authors' hypothesis that the *sexually abused offender* would construe themselves in the role of an 'abuser' rather than as a 'victim'. This position is associated with intense guilt and self-denigratory feelings, in which the self-perception of being a perpetrator allows the individual to confirm their belief about the malevolence of their personality. To perceive the individual as an 'abused victim' rather than a 'guilty abuser' may therefore dislodge them from their core role structure, which would elicit further guilt in the Kellian sense. Both women felt that to see themselves in an abused role highlighted the harmful actions of others, and represented an attempt to blame others for their own offending. Pollock & Kear-Colwell (1994) describe the use of Cognitive-Analytic Therapy (Ryle, 1990) to enable the women to progress towards a rational analysis both of their actions and of their guilt (see further discussion in Chapter 3). Interestingly, as discussed in Chapter 7, the authors' hypotheses are not always supported in the case of sex offenders who themselves have been victims of abuse.

Construal of Others

One of the characteristics often ascribed to psychopaths, if not necessarily to other personality disordered offenders, is a lack of regard for others. However, in Klass's (1980) study, both sociopathic *and* non-sociopathic drug users expected to react less negatively to harming *disliked victims* than compared to those that they liked. In contrast, the student group expected to react equally negatively to harming someone, whatever their attitude towards the victim. Since normal individuals believe that harming another person creates negative feelings even if they dislike the person, Klass (1980) suggests that most people are likely to show self-restraint in a wider range of interpersonal situations than the clinical groups. However, although the fact that an individual client has a lack of regard for other people may help to make sense of their particular behaviour, the evidence to date does not suggest that personality disordered offenders as a group construe other people in more negative ways than do other clinical groups.

Although Widom's (1976) study did not compare the construing of psychopaths to that of another clinical group, she found that psychopaths showed a significant degree of misperception about the construct systems of people in general. As mentioned earlier, both primary and secondary psychopaths frequently characterised situations in the repertory grid as dull rather than exciting, and wrongly assumed that this was also the way in which people in general (i.e. the control group) would also think. Thus as well as responding physiologically as if stimuli and/or events are dull and unexciting (Hare, 1976), psychopaths are also more likely to perceive situations in that way. In other words, psychopaths may not think that other people think differently to themselves, and therefore see no need to modify their own construct systems. The ability to construe the construction processes of other people is essential for successful social relating (Kelly's Sociality Corollary), and it is therefore likely that individuals who have a deficit in this area will be impaired in their ability to make interpersonal relationships. It is interesting to compare this PCP perspective with the theoretical approach to the understanding of autism, in which such individuals are seen to lack a 'theory of mind' (Baron-Cohen et al., 1985).

The Meaning of the Behaviour

Personality disordered offenders commit a range of types of offences, and one might therefore expect even less commonality in the personal meaning of their behaviour than among offenders whose behaviour is more similar. However, as with other offenders, their behaviour is construed by society as deviant or antisocial, and it is therefore useful to understand how offender clients who have also been diagnosed as personality disordered, construe being deviant. The above studies indicate how aspects of the structure and content of an individual's construct system may provide some insight into this. Case studies have illustrated the construing of personality disordered individuals who do not see their deviant behaviour as harmful (Fransella & Adams, 1966) or even see it as overtly positive (Howells, 1978). A further study suggests that what is viewed as exciting to normal individuals is seen as dull by psychopaths, and what elicits unpleasant feelings in the former can elicit pleasant feelings in the latter (Widom, 1976). However, there has been little published research about the construing of personality disordered offenders other than those detained in a maximum security hospital, and it is therefore inappropriate to assume commonality of construing with other populations or clinical types. Following the philosophy of personal construct psychology, it is important to take the idiographic approach and examine case examples to understand the personal meaning of offending to different individuals.

The case examples below describe the construing of three women diagnosed with borderline personality disorder, two of whom had a history of arson. Although there are some common features in both the structure and content of their construing, the variety of meanings of their deviant behaviour are clearly illustrated. Characteristics of the womens' construct systems are also reflected in both the nature and severity of their pathology.

In her early twenties Frances was convicted of arson, which involved a number of serious episodes of fire-setting. She then spent 10 years in a maximum security hospital. She had particular difficulties with interpersonal relationships, and a tendency to be impulsive, verbally aggressive and hostile in her interactions. She was assessed at the start of the process of rehabilitation back into the community. On the repertory grid her main discriminating constructs were 'Good at communicating vs Poor at communicating', 'Confident vs Not confident', 'Calm vs Angry' and 'Thinks before acting vs Acts before thinking'. A second component primarily reflected the use of the construct 'Sensitive vs Insensitive'. Frances rated herself as she was 10 years earlier at the extreme negative end of the first component, with her current self slightly more positive. She no longer construed herself as the type of person who was likely to set fires and her ideal self was identified with her previous key nurse. Her constructs illustrated that she had insight into her impulsiveness and communicative difficulties. The content of her construing clarified the clinical hypothesis, which was that Frances set fires when she felt stressed, frustrated, angry and unable to communicate how she felt. After a few initial setbacks, Frances' rehabilitation proceeded well, and she progressed to a hostel.

Sarah was a 22-year-old woman on probation for assault, who also had a history of shoplifting, self-harm, and abuse of alcohol and drugs. She had been abused by her father as a child but still had limited contact with her family. Her repertory grid was completed extremely quickly, with most of her ratings being at the extremes of the poles. Her tendency to either idealise or denigrate others was reflected in the eliciting of the idiosyncratic construct 'Megastar vs Bastard', which was an important discriminator. Her ideal self, grandmother, sister, and previous probation officer were all construed identically, as not aggressive, confident, able to trust others and as not drinking heavily. Her current self, father and brother were all construed as the complete opposite to that. The large discrepancy between her current and ideal self and the cognitive simplicity of her construct system made therapeutic work difficult, as she set herself unrealistic goals and found it difficult to perceive progress. She had a long-standing self-identity which involved being 'deviant' rather than a 'victim', and found it difficult to construe an alternative which was more positive, even in hypothetical 'experiments'. She rejected the idea of fixed role therapy, saying that it was 'too difficult'. Consequently, although she managed to live in the community, she continued to behave in a very self-destructive and deviant way. From the PCP perspective, this pattern of behaviour clearly provided her with more certainty in her life than the anticipation of change.

Interestingly, Diane, another young woman with a borderline personality disorder, had a construct system with some similar features. She had a history of arson, assaultative behaviour, substance abuse and self-harm, and had had a number of unsucessful attempts at moving to a less secure environment than a maximum security hospital. The main ways in which she construed herself and others were whether they were 'Caring vs Obnoxious', 'Kind and generous vs Bastard' and 'Physically affectionate vs Cold'. An important second component was represented by the constructs 'Impulsive and aggressive vs Not impulsive and aggressive', 'Confident vs Not confident' and 'Been abused vs Normal'. Again there was the tendency to construe others in a polarised way—if they were not kind and generous then they were a 'bastard'. However, for Diane, her way of construing her prolonged abuse as a child meant that although she did not see herself as the type of person to set fires, she was unable to construe herself as 'normal'. This key feature of her construct system made it difficult for Diane to progress with rehabilitation. She was terrified of life outside hospital and construed fire-setting as a way of ensuring that she could always return to the psychological security of a secure hospital environment.

IMPLICATIONS FOR ASSESSMENT AND TREATMENT

In working with personality disordered offenders, one of the advantages of using the PCP perspective is its emphasis on understanding the individual, which offers a positive framework with which to deal with the frustration that is often generated by this client group. Implications for the idiographic assessment and treatment of an offender with a personality disorder are outlined below. These should be seen as complementary to the standard nomothetic assessment and treatment of choice. Suggestions for elements and constructs to include in repertory grids are shown in Figures 8.5a,b and 8.6.

What are the Important Structural Characteristics of the Client's Construct System?

One reason that personality disordered offenders may get into such entrenched patterns of deviant behaviour, is that the whole structure of their construct system lacks order. It is therefore useful to assess the

Self now
Self when offending
Ideal self
Self as seen by others
Self as a child
The type of person to ... (set a fire, harm others)
A person I respect
A person I dislike
Male friend
Female friend
Key staff member
Mother
Father
Victim

Figure 8.5a. Suggested elements to use in assessment: persons grid

Betraying a close friend or relative
Driving a car at 100 miles an hour
Getting caught for a crime you committed
Attempting to beat a train at a level crossing
Being sober talking to a drunk man
'Shooting your mouth off' at someone
Being aggressive and attacking someone

(Widom, 1976)

Taking advantage of ... (a liked and disliked person)
Giving ... a black eye
Breaking a promise to ...

(Klass, 1980)

Figure 8.5b. Suggested elements to use in assessment: situations grid

tightness of their construing, the cognitive complexity and lopsidedness of their construct system, and the polarisation of elements on individual constructs. For example, many offenders with borderline personality disorders think in extreme black-and-white, all-or-nothing terms, often related to notions of 'good' and 'bad'. People and events are either idealised or denigrated, and their way of construing allows for little flexibility. It is also useful for the clinician to observe both how quickly clients make their judgements when rating elements on grids and

Accepts authority vs Does not accept authority
Responsible vs Irresponsible
Socially normal vs Socially abnormal

(Howells, 1978)

Good vs Bad
Active vs Passive
Weak vs Strong
Makes you feel anxious vs Doesn't make you feel anxious
Dull vs Exciting
Frightening vs Not frightening
Makes you feel depressed vs Doesn't make you feel depressed
Typically me vs Typically not me

(Widom, 1976)

Makes me feel uncomfortable vs Does not make me feel uncomfortable
Makes me feel guilty vs Does not make me feel guilty
Would not like to do vs Would like to do
Not like me vs Like me
Not like other people vs Like other people

(Klass, 1980)

Figure 8.6. Suggested constructs to use in assessment

whether or not they show a deficit in the use of moderate response categories, which may reflect a construct system dominated by superordinate constructs (Thomas-Peter, 1992).

How Does the Client See Themself?

Personality disordered offenders are not a homogeneous group, and as with other offenders there is wide variation in the way in which they perceive themselves and their ideal. However, there appears to be a tendency for some such offenders either to perceive no difference between their current and ideal self, or for these to be polar opposites. Both pose different problems for treatment. In the former case the client may have a deviant self-identity which is an established part of their core role structure. They may either see no need for change, or be unable to construe an alternative and perceive change as extremely threatening. In the latter case, self-esteem is so low that the client cannot allow themselves to make a success of anything and do not think that they deserve to do well. Self-destructive behaviour is therefore common, and therapeutic attempts are apparently sabotaged in order to maintain the core role structure with which they are familiar. In addition to the self/ideal discrepancy, the relationship between how the client sees themself compared to how they see the type of person likely to commit that kind of offence, can also be a useful indicator of prognosis (Fransella & Adams, 1966).

How Do They See Other People?

A repertory grid enables the clinician to assess whether the client construes other people in a polarised way, for example in terms of good and bad extremes. If they have a victim, a grid will also elicit further information about their empathy with that person. Given that there is some evidence to suggest that psychopathic offenders may assume that other people think in the same way as they do (Widom, 1976), an educative component is often an important part of treatment, as is encouraging the development of sociality (i.e. the ability to construe the construction processes of others).

How Do They See Their Behaviour?

As well as assessing how personality disordered offenders construe themselves and others, it is important to assess the way in which such clients construe their offending behaviour, as this has implications for their response to treatment. Most offenders construe their offending behaviour in ways which enable them to minimise its seriousness and harmful consequences. However, some clients with a personality disorder may overtly construe their behaviour as harmful, but either do not perceive this as self-discrepant, or are unable to envisage the possibility of change. In this case a major component of treatment may involve encouraging the client to construe alternatives for their core role structure—not an easy task. Working with personality disordered offenders who construe their offending as overtly positive is likely to present an even greater challenge to the clinician.

Facilitating Treatment

Thomas-Peter (1992) points out that many of the personality disordered offenders in his study also experienced extreme chronic anxiety. Although this may be caused by problems within the construct system, it also prevents change. He suggests that in such a case it may be helpful initially to try to control the symptoms with relaxation, anxiety management training or medication, in order to facilitate changing the source of the anxiety.

Promoting Thinking Skills

The process of completing a repertory grid often confirms the research evidence that psychopaths to make extreme judgements and show an impairment in their ability to make moderate responses. Problem-solving skills and cognitive-behavioural oriented treatments have been used to try to address these difficulties (Beck & Freeman, 1990; Turkat, 1990). The authors report encouraging results from these approaches, although there is not yet firm empirical support.

Constructing Alternatives

Like other offender clients, it is likely that the PCP assessment of a personality disordered offender will identify areas of construing which are maintaining and validating their offending. For those who wish to examine alternatives, aspects of the schema-focused approach to therapy with people with personality disorders (Layden et al., 1993) may be useful.

Encouraging Experimentation

Taking a more strategic view, one of the aims of treatment is to encourage the development of new constructs by testing them out in a safe environment, such as in therapy. Winter (1992) suggests that the therapist's basic task in working with a client who has a 'disorder of control', which is reflected in a failure to complete the CPC cycle adequately, is to facilitate experimentation with new ways of construing. However, Thomas-Peter (1992) also points out that very damaged individuals may need considerable assistance to do this and notes the advantages of diary-keeping by the client. This would focus on the relationship between the information used to make a judgement and the subsequent emotional and behavioural consequences of that. The diary allows the relatively safe exploration of alternatives by the therapist, with the use of prompting, practice and constant feedback.

Understanding Resistance to Change

The way in which some personality disordered offenders construe themselves and their behaviour means that deviant, self-destructive or offending behaviour is part of their whole core role structure. Change means uncertainty, which from the PCP perspective is to be avoided at all cost. For some personality disordered clients, this means that the threat that no longer offending poses to their core role structure is too great to anticipate. For others, even change to a different hospital environment may be extremely threatening and must be avoided. What otherwise may appear to the clinician as resistance to change or even sabotage of a treatment plan, is therefore likely to be an attempt by the client to avoid threat and maintain predictability. Understanding resistance to change therefore requires the clinician to understand the personal meaning of the behaviour to the client.

Communicating Understanding

As discussed at the beginning of the chapter, one of the characteristic features of working with clients with personality disorders is that their persistent deviant behaviour can often make professionals working with them feel frustrated and deskilled. It can therefore be important to communicate to other professional staff the meaning of that behaviour to the particular individual, and to foster a therapeutic environment in which such behaviour is not merely construed by professionals in a perjorative way.

Issues for the Clinician

As illustrated in the earlier case examples, the cognitively simplistic thinking of some borderline personality disordered offenders can lead them to see their ideal self as similar to their therapist or key member of staff working with them. This idealisation can be extremely uncomfortable for the clinician, particularly when they invariably fail to live up to expectations and are then denigrated. Dalton & Dunnett (1992) suggest that problems are also likely to occur when an individual comes to depend on only one other person for the validation of all their social constructs. Again, this is sometimes seen in the therapeutic relationship with clients diagnosed with borderline personality disorders. Having an understanding of the processes that are going on, resisting the temptation to feel 'special', and open discussion with colleagues are all important coping strategies for the clinician to try to avoid therapeutic burn-out. Main's (1957) classic article 'The ailment' explores these processes in the institutional setting, but they should also be borne in mind when working with out-patients.

The following case example illustrates in more detail the implications of working from the PCP perspective with an offender diagnosed as personality disordered. Identifying the apparent cognitive simplicity of the young man's construct system helped to understand the way in which some of his specific difficulties had major ramifications for his perceived ability to cope with life in general.

Peter, aged 24 years, was an in-patient on trial leave in a medium secure unit. He had been admitted to a maximum security hospital five years earlier after being convicted of arson with intent to endanger life, and was detained under the Mental Health Act (1983) as suffering from psychopathic disorder. He had experienced a disruptive and disturbed childhood, and had already been under the care of psychiatric services from the age of 14 years, with problems mainly relating to aggression. As a teenager he had found it difficult to establish therapeutic relationships or talk about his feelings, and was a very secretive adolescent. Clinicians never felt they had a comprehensive understanding of the nature of his difficulties. Peter eventually set a fire in a work-training centre and later told staff that this was an attempt to get across how desperate he was feeling. Peter was diagnosed as suffering from both antisocial and borderline personality disorders. Whilst in hospital he engaged in individual psychotherapy, where it emerged that his prime concern was confusion about his sexuality.

Peter completed a repertory grid shortly after his move from Special Hospital. This aimed to explore how he construed himself now compared to at the time of his offence, so clearly it was crucial to include different 'self' elements. Since sexual relationships had posed difficulties for Peter, both his previous partners, male and female, were also included as elements. He did not have an identifiable victim as such, nor was he able to identify anyone in the role of a 'friend'. His current 'key' nurse and a doctor whom he had known well were therefore also included as elements to ensure that there was a range of elements to contrast in the grid. As two constructs relating to sexuality were elicited from Peter, there was no need to supply additional constructs.

After analysis (using the INGRID programme; Slater, 1972), the most striking feature of Peter's grid was the cognitive simplicity of his construct system, with over 75% of the variance being accounted for by the first component (see Figure 8.7). The main way in which he discriminated between people was in terms of the constructs 'Secure vs Insecure', 'Trusts others vs Has difficulty trusting', 'Able to cope with life vs Unable to cope with life' and 'Satisfactory sex life vs Unsatisfactory sex life'. This latter construct was tightly associated with being able to cope with life in general. The unidimensionality of his construing made it difficult to identify the second component, and so the plot was drawn up as shown in Figure 8.7, without any constructs labelled on the vertical axis. The second component was actually accounted for by the construct 'Confident of sexual identity vs Unsure of sexual identity'. Peter tended to construe other people as either towards the positive 'coping' end of the construct poles or towards the negative 'not coping' end. He rated himself at the time of his offence at the most extreme negative pole. His current self was also towards the negative side, although not as extreme. There was still a considerable distance between the ratings of his current and ideal selves, reflecting remaining concerns about his sexuality and consequent emotional and interpersonal difficulties.

The grid helped to clarify the clinical team's hypothesis about Peter's fire-setting, that it represented an attempt to communicate the confused feelings which he was unable to express verbally, relating primarily to his sexual identity. However, it also helped to understand why this caused him such severity of distress. As discussed above, Peter's construct system was very tightly organised, with all of the constructs being interrelated, a reflection of his cognitively simple thinking. Because of this interrelationship between constructs, being uncertain about his sexuality and dissatisfied with his sex life also meant being insecure, having difficulty trusting others, and being unable to cope with life in general. In addition, he construed people (including himself) in very 'all-or-

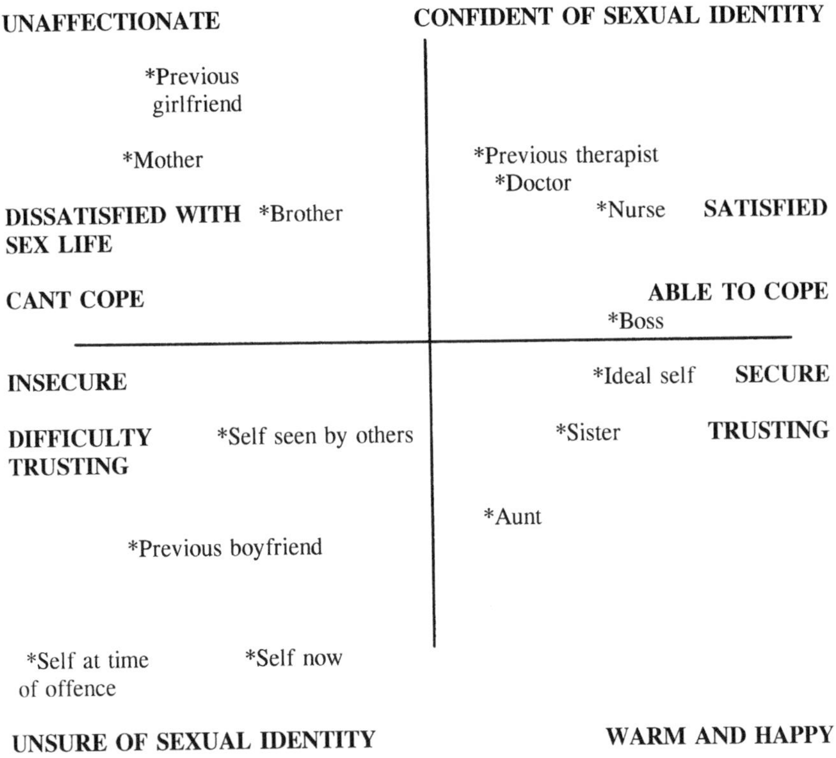

UNAFFECTIONATE   CONFIDENT OF SEXUAL IDENTITY

       *Previous
        girlfriend

    *Mother   *Previous therapist
           *Doctor

DISSATISFIED WITH *Brother   *Nurse   SATISFIED
SEX LIFE

CANT COPE   ABLE TO COPE
                                *Boss

INSECURE   *Ideal self   SECURE

DIFFICULTY   *Self seen by others   *Sister   TRUSTING
TRUSTING

                    *Aunt
    *Previous boyfriend

*Self at time   *Self now
of offence

UNSURE OF SEXUAL IDENTITY   WARM AND HAPPY

Figure 8.7. Plot of elements in construct space from Peter's initial grid

nothing' ways, so that they were either confident and able to cope or not, with no middle ground.

Peter was seen in further individual treatment for a year. Psychologically, the aim was to change his self-concept, with the social aim being to reduce his risk of reoffending. Treatment involved helping him to loosen the association between the satisfaction with his sex life and other positive personal characteristics, including coping with life in general. He was encouraged hypothetically to experiment with different situations, and keep a record of his daily mood and levels of anxiety in order to increase his understanding of his processes of construing. He was encouraged to engage in new activities at which he was good (e.g. being a volunteer with elderly people, producing art work for the patients' social centre) in order to build up a new and positive core role structure.

Peter progressed well and moved to a supported hostel. He was reassessed with the repertory grid a year after initial administration (see Figure 8.8). Although he still construed the world very much in a cognitively simple, black-and-white way, there were some interesting changes. There was still a close association between positive personal characteristics and an ability to cope with life. However, general coping ability was not now also associated with an ability to trust others and having a satisfactory sex life. Coping and security were more associated with being confident about one's sexual identity. In other words, Peter now accepted that although his sex life was less than perfect, he may still be able to progress in other areas of his life. There therefore appeared to be a loosening of the association between trusting and coping. This can be interpreted in two ways. Either Peter still perceived himself to have some difficulty in trusting others but was more able to cope with life in general, or he was able to trust people more easily, but acknowledged that he had not yet made similar changes in other domains. Future oriented constructs also now

DIFFICULTY TRUSTING   **SATISFIED WITH SEX LIFE**

*Sister

*Self at time of offence

*Self seen by others

CANT COPE

ABLE TO COPE

*Previous girlfriend   *Ideal self

SECRETIVE

OPEN

*Self now

DONT CARE   *Self a year ago   **CARE ABOUT FUTURE**
ABOUT FUTURE

*Mother

UNSURE OF   *Previous boyfriend   *Aunt   **CONFIDENT OF**
SEXUAL IDENTITY   **SEXUAL IDENTITY**

*Previous therapist

*Current girlfriend

*Brother

DISSATISFIED WITH SEX LIFE

TRUSTING

Figure 8.8. Plot of elements in construct space from Peter's second grid

appeared to be more discriminative. Peter was now thinking more about planning for the future, and whether or not people cared about the future and had a career ahead of them were now important ways in which he discriminated between them.

There were also changes in the construing of individuals in the grid. Peter saw himself as coping much better with life than he had done a year ago, although there was still some distance between his current and ideal self. There was some change from his previous tendency to rate people as either good or bad. As well as the 'ideal' group of people (including nursing staff and a previous therapist) and the 'negative' group (including his mother, previous boyfriend, and self at the time of his offence), there was now a 'middle' group who had a balance of positive and negative qualities. This group included his current self, first girlfriend (who was previously perceived more negatively) and current girlfriend. This may reflect developing feelings of confidence in a heterosexual relationship, while not idealising this.

SUMMARY AND CONCLUSIONS

Personality disordered offenders are a heterogeneous group in terms of both clinical personality type and offending behaviour. However, there are commonalities in the way this client group is itself construed by many clinicians. Because of their apparent resistance to change, offenders who are also diagnosed with personality disorders are often seen as particularly difficult to work with and treat. The personal construct perspective on deviancy and guilt enables the behaviour of this client group to be seen as entirely consistent with their way of construing the world, and as such, offers a positive framework within which to work.

Research has indicated a number of ways in which both the structure and the content of construing of some personality disordered offenders are different from those of non-offenders and non-personality disordered offenders. There particularly appears to be more evidence for idiosyncrasies in *structural* aspects of their construing. There is some evidence that psychopathic personality disordered offenders show lopsided construing (i.e. biased towards one construct pole), and that they make more extreme and less moderate judgements, faster than most people. Cognitively simple construing has also been observed in psychopathic and borderline personality disordered offenders. Individuals who show this type of construing are likely to have a view of the world in which themselves, other people and events are seen in polarised, 'all or nothing' terms.

The *content* of the construing of many offenders who are diagnosed with personality disorders also differs from that of other types of offenders. Some psychopaths may construe little difference between their actual and ideal self, and although antisocial activity is seen as harmful, it is entirely self-congruent. In contrast, although there are no empirical research studies with borderline personality disordered offenders, case examples suggest that some clients with this diagnosis may have such a large discrepancy between how they perceive their current and ideal self, that they find it difficult to construe an alternative.

The characteristics observed in the construing of personality disordered offenders may go some way to understanding why individuals from this client group are often seen by clinicians as particularly difficult to work with. Repetitive and self-destructive behaviour patterns, which frustrate the best therapeutic attempts of the clinician, can be more easily understood in the context of the above features of their construct systems. If a deviant self-identity is part of their core role structure, change is likely to be extremely threatening, regardless of whether the client construes themself in a positive or negative light. Furthermore, as suggested by Widom (1976) in relation to psychopaths, the idiosyncrasies in the patterns of their construing are likely to reduce the possibility of effective personal communication, and place the individual in a subjectively unusual world in which unpredictable behavioural reactions become more understandable. In other words, for some personality disordered offenders not only does the content of their construing relate to their behaviour, but the whole structure of their construct system is different from that of other people. This may go some way towards understanding why the very process of relating to others is difficult for such individuals.

Finally, it is important to note that, with one exception (Klass, 1980), the research into processes and patterns of construing in personality disordered offenders has been carried out with in-patients detained under the legal category of psychopathic disorder (Mental Health Act, 1983), which itself comprises a clinically heterogeneous group. Clinicians need to be cautious about assuming that this client group shows commonality of construing with out-patient populations, or other single clinical types of personality disordered offenders. An individual case-oriented approach to assessment and treatment is therefore of particular relevance with this client group.

CHAPTER 9

Alcohol, Drugs and Offending

Alcohol and drug dependence often coexist with offending, and in some individuals there is a particular association between alcohol and aggression. In this chapter, the PCP perspective on drug and alcohol problems is explored in relation to offenders. This suggests that the link between alcohol and/or drugs and offending in some clients can be understood in terms of the interaction between the person's *pre-existing* patterns of construing and the effects of alcohol and/or drugs on the *process* of their construing.

INTRODUCTION

Most research on the relationship between offending and alcohol use has focused either on delinquency or adult violence. Taking into account methodological differences, studies of young offenders are broadly consistent and suggest that there is an association between alcohol and general delinquency (e.g. McMurran & Hollin, 1989; Cookson, 1992). However, the association between alcohol and violence in adults is more complex. Blackburn (1993) notes that most concerns about the potential effects of alcohol relate to *psychopharmacological violence* (Goldstein, 1989), in which the effects of the drug itself facilitate violent acts. In the 1988 British Crime Survey, the offender was drunk in over 60% of non-job-related violent offences, and in 83% of job-related assaults on males (Mayhew et al., 1989). These findings do not establish a causal relationship, since data are not available from comparable groups of non-offenders, and most studies rely on police records and self-report. None the less, it is recognised that drink-related problems are common among both adult prisoners and young offenders, with several studies suggesting that a third or more of inmates have serious drink problems (e.g. McMurran et al., 1990).

Clearly not all people with alcohol problems offend, and alcohol-related offences are not all violent. Whether the ingestion of alcohol leads to aggression appears to depend on an interaction between the characteristics of the drinker, the psychological effects of alcohol, and provoking and constraining factors in the situation (Blackburn, 1993). Throughout the chapter a sub-group of individuals are identified who show similarities in their construing to people diagnosed with person-ality disorders (see Chapter 8), and Coid (1982) suggests that alcoholism is probably not related to violence, but that personality disorder in a sub-group of alcoholics predisposes them to both drinking and violence. As seen later in the chapter, alcohol may also facilitate other types of offending in some individuals.

The relationship between illicit drug use and offending is less clear. The evidence suggests that amphetamines and barbiturates are more likely to facilitate violence than marijuana, opiates and tranquillisers, although as with alcohol, predispositional and situational factors are important (Goldstein, 1989). It is also unclear how far drug-related offending results from the effects of the drug itself, rather than from instrumental crime to support drug use, or conflict about dealing which is resolved by violence (Blackburn, 1993). This chapter therefore focuses primarily on alcohol, rather than drug dependence, although studies of the latter are described where particularly relevant.

THE PCP PERSPECTIVE ON ALCOHOL AND DRUG DEPENDENCE

Although there has been no previous attempt from the PCP perspective to examine the meaning of alcohol and/or drug dependence in an offend-ing population, there has been a substantial body of work which has explored the development and maintenance of alcohol and drug depen-dence *per se*. Burr & Butt (1992) construe alcohol dependence in psy-chological terms, focusing on the function and meaning that alcohol (or other) dependence has for the person. However, the PCP perspective on the aetiology of alcohol dependence and its effect on the construct system has primarily been developed by Rivers & Landfield (1985). These authors suggest that alcohol dependence often occurs within the context of ordinary social situations in which a person may feel anxious. The effects of alcohol allow a person to make superficial conversation and feel that their role is being supported by others' responses. Their expectations or constructs therefore appear to be fitting the occasion and they become less anxious. In this way alcohol can serve as a 'social lubricant' by loosening the personal construct system and reducing social anxiety. Rivers & Landfield (1985) suggest that this is more likely to occur in individuals who already have difficulties in social relationships and are uncertain about their own social role. What may begin as a socially acceptable process can shift to a perpetual and abusive use of alcohol.

In PCP terms, therefore, Rivers & Landfield (1985) view the disinhibiting effect of alcohol as involving the two processes of dilation (in which a person broadens their view of the world and sees new links between events) and loosening (in which a person shows a lack of consistency in applying constructs and a lessened need to be accurate about predictions). Alcohol therefore serves as 'an agent for a temporary feeling of conceptual expansion' (Rivers & Landfield, 1985, p. 171). It may lead to a temporary loosening of the relationship between a person's ideas and conclusions about themselves and others, and the data used to validate these. In other words, almost any response can be construed as supportive of one's anticipations, either positive or negative. Anxiety is lessened, and the person's construct system appears to work better. Although the person is not able to be aware of or understand the viewpoints of others (in Kelly's terms, to play a social role), to them the alcohol instantly reduces social distance and allows them to create new temporary and fantasy roles and constructs.

Dawes (1985) similarly suggests that one of the functions of drug dependence is to allow the person to avoid the anxiety of confronting situations which they cannot anticipate. This problem occurs when a person's construct system is insufficiently defined or elaborated (i.e. does not confirm their previous experience). Dawes (1985) notes that the PCP approach would be most consistent with the Automedicative theory of drug dependence. This focuses on the notion that drug dependence is an active choice as a way of coping with stress, becoming personally adaptive to the individual as it helps them to cope with life in a less distressed manner. Supporters of this view suggest that the individual had psychological difficulties prior to the onset of dependence. Dawes (1985) proposes a PCP model of drug dependence in which drug-taking is seen as an *elaborative choice* by the individual. He suggests that the ways in which initial contacts with drugs are construed are important determinants in whether a person goes on to become dependent. A person is more likely to go on to become dependent on drugs if they construe their initial experiences in a way which enables them to anticipate some aspects of life more satisfactorily. Therefore, from the individual user's point of view, drug dependency may be seen as adaptive, in the sense that it helps to elaborate (i.e. makes sense of) aspects of their construct system which would not be possible in the drug-free state. In order to become drug-free, the person has to be enabled by treatment to reconstrue the situations or aspects of themselves which initially facilitated the use of drugs.

Both Rivers & Landfield (1985) and Dawes (1985) discuss the way in which the roles of one's 'sober self' and 'intoxicated self' become very separate in people who are dependent on alcohol and drugs. As the user begins to appreciate the effects of drug use, Dawes suggests that a separate construct system begins to emerge (according to the Fragmentation Corollary), which can be regarded as a new construction of the self when intoxicated or 'high'. This new subsystem becomes associated with certain important events, which then become difficult for the person to negotiate when sober (e.g. actual situations such as social events, or states of mind such as depression). The role of the 'intoxicated self' gradually becomes more elaborated, so that increasing numbers of relationships and activities become associated with or dependent on the person being in that role. The more that this is so, the more difficult it is to return to being sober or drug-free. G. Kelly (1955/1991) suggests that a person's maintenance in the role of an 'alcoholic' can be understood in relation to the PCP concept of guilt, i.e. 'the awareness of dislodgement of self from one's core role'. He suggests that a person whose core role structure included being 'alcoholic' would try to prevent the guilt experienced by departing from that role by resisting change, and that for some people Alcoholics Anonymous may therefore be helpful in maintaining the role with which they are familiar.

The limitations in applying Rivers & Landfield's (1985) model to alcohol use in offenders lie primarily with the authors' suggestion about aetiology. Although many offenders with alcohol problems may have started to drink in social situations, it is likely that alcohol consumption is an essential part of group membership among peers, rather than a way of coping with anxiety. Heavy use of alcohol may then become part of a young offender's core role and self-identity for the same reasons as they behave in other deviant ways—because this makes sense to them and confirms their previous experience. Having role models within the family who are substance-abusers may also mean that, for some offenders, becoming dependent on alcohol or drugs provides the most predictable way of anticipating future events. In this aspect, there is some consistency with Dawes' (1985) suggestion about the contributory factors to the development of drug dependence. Other offenders' use of alcohol or drugs may have initially developed as a way of blocking out or coping with negative feelings and moods, which is also consistent with Dawes' model.

There are therefore a number of other aspects of these PCP models of alcohol/drug dependence which *are* relevant to offenders. In terms of understanding the link between alcohol and/or drug use and offending, it is likely that the *existing patterns* of construing of the individual interact with the effect of alcohol and drug intake on the *process* of construing. For example, a person may have a core role structure in which being 'tough' is an essential component. When drunk, the loosening and dilating effects of alcohol mean that they may be more likely to construe the behaviour of others as threatening to their core role, and therefore act aggressively to maintain it.

Since not all people with alcohol and drug problems offend, pre-existing patterns of construing are therefore likely to exist which facilitate offending when intoxicated. The earlier chapters in Part II of the book have reviewed what is known about patterns of construing in different types of offenders, some of whom may use the dilating and loosening effects of alcohol as one way of 'allowing' themselves to offend. However, there is also a substantial body of research which has explored the characteristics of construing in people with drug and alcohol problems *per se*, and which it is relevant briefly to consider. Although clinicians working from the PCP and from other theoretical perspectives agree that it is not helpful to label clients (Dawes, 1985; McMurran & Hollin, 1993), the term 'alcoholic' is retained where it has been used by other authors. Elsewhere, while accepting that this is a construction made by the clinician, clients are described as having an alcohol and/or drug problem or as being dependent on those substances.

PATTERNS OF CONSTRUING IN PEOPLE WITH ALCOHOL AND DRUG PROBLEMS

The Structure of the Construct System

The degree of *cognitive complexity* of their construct system has been the main structural feature of construing that has been the focus of studies with this client group. Research has suggested that people who are dependent on alcohol have construct systems which are *either* very loosely (Chambers & Sanders, 1984) *or* tightly organised (Landfield, 1971; Rollnick & Heather, 1980; Bailey & Sims, 1991). The implications are that the construct systems of people who become dependent on alcohol may be structured in ways which tend to make it difficult for them to relate to others. A tight construct system means that the person's predictions are inflexible, they have a rigid way of relating to people and situations and are resistant to change. A loose construct system means that the person has no sense of predictability or certainty about relating in the world.

The apparent contradictory findings of both loose and tight construing in this client group may be accounted for by research which has suggested that the cognitive complexity of the construct systems of people with alcohol/drug problems may relate to underlying personality characteristics. In a study of alcoholics in a half-way house, Orford (1974) found that those who dropped out early were more likely to show a comparatively simple cognitive style for construing other people, compared to those who completed their rehabilitation. He proposed that the personality variable of 'cognitive complexity–simplicity' in social construing may be related both to early drop-out from treatment and to the clinical concept of personality disorder (see also Chapter 8). Similarly, Penrod et al. (1981) also found a difference between the cognitive complexity of different drug-users, and suggested that the preferential abuse of certain drugs provides pharmacological effects which are consonant with the underlying cognitive, defensive style of the drug-abuser.

Construing of the Self

Grids have been used to explore both the self-esteem and the self-concept of people with alcohol and drug problems. Although higher self-esteem is generally found at the end of treatment (Heather et al., 1975; Rollnick & Heather, 1980; Preston & Viney, 1984), there is no direct relationship between this and the success of treatment, with overconfidence being related to a higher rate of relapse. However, those patients whose self-respect *failed* to increase were also likely to relapse, and tended to be the ones labelled as 'psychopathic' (i.e. personality disordered) by staff. Furthermore, Preston & Viney (1984) found that even after completing treatment, drug addicts still had unusual perceptions of their ideal selves, involving notions of being helpless and self-critical. The authors suggested that the addicts were ambivalent about their goals, and may be fearful of returning to the outside world where they have to take control of their own lives. The drug addicts seemed unable to believe that they would eventually be worthwhile individuals, able to take on responsibility and handle difficulties. This pattern of construing has also been observed in some offenders with borderline personality disorder (see Chapter 8), who are unable to anticipate success in treatment.

Another major focus of study has been whether or not people who have drug and alcohol problems construe themselves in this way, since people generally tend to dissociate themselves from the stereotype of the group to which they belong (Hudson, 1970). People receiving treatment for alcohol problems have been shown to distance themselves from the concept of both 'an alcoholic' (Hoy, 1973, 1977; McCartney & O'Donnell, 1981) and 'a problem drinker' (Potamianos et al., 1985), although with the latter role being construed in a more neutral way compared to the former. McCartney & O'Donnell's (1981) study found that problem drinkers tended to identify themselves as being psychologically closest to the role of 'heavy controlled drinker' (defined as a limit of four or five pints of beer or equivalent, two or three times a week). with the roles of both 'light controlled drinker' (a limit of two pints of beer or equivalent, two or three times a week) and 'total abstainer' being alien to them. For some problem drinkers the psychological connotations of being abstinent or even a light controlled drinker may therefore create a conflict with their own self-concept. Heather et al. (1982) suggested that the abstinent patient's dilemma is that of the 'marginal deviant', in that being abstinent excludes him or her both from the conventional world and from the deviant alcoholic subculture. This situation is likely to be extremely uncomfortable, and there are two ways of reducing this: to join the conventional world and return to social drinking or to join the deviant subculture and relapse into alcoholism.

People who abuse alcohol do not therefore relate their self-concept at all closely to the stereotype which they themselves use, irrespective of whether or not that stereotype is negative. However, as discussed earlier, the nature of drug and alcohol use means that the person is likely to have a very different sense of 'self' when they are intoxicated. Indeed, Partington (1970) found that, when drunk, alcoholics construed themselves as different from their sober self and more similar to 'an alcoholic'. The way in which the person construes themself when drunk and sober also has implications for treatment, as for some individuals their 'drunk' or 'drug-using' self is closer to their ideal (Ryle, 1975; Eastman, 1978). Similarly, those clients whose self-concept does not match that of the treatment philosophy are less likely to complete rehabilitation (Bennett et al., 1992).

The Meaning of Alcohol and Drug Dependence

The above studies have illustrated that the meaning of drug and alcohol abuse to the clients is not universally negative, but is likely to relate to the person's view of themself and their dependence. However, Glantz et al. (1981) drew some conclusions about the meaning of alcohol abuse from their grid study of alcoholics. The alcoholic group used few constructs concerning interpersonal and emotional issues and tended to persist in the use of constructs with only marginal applicability, which the authors linked to a likely difficulty in predicting and controlling events. They concluded that alcohol therefore served a number of functions for alcoholics: (i) an attempt to change their world by altering their own perceptions, (ii) an attempt to increase the efficiency of their own behaviour, or (iii) an attempt to reduce the negative feelings resulting from a lower level of coping ability.

The Construing of Offenders with Alcohol Problems

Having reviewed some of the characteristic patterns of construing in people with alcohol and drug problems, it is pertinent to consider the relevance of these in such individuals who also offend. There may be some commonality of construing in this sub-group, as, unlike other types of offenders, those with a drink problem have been able to be identified by their grids alone in terms of the way in which they would respond to a stressful situation (Watson et al., 1976). However, understanding the behaviour of an individual offender with an alcohol problem involves exploring how their sober, drunk and ideal selves relate to that of their 'offending self', and the degree to which the offending behaviour and use of alcohol are linked in their core role structure. The case examples below illustrate the variety of ways in which offenders with additional alcohol problems construe the two behaviours, and the implications of this for treatment and risk of reoffending.

Bob was a 38-year-old unemployed labourer who had a long history of anxiety and depression. He started drinking and taking drugs in his late teens, initially to block out negative feelings about himself, which originated from his sense of being neglected as a child. A well established pattern developed over his adult years; when feeling low, Bob drank alcohol. When drunk, he then searched for opportunities to take drugs, which he also construed as a 'bolster' to his ability to cope with life. Bob was aware from his teenage years that he was sexually attracted to young boys, and when sober, was clear that acting on his attraction was wrong. However, at times when his relationships with adult male partners broke down, he was aware that becoming intoxicated would alter his perception of both the reasons why sexual contact with children is illegal, and his concern about the consequences of being caught. Bob therefore construed himself as both an offender and a 'problem drinker'. However, although he was motivated to prevent reoffending, he was ambivalent about giving up alcohol and drugs, as he could not anticipate being able to cope with life without them. Although he worked hard in treatment to explore the ways in which his patterns of construing contributed to his sexual offending, his continued drinking at times of stress meant that he remained at high risk of reoffending.

Matthew, a 25-year-old single man, had a longstanding drink problem and a clear self-identity as an 'alcoholic', which pre-dated his offending. He began to drink alcohol with peers in his late teens, and quickly found that drinking reduced his anxiety in social situations, particularly when talking to girls. Having grown up in a male-dominated household and attended a single-sex school, Matthew's construct system did not provide him with a basis from which he could anticipate social interactions with the opposite sex. The loosening effect of alcohol enabled him to see himself as confident at parties, and he came to construe alcohol as his 'friend'. However, although Matthew used alcohol initially in an attempt to increase the efficiency of his own behaviour, he soon became physically dependent and established a pattern of binge drinking interspersed with brief periods of abstinence. While intoxicated, he indecently assaulted an adult woman in the street and received a custodial sentence. Matthew attended a treatment group in prison, and went through a number of different stages before seeing himself in the role of an 'offender'. He initially denied the sexual nature of the offence, claiming that he accidentally brushed up against the woman. It appeared that seeing himself as an 'offender' was not consistent with his view either of himself or of a typical alcoholic. While his family and friends accepted his drink problem, they made it clear that they would not accept him in the role of a 'sex offender'. He gradually came to acknowledge that he had sexually assaulted the woman, but construed this as the disinhibited behaviour of a drunken man, which would never have been perpetrated by his 'sober self', and for which he therefore did not have to take responsibility. He appeared to reconstrue his view of an 'alcoholic' (and therefore also of his 'drunk self'), to include the potential for offending while intoxicated. However, at this stage, he still showed no guilt in either the Kellian or the conventional sense, as he did not see his offending as inconsistent with his core role. Over time, Matthew eventually came to acknowledge that he had intentionally sexually assaulted the woman, but had convinced himself that his behaviour was not serious or harmful, construing his offending as 'a schoolboy prank'. He described the alcohol as giving him 'Dutch courage', in the same way that it had earlier enabled him to feel validated at social events. On completing treatment, Matthew recognised that aspects of his 'sober self', 'drunk self' and 'offending self' were actually very similar, in terms of his way of construing women as enjoying 'sexual pranks'. Although abstaining from alcohol was important in reducing his risk of reoffending in the future, he acknowledged that this was not the only contributor, and that it was also necessary for him to re-examine his ways of construing interactions with women.

In both the above case examples, the individuals construed their use of alcohol as problematic, and perceived that abstaining from alcohol was important in reducing their risk of reoffending. This contrasts with the following case, in which the client construed his use of alcohol as non-problematic, and could not therefore anticipate the role of an 'abstainer' or really see the need to control his intake.

Stuart, a 28-year-old man, was on remand in prison after seriously stabbing his brother in a family feud. He had been drinking heavily on the day of the offence. Stuart had a history of regular, heavy drinking, and had a number of convictions for violent offences, all of which had been committed after drinking alcohol, mostly resulting from 'pub fights'. From the PCP point of view, Stuart's difficulties could be formulated in terms of both the structure and content of his construing. The clinical interview suggested that Stuart construed himself and others primarily in terms of whether they were a 'drinker' or 'not a drinker'. He demonstrated very tight and impermeable construing around this construct, in that to be a 'drinker' implied craving for alcohol, drinking every day and being unable to resist drinking alcohol. He therefore did not construe himself as having an alcohol problem, or being a 'drinker', and did not see any need to take on the role of 'abstainer' in future. Stuart did acknowledge that he had drunk heavily at times in the past, and that this had contributed to his violence. However, he saw this as resulting from provocation by others, when venturing into a certain 'rough' part of the town. In addition, Stuart continued to perceive physical violence as sometimes required as a 'last resort'. The content of his construing, in which neither his drinking nor his aggression was a problem, meant that he was unable to engage productively in therapy, and he was not recommended for a hospital disposal. However, his probation officer continued to use the PCP perspective to engage with Stuart and discuss his resistance to change (see Chapter 3).

IMPLICATIONS FOR ASSESSMENT AND TREATMENT

The personal construct psychology approach to understanding drug and alcohol abuse and studies about the nature of such individuals' construing raise a number of implications for clinical assessment and treatment. A standardised assessment enables the clinician to compare the client with others with similar difficulties, and form a view about the severity of dependence and possible treatment options. However, it is also important to assess the individual aspects of the client's behaviour, in order to design 'an individualised programme of intervention to be carried out within the treatment context defined by nomothetic considerations' (Dawes, 1985, p. 192). Techniques for the assessment of the client's construing can include the self-characterisation and a repertory grid, as well as the clinical interview (see Chapters 2, 4). Figure 9.1 suggests useful elements to include in a grid, and examples of possible supplied constructs are shown in Figure 9.2. In addition to the usual framework within which the clinician is working, the PCP perspective therefore emphasises the importance of the following issues and questions.

How Does the Client See Themself?

It is useful for the assessment of an offender with a drug or alcohol problem to include the way they construe the relationship between their sober, drunk, and offending 'selves' and their ideal self. Clearly if their ideal self is seen as similar to themselves when offending and/or intoxicated, then this does not bode well for the success of treatment, and would need to be addressed with the client before expecting them to be able to achieve or maintain sobriety. Similarly, if they construe themselves when intoxicated more positively than when sober, this needs to be addressed before change will be maintained. Motivational

Self now

Ideal self

Self as seen by others

Drunk/intoxicated (or drinking) self

Sober/drug-free (or non-drinking) self

Someone who uses drink/drugs heavily (supply name)

Someone who is in control of their drinking/drug-taking

Someone who does not drink/take drugs

Victim (if applicable)

Mother

Father

Close friend

Partner

Figure 9.1. Suggested elements to use in assessment

A responsible person vs An irresponsible person

Making a success in life vs Achieving little in life

Has self-respect vs Despises self

Respected by people vs Held in contempt by people

Able to hold down a good job vs Unable to hold down a good job

Close to family vs Cut off from family

(Rollnick & Heather, 1980)

Confused vs Not confused

Disturbed vs Not disturbed

A failure vs Not a failure

Give in easily vs Don't give in easily

Feel hopeless vs Don't feel hopeless

Feel worthless s Don't feel worthless

Unreliable vs Not unreliable

(after Preston & Viney, 1984)

Not in control of drinking (drug use) vs In control of drinking (drug use)

Has problems related to drink (drugs) vs Does not have problems related to drink (drugs)

Figure 9.2. Suggested constructs to use in assessment

Interviewing techniques may be useful here (Miller & Rollnick, 1991). In addition, the more alcohol is an established part of an individual's life, with the role of their 'drunk' self being more elaborated than that of their 'sober' self (i.e. associated with a wider range of situations and meanings), the more difficult it will be for the client to give this role up.

How Does the Client See the Link between Their Use of Alcohol and Their Offending?

A repertory grid is particularly useful in assessing whether the client construes the role of their 'offending' self as *similar to vs different to* their 'sober' and 'drunk' self. A self-characterisation may also indicate how a client's drinking and offending are related, if at all, in their core role structure. Many offenders, at least initially, see their offending self and drunk self as similar, but both different to their sober self. Having a core role structure which includes the notion of offending when drunk, enables a person to avoid experiencing guilt in both the Kellian and the conventional sense. For example, a man who becomes violent to his partner after drinking, may see himself as an easy-going person when sober, and therefore blame his violence solely on 'the drink'. Although the Fragmentation Corollary allows for an individual to show apparently inconsistent construing in different areas of their life, construing their sober self and offending self as very different allows the individual to attribute all responsibility for their offending to the alcohol, and see little need for any exploration of their pre-existing patterns of construing. This would be an issue to explore in treatment. Other offenders may see much more of a similarity between the three roles, and acknowledge that their way of construing the world sets the scene for their offending, which alcohol then facilitates.

How Do They See Different Drinking Roles?

It is important to assess this in order to set realistic goals for treatment and to understand resistance to change. For some clients, their degree of dependence or potential dangerousness when intoxicated may mean that, in the clinician's view, abstinence is the only appropriate goal. However, this role may be completely alien to the client and would require a total restructuring of their core constructs. Unless the individual can accept the role of an abstainer as positive, this will be both difficult to achieve and maintain.

The Treatment Setting

Because the use of alcohol and/or drugs often becomes a feature of many different roles in the client's life, treatment necessarily involves major reconstruction of their core self, with consequent threat and anxiety at the anticipation of change. For offenders with a problem of alcohol dependence which is independent of their offending, treatment is likely to have a greater chance of success if it occurs within a supportive environment, such as a residential therapeutic community. Research also highlights the clients' sensitivity concerning the views of others towards them (Rollnick & Heather, 1980), which is likely to contribute to the success of treatment. This suggests that treatment is therefore more likely to be successful in specialist settings, or at least from specialist clinicians, rather than in general psychiatric in-patient wards. However, it is also important for additional, individually based treatment approaches to exist, and for the person themself to recognise their need for treatment. Residential facilities are therefore helpful, but must also provide support in the crucial follow-up period, when the person is trying to maintain their new sober role. Dawes (1985) also notes one problem with intensive therapeutic community programmes: the new ways of construing that residents learn while embraced by the community, may not be sufficiently elaborated for use outside, i.e. they are too context-dependent. He therefore emphasises the importance of planning the individual's return to the community as an integral part of treatment.

Accepting the New Sober Role as Positive

Treatment of offenders with problems of alcohol or drug dependence has to help them to accept *two* new roles as positive—a non-offending self and a sober self. This requires them to elaborate and experience validation in those new roles (i.e. by successfully participating in life when sober *and* not offending), and cope with the threat of change. Following from G. Kelly's (1955/1991) hypothesis that a more hopeful view may facilitate change, Rivers & Landfield (1985) describe the importance of addressing the implications of change in treatment. For example, this might involve addressing the questions 'In what ways do I need to change and in what ways do I need to remain the same? What will I find most difficult about a sober (non-offending) life?'

Addressing Difficulties in Social Interaction

Rivers & Landfield (1985) note that many alcoholics have major difficulties in social interaction, applying inappropriate constructs in their attempt to understand and predict people. The person therefore experiences a continual lack of validation and feels anxious in social interactions when sober. The authors developed a group treatment approach for alcohol dependence known as the Interpersonal Transaction group (Landfield & Rivers, 1975), which aims to provide an opportunity for a validating social interaction. A detailed description of this approach is beyond the scope of this chapter, but can be found in Winter (1992).

Maintaining Change and Preventing Relapse

Some clients find the structured framework of Alcoholics Anonymous (AA) helpful in providing a clear role with which they are familiar, and Rivers & Landfield (1985) suggest that the admonitions of AA could be reconstructed as 'new constructs' for the recovering alcoholic. In this way statements such as 'one day at a time', which are often seen as trite by professionals, could 'provide *temporary* constructions to help the alcoholic deal with the immediate sense of chaos and fragmentation that can occur within the early stages of recovery' (Rivers & Landfield, 1985,

p. 180). As G. Kelly (1955/1991) suggests, AA also enables the client to remain in the role of the 'alcoholic', and therefore avoid the anxiety resulting from the uncertainty of change. However, many abstinent clients will not share the philosophy of AA (i.e. have a lack of commonality) and the clinician will therefore have to help them to reconstrue a new positive sober role as described above.

Understanding Relapse and Resistance to Change

Finally, the PCP approach can help in understanding why many people who are dependent on alcohol and/or drugs are resistant to change, and have high rates of relapse. Many people with alcohol problems have a relatively tight construct system which will therefore be more resistant to change (Bailey & Sims, 1991), and change will also be seen as threatening and generate considerable anxiety. Burr & Butt (1992) suggest that any dependence should be construed as 'part of the fabric of (your) life' (p. 102) and that the implications of its loss for a person are similar to the loss of important people from their life. To this extent it is important for the clinician to help the client anticipate and plan for long-term difficulties in giving up drinking.

The following case example illustrates the contribution of the PCP perspective to the assessment process.

George was a 25-year-old man who seriously stabbed an acquaintance while under the influence of alcohol. When first seen he was paranoid and hearing persecutory voices, and was diagnosed as suffering from alcohol-related hallucinations. He had started drinking heavily after the sudden death of his wife and his father, and had quickly become physically dependent on alcohol and reluctant to give this up.

At initial assessment, George described his 'drinking self' as 'anaesthetised'. He said that although he was aware of the problems resulting from drinking alcohol, including his own potential dangerousness, he could not imagine being able to cope with life without drink. The loss of both his father (from a sudden heart attack) and his wife (from a drugs overdose) in the same year, had confounded his sense of what was predictable about the world, and he had been unable to reconstruct his life and move on. Alcohol was a way of both numbing his feelings of sadness, and finding a new social role for himself, with other heavy drinkers. A repertory grid was administered to George as part of the initial assessment, and the plot of his grid is shown in Figure 9.3.

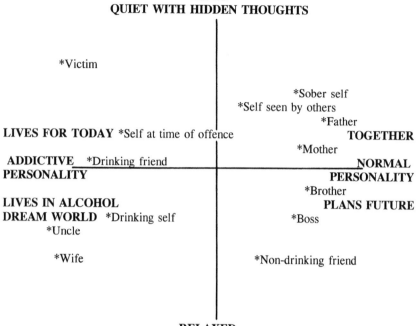

Figure 9.3. Plot of elements in construct space from George's grid

During the process of completing the grid with George, the most pertinent feature was the way in which he frequently discriminated between people using constructs relating to drink and personal stability. His plot illustrates the cognitive simplicity of his construct system, with the main discriminating constructs relating to the implications of either drinking or not drinking. In fact, a massive 67% of the variance (on the 15 × 16 grid) was accounted for by this first component. The elements tended to be rated at extreme poles of the constructs. At one end were drinkers, who were construed as living from day to day in an 'alcohol dream world'. At the other pole were non-drinkers, who were construed as sensible and stable. He had different views of himself, related to whether or not he was drinking alcohol, seeing his drinking self as more relaxed and talkative. George saw his offending self as more similar to himself when he was drinking than when he was sober, but also as more tense and secretive. Although his ideal self was not rated as an element, he said that he saw this as being similar to his non-drinking friend, who could be relaxed and sociable without the use of alcohol.

The plot from George's grid illustrates some of the findings from the research, particularly the cognitively simple construct system and the different perception of self when drunk or sober. One could hypothesise that, although alcohol initially served the purpose of blocking out unpleasant feelings and memories, the role of his drinking self had now become elaborated, and alcohol-related constructs were an integral part of his way of construing the world. In addition, George was currently unable to anticipate the possibility of being relaxed and open about his thoughts while remaining sober. This would be a potential issue to explore in treatment. The grid helped the clinician to understand George's resistance to change, and suggested that he was not likely to remain abstinent until he could both anticipate life whilst in the sober role, and have a more positive view of this role and its accompanying life-style.

SUMMARY AND CONCLUSIONS

A significant proportion of offenders also have problems in relation to their use of alcohol and/or drugs, and there is an established association (although not a causal relationship) between alcohol and delinquency, and between alcohol and aggression in some individuals. However, although there are characteristic patterns of construing in people with drug and alcohol problems *per se*, clearly not all such individuals go on to offend. From the PCP perspective, the relationship between a client's offending and their use of alcohol can be understood in terms of the interaction between *pre-existing* patterns of construing and the dilating and loosening effects of the alcohol on the *process* of construing. Although some offenders may construe their behaviour as resulting solely from their alcohol intake, it is important to explore with them the contribution of the existing content of their construct system.

The research suggests that there is a sub-group of people with alcohol and drug problems who are more resistant to treatment, in terms of dropping out early from programmes or having unusual perceptions of their ideal self. Some of the characteristic patterns of construing of these individuals have much in common with those of people who have been described as personality disordered, for example, particularly tightly organised and cognitively simple construct systems. It may be that amongst a population of people with alcohol and drug problems, this sub-group are more likely to offend.

One of the main implications of the PCP perspective for the assessment of offenders with alcohol/drug problems, is to establish the extent to which the clinician and the client construe the similarity (and subsequent relationship) between the offender's drunk (or drinking) self, sober (or non-drinking) self and offending self. Allowing for the fact that an individual's construct system may be 'fragmented', people still have superordinate constructs which maintain continuity between apparently different experiences. Some clients who offend when drunk may initially have difficulty ackowledging the significance of their construing when sober, and this relates to the degree of responsibility that the client accepts for their offending. However, even if the client is keen to explore their offence-related construing, if they have a clear self-identity which involves using alcohol, they are likely to remain at higher risk for reoffending compared to a similar client whose offending is not drink-related. Offenders who are dependent on drugs or alcohol therefore have to anticipate the loss of two roles if they are engaging in treatment. Not suprisingly, they are likely to experience particular threat and anxiety at this anticipation of change, and it is therefore important to set realistic goals.

CHAPTER 10

Mental Illness and Offending

Offenders who are diagnosed as having a mental illness are only one sub-group of those who are more commonly referred to in both clinical and legal settings as 'mentally disordered offenders'. This generic term includes offenders with psychopathic or other severe personality disorders (see Chapter 8), or with a learning disability. The PCP approach to mental illness has a long tradition, beginning with pioneering studies by Bannister and colleagues into the structure of construing in schizophrenic thought disorder. However, clearly only a minority of people with a mental illness go on to offend. Case examples are used to illustrate how both longstanding (or premorbid) and current (or illness-related) patterns of construing can contribute to the understanding of offending in clients with a mental illness.

INTRODUCTION

Offenders diagnosed with a mental illness have historically been treated differently by the legal system than those who are considered to be 'responsible' for their behaviour, and most such offenders receive a psychiatric, as opposed to a custodial disposal at court. In most Western and many other countries, the provision of secure hospital facilities for mentally ill offenders is now well established. In the UK, about 2000 mentally disordered offenders are detained in the four maximum security ('Special') hospitals and there are also about 1500 beds in smaller, medium-secure psychiatric units. The Reed Committee review of services for mentally disordered offenders recommended the provision of a further 1000 medium-secure beds, and accepted that this figure may need to be reviewed to meet the 'hidden demand' (Reed, 1993). Other mentally disordered offenders are managed in open psychiatric hospitals, therapeutic communities or hospital wings in prison or in the community. Similar provision for mentally disordered offenders is found in the United States (Kerr & Roth, 1986) and Europe (Koenraadt, 1992).

The relationship between different kinds of mental disorder and criminal or violent behaviour is complex, and studies are fraught with definitional and methodological problems. Until recently, even the reviews of this relationship reached different conclusions. Blackburn (1993) concluded that none of the major categories of mental illness seemed strongly associated with a propensity for violence. In comparison, Mullen et al. (1993) concluded that, for people with a psychotic illness, the illness itself *was* an important factor in the precipitation of most violence. The most recent research evidence suggests that the *current* experience of *certain* psychotic symptoms is a modest risk factor for the prediction of violence (Monahan, 1997). However, both these authors and others have also noted the importance of social, interpersonal or environmental factors as contributors to violence. For example, violence between psychiatric in-patients often results more from altercations about personal space or food than from psychotic symptoms *per se* (Pearson et al., 1986). Perhaps suprisingly, therefore, there has been little exploration of the contribution of individual personality factors to the offending of people with a mental illness. However, Blackburn (1968a, b) found that differences in aggression between paranoid and non-paranoid schizophrenics were related to personality traits such as emotionality and extraversion, and Howells (1983) also noted that deluded patients who were violent showed attributional processes which were more commonly associated with aggression in general. Studies of criminal and assaultative behaviour in psychiatric patients (Lindqvist & Allebeck, 1990) have also indicated that the same variables, such as deviant family background or previous history of offending, are predictive of violence or crime as in non-psychiatric populations. It is therefore important for clinicians working with mentally ill offenders not to assume a causative relationship between the mental illness and the offending, and to assess the contributory role of relevant personality factors.

THE PCP PERSPECTIVE ON MENTAL ILLNESS

G. Kelly (1955/1991) was very critical of the medical model. As discussed earlier (see Chapter 2), he did not construe clients' difficulties in terms of pathology or traditional nosological categories as he considered this to represent pre-emptive construing by professionals (i.e. assumptive and rigid). However, he accepted that clients' difficulties *could* be construed in physical, as well as psychological, terms, and suggested that clinicians might be more effective if they routinely applied both psychological and physiological construct systems at the outset of assessment, rather than applying one only after the other has been shown to be inadequate. His view was that the primary determinant of whether a problem should be approached physiologically or psychologically should be pragmatic, and relate to the client's likely response to the different types of intervention.

The PCP perspective not does not therefore discount the potential contribution of physiology or biochemistry to symptoms which are considered diagnostic of mental illness. However, personal construct theorists emphasise the ways in which the structure and content of a person's construing have led to them behaving in such a way as to be diagnosed as mentally ill. For example, much of the work from the PCP perspective on the nature of construing in people with a mental illness has focused on clients diagnosed with schizophrenia. Personal construct psychology suggests a theoretical model of thought disorder, developed from Kelly's original proposal that the thinking of some clients diagnosed as schizophrenic is characterised by loose construing. Loose constructs are those which lead to variable predictions, and schizophrenic thought disorder is seen as a state in which constructs have largely ceased to have strong stable relationships with each other. This means that 'meaning' is changeable and verbal labels simply become 'noise'. Bannister (1962) states that the lack of any pattern in construing means that 'the thought-disordered schizophrenic is left occupying a fluid, undifferentiated, subjective universe' (p. 833). The lack of constellation between constructs means that it is difficult for the person with schizophrenia to make useful unidirectional predictions about future events. However, this very looseness also means that the person cannot be wrong, as the lack of association between constructs means that apparent inconsistencies can always be 'explained' or accommodated.

The PCP perspective has also been applied to other diagnoses of mental illness. For example, clients diagnosed as paranoid have been viewed as having a structural disorder involving dilation of the construct system (Winter, 1992). As discussed in the opening chapter, dilation is a means by which a person deals with apparent incompatibilities in their construing, by broadening their view of the world and seeing new links between events or aspects of their life. However, this is only possible if the person has an existing superordinate structure in their construct system which can accommodate the new dilated field. The delusions of people who are diagnosed as paranoid may therefore represent a sweeping elaboration of a persecutory or grandiose construction. In other words, as proposed by G. Kelly (1991), the so-called fictitious perception of the client may often turn out to be a distorted construction of something that really does exist.

PATTERNS OF CONSTRUING IN PEOPLE WITH A MENTAL ILLNESS

The Structure of Construing

A detailed review of the literature on the structure of construing in people diagnosed with schizophrenia is beyond the scope of this chapter and can be found elsewhere (Winter, 1992; Pierce et al., 1992). However, it is relevant to note that the origin of this work was in the series of studies carried out by Bannister (1960, 1962), which defined thought disorder operationally in terms of repertory grid methodology. Most of this work used a specially designed repertory grid, the Bannister–Fransella Grid Test. This required subjects to rank eight photographs of people on six supplied constructs (e.g. kind, selfish) and then to repeat the task again as if they were doing it for the first time. Studies showed that the performance of thought-disordered schizo-phrenics could be differentiated both from people without a mental illness and from other patient groups (Bannister & Fransella, 1966, 1967). The grids of thought-disordered subjects were characterised by both low correlations between constructs and low consistency of the pattern of relationships between constructs when the grids were repeated. Thought disorder was therefore defined as grossly loosened construing, with the inevitable and simultaneous lowering of both *Intensity* (i.e. how tightly the construct system is organised) and *Consistency* (i.e. the relationship between constructs over time). Later studies indicated that looseness of construing was more evident with psychological constructs (e.g. 'Trusting vs Not trusting') than with non-psychological (e.g. 'Old vs Young') and that it is particularly *people*, rather than objects, that the thought-disordered person finds difficult to understand and predict (McPherson et al., 1973).

Having established that loose construing was a characteristic feature of thought disorder, Bannister (1963, 1965) then used the Grid Test to test his *serial invalidation* hypothesis of how people become thought-disordered. He found that if a person is faced with repeated invalidation of part of their construct sub-system for viewing people, they begin to alter, and eventually loosen, the pattern of relationships between their constructs (or, as Bannister puts it, 'to go out of the theory holding busi-ness'). Conversely, repeated validation (i.e. confirmation of expecta-tions) leads to an intensification of the the linkages between constructs until the system becomes simple and monolithic. Bannister & Fransella (1986) noted that the serial invalidation hypothesis could be related to those psychological theories of the origins of schizophrenic thought disorder which emphasise the role of inconsistent and incompatible messages within the family (e.g. Lidz, 1964). The serial invalidation hypothesis could also be considered relevant to the more recent emphasis on the role of expressed emotion (EE) in families as a predictor of schizophrenic relapse (e.g. Kavanagh, 1992).

Much debate in the literature has focused on Bannister's interpretation of his results in terms of loose construing. Although many studies have since supported his earlier work (see Winter's 1992 review), critics have suggested that the performance of thought-disordered schizophrenics on the Grid Test is merely a reflection of their inconsistency of performance on all cognitive tasks due to attentional deficits (Harrison & Phillips, 1979). Other authors have suggested that thought-disordered schizophrenics lack the superordinate linkages (i.e. more complex constructs which are higher up in the hierarchical structure) which allow most normal people to resolve inconsistencies in their experiences (Space & Cromwell, 1978). However, despite the differing views of authors about the precise nature of the structural characteristics of construing which contribute to the schizophrenic process, there are areas of agreement which link the different interpretations together. Another important finding from the Bannister studies was that the construct systems of thought-disordered schizophrenics were also *socially deviant* in terms of *content*. The clinical histories of the research patients indicated that they had not moved straight from 'normality' to 'thought disorder', but had progressed first through a phase in which they were described as 'paranoid' or 'deluded' or 'manifesting bizarre behaviour', indicating that gross disturbances of content in the construct system had occurred before the final disintegration of the structure. In other words, the nature of the process underlying the development of thought disorder is that the construct system becomes odd before it becomes weak. There are therefore different responses to the experience of invalidation. Some individuals remain at the stage in which merely the content of their construing is altered, and maintain a 'paranoid integration', while others proceed to structural breakdown. Lorenzini et al. (1989) suggest that, in contrast to the thought-disordered individual, the construct system of a person who is paranoid tends to become more and more monolithic, or unidimensional, as they experience repeated invalidation. These authors suggest that whereas the client with schizophrenia responds to invalidation with a sense of *threat* (i.e. the awareness of an imminent change in their core role structure), the client who is paranoid responds with *hostility*, i.e. the continuous effort to extort validational evidence for predictions that have already been shown to be a failure. The choice of a schizophrenic or paranoid 'solution' to predictive failure, may depend on the combination of premorbid personality, type of invalidation, and the existing structural state of the individual's construct system.

The Content of Construing

There has been less focus on the content of construing in people with a mental illness. Until recently, the only difference found between how schizophrenics and other clients construed themselves was that the former showed a greater tendency to identify with the opposite sex parent (Winter, 1975; Space & Cromwell, 1978). This is consistent with early work which suggested that the families of schizophrenics may be characterised by patterns of construing which are different from the usual social norm (Lidz, 1968). However, recent work by Gara et al. (1987, 1989) on the personal identity of people with schizophrenia has suggested that such clients have both poorly elaborated views of themselves and stereotyped perceptions of themselves and other people. It remains to be seen whether these results are specific to people with schizophrenia or indicative of psychopathology in general.

The Meaning of Offending to People with a Mental Illness

As seen in the preceding chapters, in offender clients the content of their construing is very relevant. However, the only empirical study of construing in mentally abnormal offenders (Howells, 1983) did not break down its overall results in terms of legal category (i.e. 'mental illness' or 'psychopathic disorder', Mental Health Act, 1983). Individual meanings must therefore be understood from case examples:

John was a 25-year-old man who had no contact with either the police or psychiatric services prior to a violent assault upon his neighbour. He was diagnosed as suffering from paranoid schizophrenia, and held an encapsulated delusion about being persecuted by his victim. In interview he described how this woman had 'held a grudge' against him ever since he had moved into the flat two years earlier, and described a range of activities which he saw as 'evidence' to support his construction. He maintained that she constantly found fault with him and 'deliberately' set out to have him moved from the flat. Although there may have been some initial reality to the mutual dislike between John and his neighbour, his construing over the years had developed to the point where any aspect of ordinary living was interpreted within a construct system that was dominated by whether or not people were 'out to cause trouble'. Assessment with a repertory grid showed a striking pattern of tightly organised, cognitively simplistic construing, in which nine of the ten constructs were clustered into a massive first component, which accounted for 91% of the variance.

This primarily reflected positive versus negative personal characteristics (See Figure 10.1a). John rated eight of the ten elements (including his current and ideal self) as being very similar, towards the positive pole of the constructs, with only 'self at the time of the offence' and his neighbour being construed at the opposite pole (See Figure 10.1b).

The information from John's grid was consistent with the hypothesis based on clinical interview: that his offending was directly related to his delusional beliefs, or in PCP terms, to the content of his construing. Similar features were also seen in one of the case examples described by Howells (1983). The structural characteristics of John's construing were clearly consistent with the literature which suggests that clients diagnosed as paranoid tend to show far greater patterns of tightly organised, or monolithic, construing (Lorenzini et al., 1989). However, from a *clinical* perspective, it was important to note that although John accepted that what he had done was 'violent' and 'bad', he still held the same persecutory beliefs about his neighbour. Given the potentially harmful consequences of the persistence of such construing, pharmacological treatment was clearly important.

In contrast, for other offenders with a mental illness, the relevant aspects of their construing which contribute to their offending may pre-date the onset of their illness. In such clients, an interaction between premorbid patterns of construing and the disinhibiting effects of illness may contribute to their offending. This may particularly occur when the client is diagnosed as having an affective component to their illness, or as being thought-disordered, as in such cases it appears that

Causes trouble vs Causes no one trouble

Not nice vs All right

Violent vs Good

Don't behave well vs Well behaved

Tell you what is wrong vs Tell you what is right

Unhelpful vs Helpful

Unkind vs Kind

Gives no encouragement vs Encourages you

Ungrateful vs Grateful

Bad vs Good

Figure 10.1a. Constructs elicited from John during assessment

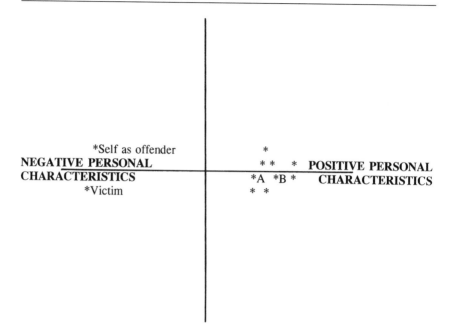

Figure 10.1b. Plot of elements in construct space from John's grid. A indicates 'self now' and B indicates 'ideal self'

the loosening of construing may contribute to the client making poor judgements. Furthermore, if the client is diagnosed as having a personality disorder in addition to their mental illness, it is again likely that premorbid characteristics of construing contribute an important part to the understanding of their offending. The following case example illustrates the complexity of such interactions.

Barry, a 27-year-old man, had a history of inpatient admissions to psychiatric hospital, and had received a diagnosis of schizo-affective disorder, with additional alcohol and drug dependence. He showed marked mood swings, but also experienced visual hallucinations and ideas of reference. He had a history of criminal convictions dating back to his early teens, ranging from car theft to Grievous Bodily Harm (GBH). Barry was transferred to hospital from prison while serving his most recent sentence, but continued to be both verbally and physically aggressive to staff and patients. In interview with Barry it emerged that he had been both physically and sexually abused as a child, and that his conduct disorder dated from this time, escalating into delinquency as a teenager and more serious offending in adulthood. Although he established a good rapport in interview, he was suspicious of more formal assessment techniques. He walked out of the room while compiling the list of elements for a repertory grid after he was asked to think of the name of a 'disliked person', and later said that he would carry on with the interviews but not the grid. He would not discuss why he walked out, but one hypothesis about his reaction was that he may have assumed that he was being probed about his abuse, which he did not initially want to discuss. On exploring Barry's history of aggression, it became clear that in some episodes the content of his premorbid construing was particularly relevant, on other occasions his construing was directly related to his illness, and sometimes there was an interaction between the two. For example, regardless of his mental state, Barry construed his interactions with others as being a 'Win vs Lose' situation, and frequently talked about not letting other people 'get away with it'. He maintained that he would only use violence 'if necessary' if he thought he was going to 'lose' in the interaction, such as in an argument with a fellow patient or friend in the community. However, there were other precursors to his violence in which Barry's construing was clearly influenced by his illness, although this was not immediately obvious without detailed interviewing. For example, one of the assaults which led to a conviction for GBH immediately followed an experience in which he had 'been followed by the Devil' and in which Barry described himself as being 'completely terrified and unable to think straight'. Barry himself accepted that as well as having a mental illness, he had a number of problems which were likely to relate to his disruptive childhood and abusive experiences, and he agreed to engage in psychotherapeutic treatment in addition to receiving medication.

The above cases therefore illustrate different ways in which the offending of a client with a mental illness can be understood. There are some similarities to offender clients with problems of alcohol dependence, as seen in Chapter 9. In other words, with *some* clients, the illness (or use of alcohol) may be a 'red herring', in that its contribution to the understanding of the client's offending is not as important as their premorbid patterns of construing. It is easy to assume that offending which is perpetrated by a client with a mental illness can be accounted for by their mental state. However, as seen in the cases throughout the chapter, the offence-related construing of such a client may also be independent of any illness, or be attributed to the interaction between the process of the illness and longstanding patterns of construing.

IMPLICATIONS FOR ASSESSMENT AND TREATMENT

The main implication of the PCP perspective when working with an offender with a mental illness is to highlight the importance of individual personality factors, as well as the traditional psychiatric diagnosis, throughout the process of assessment and treatment. Clients with a mental illness who also offend are very much in the minority, and one purpose of the assessment is to determine why *this particular individual* with a mental illness has behaved in the way they have. The physiological and psychological construct systems for construing a client's difficulties have different ranges of convenience (i.e. limits of applicability). The range of problematic behaviour presented by the client (from both their own and others' perspective) may not be fully subsumed within only one system. If using a grid in assessment, it may be useful to use the elements and constructs suggested in one of the previous chapters, depending on the client's offending behaviour.

What Are the Structural Features of the Client's Construing?

The tightness or looseness of a client's construct system is likely to reflect the degree to which they are thought-disordered. Clients whose construing is very tight and unidimensional, such as in the case example of John above, are more likely to have an integrated paranoid delusion. The structural features of construing can therefore help to make sense of the way in which the symptoms of a client's illness affect all aspects of their life, as well as contributing to the understanding of their offending.

How Does the Client Construe Their Different 'Selves'?

As with other offender clients, it is still important to assess the way in which a person with a mental illness construes their actual, ideal and offending self. However, such clients may also construe themselves differently when they are ill, compared to when they are not ill, or when in hospital and in the community. An offender with a mental illness has the potential to identify with one or both of two different roles, that of an offender and that of a psychiatric patient. It is therefore useful to understand whether or not the client sees themself as fitting into the role of a 'patient', or whether they have a stereotype of a 'typical patient' from which they distance themself. If the individual has difficulty construing themself as a patient, they may have more difficulties adjusting to and complying with the practicalities of inpatient routines. For example, a person who sees themself as part of the criminal fraternity and who has been transferred to a secure psychiatric hospital from prison, may be better placed back within the prison system once their mental illness has been treated and if they are stable and compliant with medication. On the other hand, if a client construes themself as very similar to other patients, or has no difficulty in seeing themself in this way, they may be able to make good use of psychiatric rehabilitation services, and develop a new core role structure which includes the notion of being 'a patient'.

How Do They Construe Others?

As with any other offender client it is important to assess how a person diagnosed with a mental illness construes their victim(s). In addition, research has suggested that the way in which the mentally ill client both construes, and is themselves perceived by, their family may be important for prognosis (Kavanagh, 1992; Scott et al., 1993).

What is the Significance of the Client's Premorbid Patterns of Construing?

As illustrated in the earlier case examples, the degree to which the client's premorbid patterns of construing contribute to the understanding of their offending, varies considerably between individuals diagnosed with a mental illness. For example, in some individuals, it may be clear that their tendency to construe other people, or their victim, in a suspicious way has only had a recent onset, and their construct system may be dominated by the content of their delusions. Other individuals may show symptoms diagnostic of mental illness which are unrelated to their offending, and their offence-related construing (and indeed their behaviour) may pre-date the onset of their illness. With other clients, although the content of their construing may not be considered 'paranoid' or 'psychotic', the loosening effects of their symptoms may contribute to them interpreting events in ways which are facilitative of offending.

The Role of Medication

Although as discussed earlier, G. Kelly (1991) and Bannister (1985) were critical of the medical model of psychiatric illness, both authors accepted that pharmacological and physical treatments have a part to play in the treatment of such problems. This is particularly the case if the client construes their difficulties in such a way that they are more likely to respond to physical treatments. For example, Bannister & Mair

(1968) note that, 'If the patient regards his condition as an "illness" of mysterious origin, unrelated to his present outlook or past way of life, or if he has been persuaded by the hospital to accept such a view, then he may well respond to equally mysterious chemicals as the appropriate agents of recovery' (p. 213). More recently, Dalton & Dunnett (1992) provide a PCP perspective on issues relating to compliance with medication, and suggest that unless a client perceives this as something which enables them to be in control of their life, they will either fight against the need for medication or feel diminished through their need for it. Other authors have noted the positive ways in which medication may assist the client in organising their construing, particularly in relation to their view of themselves (Dawes, 1985; Gara et al., 1987).

Personal Construct Psychotherapy with Mentally Ill Clients

Although there have been recent developments in the use of psychological approaches to manage and modify a client's psychotic symptoms (e.g. Tarrier, 1992), the notion of understanding the meaning of delusional systems is well established from the personal construct psychology perspective (Bannister, 1985; Dunnett, 1988). Bannister (1985) described his work with deluded clients, in which he attempted to focus on the superordinate themes which were reflected in their delusions, and then to devise appropriate 'experiments' with the clients to test these out. However, Bannister's view was that one of the purposes served by delusions is to allow the client to maintain a distance from others, and to test out who may be trusted. Consequently, trust in the therapist may take a long time to achieve, with therapy being a lengthy process. In addition, although this approach may enable the clinician to engage with the deluded client, explore their delusions and begin to test them out, it is not clear how far it facilitates actual change in the client's symptoms. Finally, as illustrated throughout the chapter, for other clients there may be aspects of their premorbid patterns of construing which contribute a greater part to the development and maintenance of their offending. These can then be addressed in psychotherapeutic treatment which is seen as separate from, but parallel to, the pharmacological treatment of their thought disorder or delusional beliefs.

The following case example illustrates the various contributory roles of a client's thought disorder, paranoid beliefs, auditory hallucinations and premorbid patterns of construing to their conviction for indecent assault, and the use of the PCP perspective to inform assessment and treatment.

Mark was a single man in his late thirties who had a long psychiatric history, including inpatient admissions. He had been diagnosed as suffering from schizophrenia at the age of 18 years, after hearing voices and claiming that he was being influenced through telepathy. He had had no previous contact with the police before being convicted of the indecent assault of a woman whom he had tried to befriend. A pre-trial psychiatric assessment did not conclude that the offence was related to his mental state, as Mark had said that that he thought he could sexually assault the woman and get away with it. He therefore received a custodial sentence. However, he became increasingly suspicious and verbally aggressive in prison and was transferred to hospital, where he complied with medication and his mental state was stabilised.

At interview with Mark it was clear that he was thought-disordered, and was difficult to follow at times. However, he was ashamed of his offence, and saw this as being out of character. One aim of assessment was therefore to understand Mark's construing of his offending, his victim, and women in general, and the contribution of both longstanding premorbid aspects of construing and those which related more to his mental state at the time of the offence. Because of the nature of his offence, it was important to obtain a detailed history of Mark's psychosexual development and relationships. Mark's longest relationship with a woman had been in his early twenties, when he was married to a fellow psychiatric patient for just under a year. Otherwise his relationships had all been brief, or 'one night stands'. In the year preceding his offence, Mark had become more and more preoccupied with his single status. He consistently used the opposing poles of constructs to contrast himself with his siblings and friends. He described the latter as 'married', 'settled', 'have a family', in comparison to himself, who was 'not married', 'frustrated' and 'lonely'. He described trying to make conversation with women on the bus or in coffee shops, with the hope of developing a lasting relationship.

Mark said that he had stopped taking his antipsychotic medication a few weeks before his offence, as he felt it was no longer necessary. He described a subsequent deterioration in his self-care, and a gradual increase in suspiciousness. He construed delays from the Social Security in sorting out his benefits as intentional. His loose construing was illustrated by statements like, 'children kept playing in front of my flat ... I wondered why they were there and why they were picking on me? ... I wouldn't have committed my offence if they hadn't always been there.'

Mark's victim was a young woman who lived on the same estate. He first saw her in the local pub, where he construed ordinary social conversation as evidence that she was interested in developing a relationship with him. When he then bumped into her on a number of occasions, he interpreted this as her being 'provocative', deliberately coming out of her flat at the same time as him. He also said that this was a 'sign' that he was 'meant' to have a relationship with the woman. Detailed interviewing over a number of sessions therefore indicated that some of the content of Mark's offence-related construing may have been directly related to his mental state at the time. However, he also admitted to a long-standing tendency to construe men and women in gender-stereotypical ways, particularly illustrated by his use of the construct 'Women's jobs (i.e. housewives, care women) vs Men's jobs' (i.e. policeman, driver). He had also always construed some women as 'inviting' sexual assault, by wearing short skirts or tight tops, or by not resisting sexual advances, and did not think that there was anything inappropriate about approaching unknown women in the hope that this would lead to a sexual encounter. The treatment plan for Mark therefore aimed to involve a combination of both pharmacological and psychotherapeutic approaches. The latter included attempts to help him reconstrue his view of women and approach to relationships. Unfortunately, Mark tended to 'slot-rattle' quickly within the sessions, completely reversing his constructions, appearing to want to 'say the right thing'. He also maintained that he was now no longer interested in developing a relationship with a woman or getting married because it was 'too much trouble'. In PCP terms, this could be described as Mark accommodating his conviction by constricting his field of vision. From a psychotherapeutic perspective, Mark therefore made little change. However, having a long history of contact with psychiatric services meant that being 'a patient' was already part of his core role. Treatment therefore focused on encouraging Mark to accept that in order to reduce his risk of further reoffending, he would require long-term support and monitoring from mental health services, which included the need for medication.

SUMMARY AND CONCLUSIONS

Personal construct theorists have always emphasised the psychological construction of symptoms which are considered diagnostic of mental illness, and one of the most widely studied fields within PCP has been the nature and origin of construing in people diagnosed with schizophrenic thought disorder. Although there is disagreement about the precise nature of the structural characteristics of construing which contribute to thought disorder, most authors agree that this represents an attempt to resolve internal inconsistencies within the construct system, which in some cases may be characteristic of the family environment. It is now acknowledged that individuals will respond to serial invalidation of their construing in different ways. This may contribute to the understanding of why some individuals develop a relatively integrated 'paranoid' delusional system, whereas others progress to a state of thought disorder (Lorenzini et al., 1989).

Since only a minority of clients with a mental illness offend, and the relationship between mental illness and crime is not causative, there is clearly a need to focus on additional personality factors in order to understand the personal meaning of offending to a client with a mental illness. Although therefore it has been the *structural* features of construing which have been the main focus of study in clients with a mental illness, it is the *content* of construing which may be more useful in understanding why some individuals go on to offend. Furthermore, it is useful in planning treatment to distinguish between that construing which is primarily related to their illness or current mental state, and that which is primarily premorbid or longstanding. In other cases there may be an interaction, in which the client's symptoms have a loosening effect on their construing, and they interpret events in ways which are not traditionally 'psychotic', but are different from usual.

Finally, the important difference between clients with a mental illness and those who also go on to offend, is the potential harm of their behaviour to other people, as well as themselves. It is therefore particularly important to ensure that both pharmacological *and* psychological constructions of their symptoms and behaviour are applied during the assessment process, in order for appropriate treatment to be planned. Subsuming all of the offending behaviour of the mentally ill client within either one of the two approaches to construction, is to reject a potential opportunity to reduce the risk of further reoffending.

Epilogue

CONCLUDING COMMENTS: REFLEXIVE CONSIDERATIONS ON THE USE OF PCP

One of the essential concepts in PCP is that it is a reflexive theory, applicable to the whole spectrum of human experience and not just to that which is considered deviant. It is therefore useful to take a reflexive look at the potential use of PCP by clinicians working with offenders.

There are a number of factors that contribute to the way in which a clinician construes their 'professional self'. For many clinicians, their training and qualifications form an essential part of their core role. For example, such individuals may construe their 'professional self' in terms of their professional role, i.e. as 'a clinical psychologist' or 'a social worker'. However, whatever their professional background, a clinician's approach to assessment and treatment can also lie anywhere along the construct of 'Primarily informed by a single theoretical orientation (pole A) vs Primarily informed by a range of theoretical orientations' (pole B). A clinician who is at pole A may be likely to construe themselves as being 'a cognitive-behaviourist', 'a psychoanalyst' or 'a personal construct theorist', whereas a clinician who is at pole B may be more likely to construe themselves as 'eclectic'. One could hypothesise that a clinician whose professional core role structure is defined in terms of their theoretical orientation rather than their professional role, may be more likely to experience anxiety and threat (in the Kellian sense) at the prospect of 'slot-rattling' towards pole B. Furthermore, the more tightly a clinician construes both their existing and other orientations, the more resistant they are likely to be to the prospect of change. However, my own hypothesis is that the clinicians who have chosen to read this book and have reached the end are either (i) those who are already using aspects of the PCP perspective in their work with offenders and are therefore validating and elaborating their construing, or (ii) those for whom an interest in the use of the PCP perspective in their work with offenders does not pose too great a threat to their core role. Using the reflexive nature of PCP, the aims of the author have therefore been

1. To reconstrue pre-existing constructions about PCP which may have invalidated its use by some clinicians as a therapeutic approach. For example, this may involve loosening construing in some areas (i.e. 'PCP equals the use of repertory grids') and tightening it in others (i.e. 'PCP is just another cognitive theory').
2. To encourage the construing of clinicians working with offenders to 'slot-rattle' along the construct of 'Primarily informed by another theoretical orientation (pole X) vs Primarily informed by PCP (pole Y)' in the direction of pole Y.
3. To encourage experimentation with the PCP approach in the assessment and treatment of offenders.

Certainly the current focus on addressing the ways in which offenders interpret events, combined with the need to acknowledge the heterogeneity of offenders and to use multi-faceted approaches, makes this seem a timely point at which to introduce personal construct psychology to a wider range of clinicians working with offenders.

Appendices

APPENDIX I: PERSONAL CONSTRUCT THEORY

Reproduced from G. Kelly (1955, reprinted 1991)

(a) *Fundamental Postulate:* A person's processes are psychologically channelised by the ways in which they anticipate events.

(b) *Construction Corollary:* A person anticipates events by construing their replications.

(c) *Individuality Corollary:* Persons differ from each other in their construction of events.

(d) *Organisation Corollary:* Each person characteristically evolves, for their convenience in anticipating events, a construction system embracing ordinal relationships between constructs.

(e) *Dichotomy Corollary:* A person's construction system is composed of a finite number of dichotomous constructs.

(f) *Choice Corollary:* A person chooses for themselves that alternative in a dichotomised construct through which they anticipate the greater possibility for extension and definition of their system.

(g) *Range Corollary:* A construct is convenient for the anticipation of a finite number of events only.

(h) *Experience Corollary:* A person's construction system varies as they successfully construe the replication of events.

(i) *Modulation Corollary:* The variation in a person's construction system is limited by the permeability of the constructs within whose ranges of convenience the variants lie.

(j) *Fragmentation Corollary:* A person may successively employ a variety of construction subsystems which are inferentially incompatible with each other.

(k) *Commonality Corollary:* To the extent that one person employs a construction of experience which is similar to that employed by another, their psychological processes are similar to those of the other person.

(l) *Sociality Corollary:* To the extent that one person construes the construction processes of another they may play a role in a social process involving the other person.

APPENDIX II: MANUAL GRID ANALYSIS

Chris Evans

Some manual analysis is sensible and useful for any grid. This includes thinking about the elements used, thinking about the constructs used (particularly when these have been elicited) and particularly noting whether there are surprising constructs or surprising labels for opposing poles for constructs (if these have been elicited). Sometimes there are two emergent poles that sound very similar to you but which each have different opposing poles. This can be highly informative about the organisation of the client's construing. A quick look for constructs that seem synonymous should be followed by a quick scan of the element ratings on those constructs to see if the elements *are* similarly rated. Eyeball scanning often detects fairly reliably that the rating scale available has been used in a very particular way, for example all ratings at one end of the scale even for obviously negatively correlated constructs. There is nothing intrinsically 'wrong' about construct usages or ratings that look very odd to you; however, they *may* be pointers to very important differences or difficulties in the use of the grid.

More extensive 'manual' analysis of grids is really only feasible for 'yes/no' or '+/–' rated grids. Such analyses are only ways of rearranging the data in the grid you were given. This is also true for all computer analyses, no matter how sophisticated they are nor how obviously this seems not to be the case. 'Manual' analyses actually shade into computer analyses nowadays as readily available computers with cheap word processing or spreadsheet programs can facilitate the 'manual' work.

The technique is to rearrange the grid to put things that were rated similarly near to each other. This can be done for both constructs and elements. Consider the following (oversimplified) grid:

	Me now	Me as I'd like to be	Mother	Father	Girlfriend	Victim
Kind	–	+	+	–	–	–
Angry	+	–	–	+	+	+
Gets deserts	+	–	–	–	+	+
Provocative	–	–	–	+	–	–
Clever	–	+	+	–	–	+
Unattractive	+	–	+	–	+	–
Sexy	–	–	–	+	–	+

Two constructs are virtually identical, 'Provocative' and 'Sexy', and 'Unattractive' is very similar but with reversed ratings. The construct 'Kind' is also identical in ratings to 'Angry' but reversed. Two elements are identical in their ratings: 'Me now' and 'Girlfriend'.

These similarities can be made clearer by rearranging the grid, as below. The use of brackets indicates that the construct has been reversed.

	Me now	Girlfriend	Me as I'd like to be	Mother	Father	Victim
(Kind)	+	+	−	−	+	+
Angry	+	+	−	−	+	+
Gets deserts	+	+	−	−	−	+
Clever	−	−	+	+	−	+
(Unattractive)	−	−	+	−	+	+
Sexy	−	−	−	−	+	+
Provocative	−	−	−	−	+	−

This rearrangement makes it easier to see the similarities outlined above. For example, this person sees his father and his victim as being similar, and sees himself as identical to his girlfriend.

A further way in which dichotomous '+/−' ratings can be examined manually is to measure the element/construct similarities by counting the number of matching scores. Hence the matching score of '(Kind)' and 'Angry' is 6, the maximum possible given the use of only six elements. This can be shown in a matrix, as below:

	(Kind)	Angry	Gets deserts	Clever	(Unattractive)	Sexy	Provocative
(Kind)	6						
Angry	6	6					
Gets deserts	5	5	6				
Clever	1	1	2	6			
(Unattractive)	3	3	2	4	6		
Sexy	4	4	3	3	5	6	
Provocative	3	3	2	2	4	5	6

For this person, as well as the exact equivalence of 'Angry' and 'Unkind', there is also a close association between these constructs and 'Gets deserts'. The client is also using the constructs 'Sexy', 'Attractive' and 'Provocative' in a very similar way. It can be seen how these strong, simple linkages might reflect fundamental aspects of construing that may be important in a client's offending behaviour.

The elements can also be rearranged in this way, as shown below:

	Me now	Girlfriend	Me as I'd like to be	Mother	Father	Victim
Me now	6					
Girlfriend	6	6				
Me as I'd like to be	2	2	6			
Mother	3	3	6	6		
Father	3	3	2	1	6	
Victim	4	4	3	2	4	6

This makes it easy to see who the client apparently sees himself as more like (i.e. his girlfriend) and to whom he would apparently like to be more similar (i.e. his mother). Of course, this should raise the question of the extent to which the constructs that were used in the grid fully reflect his construing of himself and other people. It is therefore often helpful, after looking at a grid, whether manually or computer analysed, to go back to the person and ask about ways in which two elements rated as similar differ, and about the similarities between elements that were rated as very different.

The computer programs G-PACK (Bell, 1987; see Appendix V) and REPGRID (Shaw, 1989) both implement ways in which the elicitation of a grid can automatically take into account the patterns of similarity between elements. This interactivity is one of the advantages of using a computer to help not only with the analysis of grids but also with their elicitation.

APPENDIX III: COMPUTER ANALYSIS OF REPERTORY GRIDS

Chris Evans

Grids have been linked in many people's minds with computer analysis and it is true that computers have made possible analyses that are simply impossible or utterly impractical by hand. However, there have been disadvantages to this link. The main one is that it has prevented many people from using grids either because they had no access to computers or disliked using them. Almost as importantly, when computers and grid programs were very fixed in their options many people came to have a rather unthinking faith in the output of the programs or a blanket dismissal of their output as too rigid. Modern computers have a 'friendliness' and flexibility that makes it possible to move beyond this. To begin, I would strongly recommend that readers of this book try to locate themselves in this classification:

1. Without easy access to computers or utterly computer-phobic
2. Fairly statistics/maths-phobic
3. Pragmatic about computers and statistical/psychometric tools
4. Keen on computers and maths and/or statistics.

Group 1. Computer-deprived or Utterly Computer-phobic

Those in this group should read no further for now but should experiment with any of the 'yes/no' or '+/−' grid methods that do not require computers for analysis (see Appendix II).

Group 2. Fairly Statistics/Maths-phobic

Those in this group should probably experiment with 'yes/no' or '+/−' scored grids and experiment with a word processor which can handle 'column moves' and/or tables to ease reorganisation of their grid data to make inter-construct and inter-element similarities easier to visualise and to make it easier to discuss these similarities with the person who completed the grid (see Appendix II). They may then want to move on to use one of the grid packages (see below) that offer specific analyses. If they have access to the World Wide Web they should try using the interactive grid elicitation and analysis package derived from

RepGridII which can be found at: http://Tiger.cpsc.ucalgary.ca/WebGrid/ WGInitial.html

The RepGridII program itself, though only available for Macintosh computers at present and not cheap, is undoubtedly the friendliest of the computer options for grid analysis for people in this position. It offers a very full repertoire of analyses of the relationships between elements, between constructs and between elements *and* constructs, as well as excellent graphical summaries of the analyses and options to compare multiple grids and to allow elaboration of grids by addition of further elements and/or constructs in the light of the analysis of the first grid. Contact information is given below. Another very friendly program for someone in this group is INGRID96 which is available for PCs (see contact information below).

Group 3. Pragmatic about Computers and Statistical/Psychometric Tools

People in this group should find most of the available grid analysis packages will become steadily more and more useful and comprehensible with usage. I would recommend experimenting with INGRID96 and then Circumgrids for a learning experience (and for the latter's annotated bibliography). After that, the G-PACK package, OMNIGRID, FLEXIGRID or GRIDCOR programs are the next stop for PC users and the OMNIGRID hypercard stack or RepGridII are the options for Macintosh users (speaking from my own personal experience).

Group 4. Keen on Computers and Maths and/or Statistics

People in this group will probably feel comfortable taking any of a number of routes into computer analysis of grids. Those with some familiarity with spreadsheets will find it easy to use them to carry the simple grid reorganisation, and to make the computation of difference scores for both the elements and constructs quite easy. Some spreadsheets offer statistical or matrix tools or are amenable to 'plug-ins' which offer correlation and matrix decomposition functions which would make possible all the options of traditional grid packages. Those who are mathematically oriented might also be able to combine these or simpler functions and macros with the 'what if?' and 'goal-seeking' capacities of the more powerful spreadsheets to do a variety of analyses.

Another approach is to use the capabilities of conventional statistics packages to carry out grid analyses. Most packages, even those for personal computers, can offer construct intercorrelations and element distances. Most will also offer cluster and principal component methods of looking at both the elements *and* constructs together. Some thought has to be given to the exact methods being offered by the packages, particularly if you want to align the results with the output of traditional grid analysis packages, as the options that are appropriate for traditional nomothetic statistical datasets are not those which are most appropriate for grid data. These issues are best understood by using the G-PACK package to explore various scaling options and to compare the results with those produced by the statistical packages. Statistics packages that offer true matrix handling abilities such as the MATRIX functions in SPSSX or the IML package in SAS, enable the user to emulate the exact methods used by

Slater's G.A.P. An example of how this is done in SAS/IML is available on the World Wide Web at: http://psyctc.sghms.ac.uk/grids/ingrid2.sas.

Good statistics packages or the packages dedicated to multi-dimensional scaling will provide this facility. Analysis using ordinal scaling and allowing 'untying' of identical ratings is probably the most appropriate to the level of information provided by most grid ratings. Finally, for those who are more mathematically than statistically inclined, packages like MathCad, Mathematica, Maple, Guass, S++ and other maths programs provide extensive options to 'roll your own' analyses.

Contact Information for Grid Packages

Further information about grid packages and contact addresses can be found on the World Wide Web at: http://psyctc.sghms.ac.uk/grids/

or from:

Dr Chris Evans
Senior Lecturer in Psychotherapy and Consultant to the
  Prudence Skynner Family Therapy Clinic
Department of General Psychiatry
St. George's Hospital Medical School
Cranmer Terrace
London SW17 0RE

Email: C.Evans@sghms.ac.uk

APPENDIX IV: MEASURES OF COGNITIVE DIFFERENTIATION (ADAPTED FROM WINTER, 1992)

Intensity

This is a measure developed by Bannister (1960), of the tightness of organisation in an individual's construct system. The Intensity score is obtained by squaring the correlation between each pair of constructs in a person's grid, multiplying by 100, and summing all the scores.

Bieri et al.'s (1966) measure of cognitive complexity

The authors defined cognitive complexity as 'the capacity to construe social behaviour in a multidimensional way' (p. 185). This measure involves comparing the ratings of every element on each pair of constructs in a person's grid, and giving a score of 1 where there is exact agreement. The greater the agreement, the higher the score, and therefore the lower the degree of cognitive complexity.

Crockett's (1965) Measure of Cognitive Complexity

This measure involves simply totalling the number of constructs used by an individual when describing other people.

APPENDIX V: COMPUTER ANALYSIS OF CHANGE IN GRIDS

Chris Evans

There are a number of ways of analysing multiple grids and change in grids. All rely on at least some of the grid being alignable. The simplest situation is when exactly the same elements and constructs have been used on more than one occasion. In this situation DELTA in the late Patrick Slater's Grid Analysis Package (G.A.P.) comes into its own (see Appendix III). DELTA analyses two grids with identical elements and constructs, providing a listing of the changes in construct means (and their significance applying the logic of the *t*-test to the change), a list of the correlations between the ratings on the first occasion and the second and the again rather spurious significance of this based on applying a sampling model to the Pearson correlation coefficient that is calculated. Although the significances should be ignored, the correlations themselves are useful and not infrequently show that some constructs have remained almost unchanged (something that can often be seen by eyeballing the two grids) while others have changed very markedly. As well as these calculations, DELTA also conducts a standard INGRID-style analysis of the grid of differences between the grids (with the changes in construct means removed). This is helpful, and again, just eyeballing that grid often reveals very obvious areas of change and other areas of relative constancy.

Sometimes *either* the elements or the constructs are the same in grids. In these cases the grids can be aligned on the matching elements or constructs to create a larger grid. In G.A.P. the program PREFAN can be used to put grids with the same elements together to form one big grid. In principle this can be done whether or not the constructs are the same and can be done for any (reasonable) number of grids. The program then conducts an INGRID-style analysis of the entire grid. It can be particularly interesting to inspect the large construct intercorrelation matrix that is produced. Sometimes a construct changes its use so markedly that it correlates more closely with a different construct from a former occasion than with itself. An example might be a change in the usage of 'Provocative' so that in a post-treatment grid its use might correlate only, say, 0.11 with its usage in the pre-treatment grid, but it might correlate 0.86 with the earlier usage of 'Aggressive'. If on the second occasion 'Aggressive' still correlated fairly highly with its usage on the first occasion, and if other constructs have also shown stability, then this might be taken as encouraging evidence of positive change. This interpretation might be supported if 'Provocative' correlated 0.9 with 'Sexually attractive' on the first occasion and now correlates −0.23 with that construct, which itself stayed fairly stable.

ADELA, another program in the G.A.P. suite, carries out the same process for grids with the same constructs. Here the inter-element distance matrix is most informative and a plot of the component analysis can be annotated with trails showing how the elements moved between occasions. A third program in the G.A.P. suite, SERIES, will produce what is effectively a simple analysis of variance of changes across repetitions of a grid of fixed elements and constructs. This is probably the least useful of the four change/multiple grid programs in G.A.P.

The cluster analytic program FOCUS for the old Apple computers could be used to present cluster analyses of grids created by putting together multiple grids and its sister program CORE was particularly designed to find areas of commonality. Another sister program, SOCIOGRIDS, offered a variety of options for exploration of similarities and differences between grids using the same elements. These options included the capacity to engage the client in extending the grids to explore new constructs and to add new elements that might either help pull together differences between the grids or tease apart apparent similarities (Shaw, 1981). All these approaches are now available in the commercial Apple Macintosh program REPGRID II (Shaw, 1989) which has replaced those earlier programs.

Finally, it is possible to use the statistics packages that offer multiple matrix forms of multidimensional scaling (MDS) to carry out analyses of multiple grids. Grids which are identical on both elements and constructs can be fed in directly for a form of INDSCAL style analysis (e.g. see Everitt & Dunn, 1983; Cox & Cox, 1994, pp 142–151). Grids which have non-identical elements can be analysed by feeding in the construct correlation matrices for each occasion and grids with non-identical constructs can be analysed by using the inter-element distance matrices. MDS options are available in the big statistics packages such as SPSS, SAS, SYSTAT and STATISTICA.

Glossary

This is not a complete list of the terms specific to PCP, but defines those which are most commonly used throughout this book.

Construct: A way of discriminating between events.

Construct system: The unique way in which a person's constructs are organised.

Core constructs: Constructs which are essential to one's sense of self.

Core role structure: The way in which a person's core constructs are related to each other.

CPC cycle: A process of construing in which a person makes a decision about how to act.

Elements: The items of interest (often in a repertory grid), e.g. people, situations, events.

Permeability: The degree of flexibility with which constructs encompass new elements.

Pole: Each end of a construct, e.g. 'Caring (pole A) vs Not caring (pole B)'.

Slot-rattling: Moving from one pole of a construct to another.

Subordinate constructs: Those which are 'lower down' in the hierarchy.

Superordinate constructs: Those which are 'higher up' in the hierarchy.

Tightness/Looseness: The degree to which a construct leads to an unvarying prediction (tight construing) or varying predictions (loose construing).

Further Reading and Resources

Bannister, D. & Fransella, F. (1986). *The Inquiring Man: The Psychology of Personal Constructs (Third Edition)*. London: Routledge. This is one of the classic books about Personal Construct Psychology, which describes the theory in some detail and some of its professional applications.

Beail, N. (1985). *Repertory Grid Technique and Personal Constructs: Applications in Clinical and Educational Settings*. London: Croom Helm. Another book which describes the applications of PCP. It contains a particularly clear and comprehensive chapter about the use of repertory grids.

Button, E. (1985). *Personal Construct Theory and Mental Health*. London: Croom Helm. This book describes the theory and practice of PCP and its application in a range of mental health settings.

Dalton, P. & Dunnett, G. (1992). *A Psychology for Living: Personal Construct Theory for Professionals and Clients*. Chichester: Wiley. This is an excellent book for those who are new to PCP. Using frequent examples, the book makes PCP easily accessible to those who are unfamiliar with the ideas, and clarifies the theory for those who have had some introduction.

Fransella. F. (1995). *George Kelly*. London: Sage. This book, in the series 'Key Figures in Counselling and Psychotherapy', describes the contributions which Kelly made to theory and practice, the influences and applications of PCP, and some criticisms and rebuttals.

Fransella, F. & Bannister, D. (1977). *A Manual for Repertory Grid Technique*. London: Academic Press. Another classic and comprehensive text. As its title suggests, it focuses exclusively on the design and use of repertory grids, their underlying assumptions and limitations. However, readers who are unfamiliar with grid technique would probably be advised to come to this book after reading some of the more introductory chapters in the above books (e.g. Beail, 1985).

Fransella, F. & Dalton, P. (1990). *Personal Construct Counselling in Action*. London: Sage. This book outlines the key principles which underlie the PCP approach to counselling and psychotherapy. It includes a description of repertory grid technique and other methods for assessing construing, and describes a case-study in some detail.

Maitland, P. & Brennan, D. (1992). *Personal Construct Theory, Deviancy and Social Work, (2nd edition)*. London: Inner London Probation Service/Centre for Personal Construct Psychology. This book contains a collection of papers presented at an ILPS conference in 1988, examining the application of PCP to a range of 'deviant' behaviours.

Winter, D.A. (1992). *Personal Construct Psychology in Clinical Practice: Theory, Research and Applications*. London: Routledge. This is an excellent book for those who are already familiar with PCP or want to know more. It comprehensively reviews the clinical and research applications of PCP, together with relevant academic and theoretical issues.

JOURNALS

Journal of Constructivist Psychology (formerly *International Journal of Personal Construct Psychology*), edited by R. & G. Neimeyer. Hemisphere Publishing Corporation, 79 Madison Avenue, Suite 1110, New York, USA.

British Journal of Medical Psychology also often publishes PCP-oriented research and clinical case studies.

FURTHER INFORMATION

For further information and details about General Basic Courses in PCP and the Diploma in Counselling and Psychotherapy, contact:

The Centre for Personal Construct Psychology
132 Warwick Way
London SW1V 4JD
Tel: 0171 834 8875
Fax: 0171 828 2108

References

Adams-Webber, J. R. (1979). *Personal Construct Theory: Concepts and Applications*. Chichester: Wiley.

Agnew, R. & Peters, A. A. R. (1986). The techniques of neutralisation: An analysis of predisposing and situational factors. *Criminal Justice and Behaviour*, **13**, 81–97.

American Psychiatric Association (1994). *Diagnostic and Statistical Manual of Mental Disorders* (4th Edition) (DSMIV) Washington DC: American Psychiatric Association.

Arnold, J. (1988). Do self-ideal discrepancies and global self-esteem amount to the same thing?: An empirical investigation. *British Journal of Guidance and Counselling*, **16**, 190–202.

Aveline, M. & Shapiro, D. A. (1995). *Research Foundations for Psychotherapy Practice*. Chichester: Wiley.

Bailey, P. E. & Sims, A. C. P. (1991). The repertory grid as a measure of change and predictor of outcome in the treatment of alcoholism. *British Journal of Medical Psychology*, **64**, 285–293.

Bandura, A. (1977). *Social Learning Theory*. Englewood Cliffs, NJ: Prentice-Hall.

Bannister, D. (1960). Conceptual structure in thought disordered schizophrenics. *Journal of Mental Science*, **106**, 1230–1249.

Bannister, D. (1962). The nature and measurement of schizophrenic thought disorder. *Journal of Mental Science*, **108**, 825–842.

Bannister, D. (1963). The genesis of schizophrenic thought disorder: A serial invalidation hypothesis. *British Journal of Psychiatry*, **109**, 680–686.

Bannister, D. (1965). The genesis of schizophrenic thought disorder: Re-test of the serial invalidation hypothesis. *British Journal of Psychiatry*, **111**, 377–382.

Bannister, D. (1985). The psychotic disguise. In W. Dryden (Ed.). *Therapists' Dilemmas*. London: Harper and Row.

Bannister, D. & Fransella, F. (1966). A grid test of schizophrenic thought disorder. *British Journal of Social and Clinical Psychology*, **5**, 95–102.

Bannister, D. & Fransella, F. (1967). *A Grid Test of Schizophrenic Thought Disorder: A Standard Clinical Test*. Barnstable: Psychological Test Publications.

Bannister, D. & Fransella, F. (1986). *Inquiring Man: The Psychology of Personal Constructs*, (3rd Edition). London: Croom Helm.

Bannister, D. & Mair, J. M. M. (1968). *The Evaluation of Personal Constructs*. London: Academic Press.

Barker, M. & Morgan, R. (1993). *Sex Offenders: A Framework for the Evaluation of Community Based Treatment*. Crown Copyright. Available from Home Office Library, 50 Queen Anne's Gate, London W1H 9AT, UK.

Baron-Cohen, S., Leslie, A. M. & Frith, U. (1985). Does the autistic child have a theory of mind? *Cognition,* **21,** 37–46.

Beail, N. (1985). An introduction to repertory grid technique. In N. Beail (Ed.). *Repertory Grid Technique and Personal Constructs: Applications in Clinical and Educational Settings.* London: Croom Helm.

Beck, A. T. (1976). *Cognitive Therapy and the Emotional Disorders.* New York: International Universities Press.

Beck, A. T. & Freeman, A. (1990). *Cognitive Therapy of Personality Disorders.* New York: Guilford Press.

Beck, A. T., Rush, A. J., Shaw, B. S. & Emery, G. (1979). *Cognitive Therapy of Depression.* New York: Guilford.

Beckett, R. C. (1994). Cognitive behavioural treatment for men who sexually assault children. In T. Morrison, M. Erooga & R. C. Beckett (Eds). *Sexual Offending Against Children.* London: Routledge.

Beckett, R., Beech, A., Fisher, D. & Fordham, A. S. (1994). *A Community Treatment for Sex Offenders: An Evaluation of Seven Treatment Programmes.* London: Home Office Publications Unit.

Bell, R. C. (1987). G-PACK: A computer program for the elicitation and analysis of repertory grids.

Bennett, G., Rigby, K. & Owers, D. (1992). Assessment of psychological change within a residential rehabilitation centre for drug users. In P. Maitland & D. Brennan (Eds). *Personal Construct Theory, Deviancy and Social Work,* (2nd Edition). London: Inner London Probation Service/Centre for Personal Construct Psychology.

Bieri, J., Atkins, A. L., Briar, S., Leaman, R. L., Miller, H. & Tripodi, T. (1966). *Clinical and Social Judgements.* New York: Wiley.

Blackburn, R. (1968a). Personality in relation to extreme aggression in psychiatric offenders. *British Journal of Psychiatry,* **114,** 821–828.

Blackburn, R. (1968b). Emotionality, extraversion, and aggression in paranoid and non-paranoid schizophrenic offenders. *British Journal of Psychiatry,* **114,** 1301–1302.

Blackburn, R. (1993). *The Psychology of Criminal Conduct: Theory, Research and Practice.* Chichester: Wiley.

Blackburn, R., Crellin, M. C., Morgan, E. M. & Tulloch, R. M. B. (1990). Prevalence of personality disorders in a special hospital population. *Journal of Forensic Psychiatry,* **1,** 43–52.

Bodden, J. & James, L. E. (1976). Influence of occupational information giving on cognitive complexity. *Journal of Counseling Psychology,* **23,** 280–282.

Bonarius, J. C. J. (1965). Research in the personal construct theory of George A. Kelly. In B. A. Maher (Ed.). *Progress in Experimental Personality Research (Vol. 2).* New York: Academic Press.

Brennan, D. (1992). Deviancy as a quest for self. In P. Maitland & D. Brennan (Eds). *Personal Construct Theory, Deviancy and Social Work.* London: Inner London Probation Service/Centre for Personal Construct Psychology.

Briere, J. & Runtz, M. (1993). Childhood sexual abuse: Longterm sequelae and implications of psychological assessment. *Journal of Interpersonal Violence,* **8,** 312–330.

Burr, V. & Butt, T. (1992). *Invitation to Personal Construct Psychology.* London: Whurr Publishers Limited.

Busch, K. G., Zagar, R., Hughes, J. R., Arbit, J. & Bussell, R. E. (1990). Adolescents who kill. *Journal of Clinical Psychology,* **46,** 472–485.

Button, E. (1985). Personal construct theory: the concepts. In E. Button (Ed.). *Personal Construct Theory and Mental Health*. London: Croom Helm.

Cannell, J. E. (1985). Pastoral psychology: A personal construct perspective. In F. Epting & A. W. Landfield (Eds). *Anticipating Personal Construct Psychology*, Lincoln, University of Nebraska Press.

Carr, J. & Townes, B. (1975). Interpersonal discrimination as a function of age and psychopathology. *Child Psychiatry and Human Development*, **5**, 209–215.

Carson, R. C. (1979). Personality and exchange in developing relationships. In L. R. Burgess & T. L. Huston (Eds). *Social Exchange in Developing Relationships*. New York: Academic Press.

Chambers, W. & Grice, J. W. (1986). Circumgrids: A repertory grid package for personal computers. *Behaviour Research Methods, Instruments, and Computers*, **18**, 468.

Chambers, W. & Sanders, J. (1984). Alcoholism and logical consistency of personal constructs. *Psychological Reports*, **54**, 882.

Chetwynd, J. (1977). The psychological meaning of structural measures derived from grids. In P. Slater (Ed.). *The Measurement of Intrapersonal Space by Grid Technique. Vol. 2. Dimensions of Intrapersonal Space*. London: Wiley.

Chin-Kueng-Li. (1988). PCT interpretation of adult sexual involvement with children. In F. Fransella & L. Thomas (Eds). *Experimenting with Personal Construct Psychology*. London: Routledge & Kegan Paul.

Chin-Kueng-Li. (1992). Ethics, politics and paedophilia: The relevance of George Kelly. In P. Maitland & D. Brennan (Eds). *Personal Construct Theory, Deviancy and Social Work*. (2nd Edition). London: Inner London Probation Service/Centre for Personal Construct Psychology.

Clark, N. K. (1993). Sexual offenders: An overview. In N. K. Clark & G. M. Stevenson (Eds). *Sexual Offenders: Context, Assessment and Treatment*. DCLP Occasional Paper No. **19**. Leicester: British Psychological Society.

Clarke, S. & Llewelyn, S. (1994). Personal constructs of survivors of childhood sexual abuse receiving cognitive analytic therapy. *British Journal of Medical Psychology*, **67**, 273–289.

Cleckley, H. (1976). *The Mask of Sanity*, 6th Edition. St. Louis, MO: Mosby.

Coid, J. (1982). Alcoholism and violence. *Drug and Alcohol Dependence*, **9**, 1–13.

Cookson, H. M. (1992). Alcohol use and offence type in young offenders. *British Journal of Criminology*, **32**, 352–360.

Cox, T. F. & Cox, M. A. A. (1994). *Multidimensional Scaling*. London: Chapman & Hall.

Crockett, W. H. (1965). Cognitive complexity and impression formation. In B. A. Maher (Ed.). *Progress in Experimental Personality Research (Vol. 2)*. New York: Academic Press.

Cummins, P. (1992). Reconstruing the experience of sexual abuse. *International Journal of Personal Construct Psychology*, **5**, 355–365.

Dalton, P. & Dunnett, G. (1992). *A Psychology for Living: Personal Construct Theory for Professionals and Clients*. Chichester: Wiley.

Davis, H. & Cunningham, C. (1985). Mental handicap: People in context. In E. Button (Ed.). *Personal Construct Theory and Mental Health*. London: Croom Helm.

Dawes, A. (1985). Construing drug dependence. In E. Button (Ed.). *Personal Construct Theory and Mental Health*. London: Croom Helm.

Dodge, K. A. (1986). A social-information processing model of social competence in children. In M. Perlmutter (Ed.). *Minnesota Symposium on Child Psychology*. Hillsdale, NJ: Erlbaum.

Dolan, B. (1995). The attribution of blame for criminal acts: Relationship with personality disorders and mood. *Criminal Behaviour and Mental Health*, **5**, 41–51.

Dolan, B. & Coid, J. (1995) *Psychopathic and Antisocial Personality Disorders: Treatment and Research Issues*. London: Gaskell.

Duguid, S. (1981). Moral development, justice and democracy in prison. *Canadian Journal of Criminology*, **23**, 147–162.

Dunnett, G. (1988). Myths, methods, and technique. In G. Dunnett (Ed.). *Working with People: Clinical Uses of Personal Construct Psychology*. London: Routledge.

Eastman, C. (1978). The self identity and drinking motivation of alcoholics and social drinkers. PhD Thesis, University of Birmingham (unpublished).

Ellis, A. (1979). The theory of Rational–Emotive Therapy. In A. Ellis & J. M. Whitely (Eds). *Theoretical and Empirical Foundations of Rational–Emotive Therapy*. Monterey, CA: Brooks/Cole.

Epting, F. R. (1984). *Personal Construct Counseling and Psychotherapy*. New York: Wiley.

Everitt, B. S. & Dunn, G. (1983). *Advanced Methods of Data Exploration and Modelling*. London: Heinemann Educational Books.

Farrington, D. P. (1992). Explaining the beginning, progress, and ending of antisocial behaviour from birth to adulthood. In J. McCord (Ed.). *Facts, Frameworks and Forecasts: Advances in Criminological Theory, Vol. 3*. New Brunswick, NJ: Transactional Publishers.

Feixas, G., Moliner, J. L., Montes, J. N., Marie, M. T. & Neimeyer, R. A. (1992). The stability of structural measures derived from repertory grids. *International Journal of Personal Construct Psychology*, **5**, 25–39.

Feldman, M. P. & Peay, J. (1982). Ethical and legal issues. In A. S. Bellak, M. Hersen & A. E. Kazdin (Eds). *International Handbook of Behaviour Modification*. New York: Plenum.

Ferguson, T. J. & Rule, B. G. (1983). An attributional perspective on anger and aggression. In R. G. Geen & E. I. Donnerstein (Eds). *Aggression: Theoretical and Empirical Reviews, Vol. 1*. New York: Academic Press.

Finkelhor, D. (1979). What's wrong with sex between adults and children? Ethics and the problems of sexual abuse. *American Journal of Orthopsychiatry*, **49**, 692–697.

Finkelhor, D. (1986). Abusers: Special topics. In D. Finkelhor (Ed.). *A Source Book on Child Sexual Abuse*. Newbury Park, CA: Sage.

Fisher, D. & Howells, K. (1993). Social relationships in sexual offenders. *Sexual and Marital Therapy*, **8**, 122–136.

Fransella, F. (1972). *Personal Change and Reconstruction*. London: Academic Press.

Fransella, F. (1981). Repertory grid technique. In F. Fransella (Ed.). *Personality, Theory, Measurement and Research*. London: Methuen.

Fransella, F. (1985). Death by starvation: Whose decision? In W. Dryden (Ed.). *Therapists' Dilemmas*. London: Harper and Row.

Fransella, F. (1989). Obstacles to change. In W. Dryden, & P. Trower (Eds). *Cognitive Psychotherapy: Therapeutic Stasis and Change*. London: Cassel.

Fransella, F. (1995). *George Kelly. Key Figures In Counselling and Psychotherapy*. London: Sage.

Fransella, F. & Adams, B. (1966). An illustration of the use of repertory grid technique in a clinical setting. *British Journal of Social and Clinical Psychology*, **5**, 51–62.

Fransella, F. & Bannister, D. (1967). A validation of repertory grid technique as a measure of political construing. *Acta Psychologica*, **26**, 97–106.

Fransella, F. & Bannister, D. (1977). *A Manual for Repertory Grid Technique*. London: Academic Press.

Fransella, F. & Dalton, P. (1990). *Personal Construct Counselling in Action*. London: Sage.

Gara, M. A., Rosenberg, S. & Cohen, B. D. (1987). Personal identity and the schizophrenic process. *Psychiatry*, **50**, 267–269.

Gara, M. A., Rosenberg, S. & Mueller, D. R. (1989). Perception of self and others in schizophrenia. *International Journal of Personal Construct Psychology*, **2**, 253–270.

Glantz, M., Burr, W. & Bosse, R. (1981). Constructs used by alcoholics, non-psychotic outpatients and normals. Paper presented at the 4th International Congress on Personal Construct Psychology, St. Catharine's, Ontario.

Goldfried, M. R. (1988). Personal construct therapy and other theoretical orientations. *International Journal of Personal Construct Psychology*, **1**, 317–327.

Goldstein, A. P., Glick, B., Erwin, M. J., Pask-McCartney, C. & Rubama, I. (1989). *Reducing Delinquency: Intervention in the Community*. New York: Pergamon.

Goldstein, P. J. (1989). Drugs and violent crime. In N. A. Weiner & M. E. Wolfgang (Eds). *Pathways to Criminal Violence*. Newbury Park, CA: Sage.

Haney, C. W. (1983). The good, the bad and the lawful: An essay on psychological injustice. In W. S. Laufer & J. M. Day (Eds). *Personality Theory, Moral Development, Criminal Behavior*. Lexington, VA: Lexington Books.

Hare, R. D. (1976). Psychopathy. In P. Venables & M. Christie (Eds). *Research in Psychophysiology*. New York: Wiley.

Hare, R. D. (1979). A research scale for the assessment of psychopathy in criminal populations. *Personality and Individual Differences*, **1**, 111–119.

Hare, R. D. (1980). *Psychopathy*. New York: Wiley.

Hare, R. D. (1991). *Hare Psychopathy Checklist—Revised*. Toronto, Ontario: Multi-Health Systems Incorporated.

Harrison, A. & Phillips, J. P. M. (1979). The specificity of schizophrenic thought disorder. *British Journal of Medical Psychology*, **52**, 105–118.

Harter, S. L. & Neimeyer, R. A. (1995). Long term effects of child sexual abuse: Toward a constructivist theory of trauma and its treatment. In R. A. Neimeyer & G. A. Neimeyer (Eds). *Advances in Personal Construct Psychology, Vol 3*. London: JAI Press Inc.

Hayden, B., Nasby, W. & Davids, A. (1977). Interpersonal conceptual structures, predictive accuracy and social adjustment of emotionally disturbed boys. *Journal of Abnormal Psychology*, **86**, 315–320.

Heather, N. (1979). The structure of delinquent values: A repertory grid investigation. *British Journal of Social and Clinical Psychology*, **18**, 263–275.

Heather, N., Edwards, S. & Hore, B. D. (1975). Changes in the construing and outcome of group therapy for alcoholism. *Journal of Studies on Alcohol*, **36**, 1238–1253.

Heather, N., Rollnick, S. & Winton, M. (1982). Psychological change among in-patient alcoholics and its relationship to treatment outcome. *British Journal of Alcohol and Alcoholism*, **17**, 90–97.

Hinkle, D. (1965). The change of personal constructs from the viewpoint of a series of construct implications. PhD Thesis, Ohio State University (unpublished).

Hoghughi, M. (1979). The Aycliffe token economy. *British Journal of Criminology*, **19**, 384–399.

Hollin, C. R. & Henderson, M. (1984). Social skills training for young offenders: False expectations and the 'failure of treatment'. *Behavioural Psychotherapy*, **12**, 331–341.

Horley, J. (1988). Cognitions of child sexual abusers. *Journal of Sex Research*, **25**, 542–545.

Hoskyns, S. (1988). Studying group music therapy with adult offenders: Research in progress. *Psychology of Music*, **16**, 25–41.

Houston, J. & Adshead, G. (1993). The use of repertory grids to assess change: Application to a sex offenders' group. In N. Clark & G. Stephenson (Eds). *Sexual Offenders: Context, Assessment and Treatment. Issues in Criminological and Legal Psychology*, **19**, 43–51.

Houston, J., Thomson, P. & Wragg, J. (1994). A survey of forensic psychologists' work with sex offenders in England and Wales. *Criminal Behaviour and Mental Health*, **4**, 118–129.

Howells, K. (1978). The meaning of poisoning to a person diagnosed as a psychopath. *Medicine, Science and the Law*, **18**, 179–184.

Howells, K. (1979). Some meanings of children for pedophiles. In M. Cook & G. Wilson (Eds). *Love and Attraction*. Oxford: Pergamon.

Howells, K. (1981). Adult sexual interest in children: Considerations relevant to theories of aetiology. In M. Cook & K. Howells (Eds). *Adult Sexual Interest in Children*. New York: Academic Press.

Howells, K. (1983). Social construing and violent behaviour in mentally abnormal offenders. In J. W. Hinton (Ed.). *Dangerousness: Problems of Assessment and Prediction*. London: Allen and Unwin.

Hoy, R. M. (1973). The meaning of alcoholism for alcoholics: A repertory grid study. *British Journal of Social and Clinical Psychology*, **12**, 98–99.

Hoy, R. M. (1977). Some findings concerning beliefs about alcoholism. *British Journal of Medical Psychology*, **50**, 227–235.

Hudson, L. (1970). *Frames of Mind*. Harmondsworth, UK: Penguin.

Huesmann, L. R. & Eron. L. D. (1984). Cognitive processes and the persistence of aggressive behavior. *Aggressive Behavior*, **10**, 243–251.

Isaacson, G. S. (1966). A comparative study of the meaningfulness of personal and common constructs. PhD Thesis, University of Missouri (unpublished).

Izzo, R. L. & Ross, R. R. (1990). Meta-analysis of rehabilitation programs for juvenile delinquents: A brief report. *Criminal Justice and Behaviour*, **17**, 137–142.

Jackson, S. (1992). A self characterisation: Development and deviance in adolescent construing. In P. Maitland, & D. Brennan (Eds). *Personal Construct Theory, Deviancy and Social Work*, 2nd Edition. London: Inner London Probation Service/Centre for Personal Construct Psychology.

Jackson, S. R. & Bannister, D. (1985). Growing into self. In D. Bannister (Ed.). *Issues and Approaches in Personal Construct Theory*. London: Academic Press.

Jurkovic, G. J. & Prentice, M. M. (1977). Relation of moral and cognitive development to dimensions of juvenile delinquency. *Journal of Abnormal Psychology*, **86**, 414–420.

Kaplan, H. B. (1980). *Deviant Behavior in Defense of Self.* New York: Pergamon.

Kavanagh, D. J. (1992). Recent developments in expressed emotion and schizophrenia. *British Journal of Psychiatry*, **160**, 601–620.

Kazdin. A. E. (1987). Treatment of antisocial behaviour in children: Current status and future directions. *Psychological Bulletin*, **102**, 187–203.

Kelly, D. (1992). A personal construct psychology perspective on deviance. In P. Maitland & D. Brennan (Eds). *Personal Construct Theory, Deviancy and Social Work.* London: Inner London Probation Service/Centre for Personal Construct Psychology.

Kelly, D. & Taylor, H. (1981). Take and escape: A personal construct study of car theft. In H. Bonarius, R. Holland & S. Rosenberg (Eds). *Personal Construct Psychology: Recent Advances in Theory and Practice.* London: Macmillan.

Kelly, G. (1955/1991). *The Psychology of Personal Constructs*, Volumes 1 & 2. London: Routledge, in association with the Centre for Personal Construct Psychology. (First published 1955.)

Kelly, G. A. (1969a). Personal construct theory and the psychotherapeutic interview. In B. Maher (Ed.). *Clinical Psychology and Personality: The Selected Papers of George Kelly.* New York: Wiley.

Kelly, G. A. (1969b). Hostility. In B. Maher (Ed.). *Clinical Psychology and Personality: The Selected Papers of George Kelly.* New York: Wiley.

Kelly, G. A. (1970). A brief introduction to personal construct theory. In D. Bannister (Ed.). *Perspectives in Personal Construct Theory.* London: Academic Press.

Kelly, G. A. (1980). A psychology of the optimal man. In A. W. Landfield & L. M. Leitner (Eds). *Personal Construct Psychology: Psychotherapy and Personality.* New York: Wiley.

Kernis, M. H., Grannemann, B. D. & Barclay, L. C. (1989). Stability and level of self-esteem as predictors of anger arousal and hostility. *Journal of Personality and Social Psychology*, **56**, 1013–1022.

Kerr, C. A. & Roth, J. H. (1986). Populations, practices and problems in forensic psychiatric facilities. *Annals of the American Academy of Political and Social Science*, **484**, 127–143.

Kiesler, D. J. (1983). The 1982 interpersonal circle: A taxonomy for complimentarity in human transactions. *Psychological Review*, **90**, 185–214.

Klass, E. T. (1980). Cognitive appraisal of transgression among sociopaths and normals. *Cognitive Therapy and Research*, **4**, 353–367.

Knight, R. A. & Prentky, R. A. (1990). Classifying sexual offenders: The development and corroboration of taxonomic models. In W. L. Marshall, D. R. Laws & H. E. Barbaree (Eds). *Handbook of Sexual Assault: Issues, Theories, and Treatment of the Offender.* New York: Plenum.

Koenraadt, F. (1992). The individualising function of forensic multidisciplinary assessment in a Dutch residential setting: The Pieter Baan centre experience. *International Journal of Law and Psychiatry*, **15**, 195–203.

Koch, H. C. H. (1983). Changes in personal construing in three psychotherapy groups and a control group. *British Journal of Medical Psychology*, **56**, 245–254.

Landfield, A. W. (1971*). Personal Construct Systems in Psychotherapy.* Lincoln, NE: University of Nebraska Press.

Landfield, A. W. (1980). Personal construct psychotherapy: A personal construction. In A. W. Landfield & L. M. Leitner (Eds). *Personal Construct Psychology: Psychotherapy and Personality.* New York: Wiley.

Landfield, A. W. & Epting, F. R. (1987). *Personal Construct Psychology: Clinical and Personality Assessment*. New York: Human Sciences Press.

Landfield, A. W. & Rivers, P. C. (1975). An introduction to interpersonal transaction and rotating dyads. *Psychotherapy: Theory, Research and Practice*, **12**, 366–374.

Layden, M. A., Newman, C. F., Freeman, A. & Morse, S. B. (1993). *Cognitive Therapy of Borderline Personality Disorder*. Boston, MA: Allyn and Bacon.

Levey, S. & Howells, K. (1990). Anger and its management. *Journal of Forensic Psychiatry*, **1**, 305–327.

Lidz, T. (1964). *The Family and Human Adaptation*. London: Hogarth.

Lidz, T. (1968). The family, language and the transmission of schizophrenia. In D. Rosenthal & S. S. Kety (Eds). *The Transmission of Schizophrenia*. Oxford: Pergamon.

Lindqvist, P. & Allebeck, P. (1990). Schizophrenia and crime: A longitudinal follow up of 644 schizophrenics in Stockholm. *British Journal of Psychiatry*, **157**, 347–350.

Lockhart, W. H. (1979). Illustrations of the use of self-identity plots to measure change with young offenders. *Journal of Adolescence*, **2**, 139–152.

Lorenzini, R., Sassaroli, S. & Rocchi, M. T. (1989). Schizophrenia and paranoia as solutions to predictive failure. *International Journal of Personal Construct Psychology*, **2**, 417–432.

Main, T. S. (1957). The ailment. *British Journal of Medical Psychology*, **30**, 129–145.

Mann, R. (Ed.) (1996). *Motivational Interviewing with Sex Offenders: A Practice Manual*. Available from Carolyn Martinson, NOTA Administrator, The Office, 50 Hayburn Avenue, Hull HU4 5NA, UK.

Marshall, W. L. & Barbaree, H. E. (1990a). An integrated theory of the etiology of sexual offending. In W. L. Marshall, D. R. Laws & H. E. Barbaree (Eds). *Handbook of Sexual Assault: Issues, Theories and Treatment of the Offender*. New York: Plenum.

Marshall, W. L. & Barbaree, H. E. (1990b). Outcome of comprehensive cognitive-behavioral treatment programs. In W. L. Marshall, D. R. Laws & H. E. Barbaree (Eds). *Handbook of Sexual Assault: Issues, Theories and Treatment of the Offender*. New York: Plenum.

Marshall, W. L., Barbaree, H. E. & Christophe, D. (1986). Sexual offenders against female children: Sexual preferences for age of victims and type of behaviour. *Canadian Journal of Behavioural Science*, **18**, 424–439.

Matza, D. & Sykes, F. (1961). Juvenile delinquency and subterranean values. *American Sociological Review*, **26**, 712–719.

Mayhew, P., Elliott, D. & Dowds, L. (1989). *The 1988 British Crime Survey*. London: HMSO.

McCartney, J. & O'Donnell, J. T. (1981). The perception of drinking roles by recovered problem drinkers. *Psychological Medicine*, **11**, 747–754.

McCoy, M. M. (1981). Positive and negative emotion: A personal construct theory interpretation. In H. Bonarius, R. Holland & S. Rosenberg (Eds). *Personal Construct Psychology: Recent Advances in Theory and Practice*. London: Macmillan.

McDougall, C., Barnett, R. M., Ashurst, B. & Willis, B. (1987). Cognitive control of anger. In B. J. McGurk, D. M. Thornton & M. Williams (Eds). *Applying Psychology to Imprisonment: Theory and Practice*. London: HMSO.

McPherson, F. M., Blackburn, I. M., Draffan, J. W. & McFadyen, M. (1973). A further study of the Grid Test of Thought Disorder. *British Journal of Social and Clinical Psychology*, **12**, 420–427.

McMurran, M. & Hollin, C. R. (1989). Drinking and delinquency: Another look at young offenders and their drinking. *British Journal of Criminology*, **29**, 386–394.

McMurran, M. & Hollin, C. R. (1993). *Young Offenders and Alcohol Related Crime*. Chichester: Wiley.

McMurran, M., Hollin, C. R. & Bowen, A. (1990). Consistency of alcohol self-report measures in a male young offender population. *British Journal of Addictions*, **85**, 205–208.

Megargee, E. I. (1966). Undercontrolled and overcontrolled personality types in extreme antisocial aggression. *Psychological Monographs*, **80,** Whole number 611.

Meichenbaum, D. (1977). *Cognitive-Behavior Modification: An Integrative Approach*. New York: Plenum.

Miller, K. & Treacher, A. (1981). Delinquency: A personal construct theory approach. In H. Bonarius, R. Holland, & S. Rosenberg (Eds). *Personal Construct Psychology: Recent Advances in Theory and Practice*. London: Macmillan.

Miller, W. R. & Rollnick, S. (1991). *Motivational Interviewing: Preparing People for Change*. New York: The Guildford Press.

Monahan, J. (1997). Clinical and actuarial predictions of violence. In D. Faigman, D. Kaye, M. Saks, & J. Sanders (Eds). *Modern Scientific Evidence: The Law and Science of Expert Testimony. Vol. 1.* St Paul, MN: West Publishing.

Moos, R. H. & Moos, B. S. (1976). A typology of family social environments. *Family Process*, **15**, 357–371.

Morrison, T. (1994). Context, constraints and considerations for practice. In T. Morrison, M. Erooga, & R. C. Beckett (Eds). *Sexual Offending against Children: Assessment and Treatment of Male Abusers*. London: Routledge.

Mullen, P., Taylor, P. J. & Wessely, S. (1993). Psychosis, violence and crime. In J. Gunn & P. J. Taylor (Eds). *Forensic Psychiatry: Legal and Ethical Issues*. Oxford: Butterworth-Heinemann.

Murphy, W. D. (1990). Assessment and modification of cognitive distortions in sex offenders. In W. L. Marshall, D. R. Laws & H. R. Barbaree (Eds). *Handbook of Sexual Assault: Issues, Theories and Treatment of the Offender*. New York: Plenum.

Needs, A. (1988). Psychological investigation of offending behaviour. In F. Fransella & L. Thomas (Eds). *Experimenting with Personal Construct Theory*. London: Routledge & Kegan Paul.

Needs, A. (1992). Some issues raised by the application of personal construct psychology to the sexual abuse of children. In P. Maitland & D. Brennan (Eds). *Personal Construct Theory, Deviancy and Social Work*. London: Inner London Probation Service/Centre for Personal Construct Psychology.

Neimeyer, G. J. & Metzler, A. (1987). Sex differences in vocational integration and differentiation. *Journal of Vocational Behaviour*, **30**, 167–174.

Neimeyer, R. A. (1985). *The Development of Personal Construct Psychology*. Lincoln, NE: University of Nebraska Press.

Noble, G. (1971). Some comments on the nature of delinquents' identification with television heroes, fathers and best friends. *British Journal of Social Clinical Psychology*, **10**, 172–180.

Norris, H. & Makhlouf-Norris, F. (1976). The measurement of self-identity. In P. Slater (Ed.). *The Measurement of Intrapersonal Space by Grid Technique. Vol. 1. Explorations of Intrapersonal Space.* Chichester: Wiley.

Norris, M. (1977). Construing in a detention centre. In D. Bannister (Ed.). *New Perspectives in Personal Construct Theory.* London: Academic Press.

Norris, M. (1983). Changes in patients during treatment at the Henderson Hospital Therapeutic Community during 1977–81. *British Journal of Medical Psychology*, **56**, 135–144.

Novaco, R. W. (1978). Anger and coping with stress. In J. P. Foreyt & D. P. Rathjen (Eds). *Cognitive Behaviour Therapy.* New York: Plenum.

Nystedt, L., Ekehammar, B. & Kusinen, J. (1976). Structural representations of person perceptions: A comparison between own and provided constructs. *Scandinavian Journal of Psychology*, **17**, 223–233.

O'Keefe, B. J. & Sypher, H. E. (1981). Cognitive complexity measures and the relationship of cognitive complexity to communication. *Human Communication Research*, **8**, 72–92.

Orford, J. (1974). Simplistic thinking about other people as a predictor of early dropout at an alcoholism halfway house. *British Journal of Medical Psychology*, **47**, 53–62.

Partington, J. T. (1987). Dr. Jekyll and Mr. High: Multidimensional scaling of alcoholics' self-evaluations. *Journal of Abnormal Psychology*, **75**, 131–138.

Pearson, M., Wilmot, E. & Padi, M. (1986). A study of violent behaviour among inpatients in a psychiatric hospital. *British Journal of Psychiatry*, **149**, 232–235.

Penrod, J. H., Epting, R. F. & Waddon, T. A. (1981). Interpersonal cognitive differentiation and drug of choice. *Psychological Reports*, **49**, 752–756.

Perkins, D. E. (1987). A psychological treatment programme for sex offenders. In B. J. McGurk, D. M. Thornton & M. Williams (Eds). *Applying Psychology to Imprisonment: Theory and Practice.* London: HMSO.

Pierce, D. L., Sewell, K. W. & Cromwell, R. L. (1992). Schizophrenia and depression: Construing and constructing empirical research. In R. J. Neimeyer & G. J. Neimeyer (Eds). *Advances in Personal Construct Psychology, Vol 2.* London: JAI Press Limited.

Pollock, P. H. & Kear-Colwell, J. J. (1994). Women who stab: A personal construct analysis of sexual victimisation and offending behaviour. *British Journal of Medical Psychology*, **67**, 13–22.

Potamianos, G., Winter, D., Duffy, S. W., Gorman, D. M. & Peters, T. J. (1985). The perception of problem drinkers by general hospital staff, general practitioners and alcoholic patients. *Alcohol*, **2**, 563–566.

Preston, C. A. & Viney, L. L. (1984). Self- and ideal-self-perception of drug addicts in therapeutic communities. *The International Journal of the Addictions*, **19**, 805–818.

Quinsey, V. L. (1986). Men who have sex with children. In D. Weisstub (Ed.). *Law and Mental Health: International Perspectives*, Vol. 2. New York: Pergamon.

Ravenette, A. T. (1977). Personal construct theory: An approach to the psychological investigation of children and young people. In D. Bannister (Ed.). *New Perspectives in Personal Construct Theory.* London: Academic Press.

Ravenette, A. T. (1992). The one off interview. In P. Maitland & D. Brennan (Eds). *Personal Construct Theory, Deviancy and Social Work, (2nd Edition).* London: Inner London Probation Service/ Centre for Personal Construct Psychology.

Reed, J. (1993). *Review of Health and Social Services for Mentally Disordered Offenders and Others Requiring Similar Services*. London: HMSO Publications.

Reicher, S. & Emler, N. (1986). Managing reputations in adolescents: The pursuit of delinquent and non-delinquent identities. In H. Beloff (Ed.). *Getting into Life*. London: Methuen.

Reker, G. T. (1974). Interpersonal conceptual structure of emotionally disturbed and normal boys. *Journal of Abnormal Psychology*, **83**, 380–386.

Rivers, C. & Landfield, A. (1985). Personal construct theory and alcohol dependence. In E. Button (Ed.). *Personal Construct Theory and Mental Health*. London: Croom Helm.

Rollnick, S. & Heather, N. (1980). Psychological change among alcoholics during treatment. *British Journal of Alcohol and Alcoholism*, **15**, 118–123.

Rosenberg, M. (1965). *Society and the Adolescent Self Image*. Princeton, NJ: Princeton University Press.

Ross, R. R. & Fabiano, E. A. (1985). *Time to Think: A Cognitive Model of Delinquency Prevention and Offender Rehabilitation*. Johnson City, TE: Institute of Social Sciences and Arts.

Ross, R. R., Fabiano, E. A. & Ewles, C. D. (1988). Reasoning and rehabilitation. *International Journal of Offender Therapy and Comparative Criminology*, **20**, 29–35.

Rutter, M. (1969). *Maternal Deprivation Reassessed*. Harmondsworth: Penguin.

Ryle, A. (1975) *Frames and Cages: The Repertory Grid Approach to Human Understanding*. London: Sussex University Press.

Ryle, A. (1990). *Cognitive-Analytic Therapy: Active Participation in Change*. Chichester: Wiley.

Ryle, A. & Breen, D. (1972). Some differences in the personal constructs of neurotic and normal subjects. *British Journal of Psychiatry*, **120**, 483–489.

Safran, J. D. (1990). Toward a refinement of cognitive therapy in the light of interpersonal theory: 1. Theory. *Clinical Psychology Review*, **10**, 87–105.

Salmon, P. (1976). Grid measures with child subjects. In P. Slater (Ed.). *The Measurement of Intrapersonal Space by Grid Technique. Vol 1. Explorations of Intrapersonal Space*. London: Wiley.

Salter, A. C. (1988). *Treating Child Sex Offenders and Victims: A Practical Guide*. Newbury Park, CA: Sage.

Sarason, I. G. (1978). A cognitive social learning approach to juvenile delinquency. In R. D. Hare & D. Schalling (Eds). *Psychopathic Behaviour: Approaches to Research*. Chichester: Wiley.

Scimecca, J. A. (1985). Toward a theory of self for radical criminology. *Psychology: A Quarterly Journal of Human Behaviour*, **22**, 27–35.

Scott, R. D., Fagin, L. & Winter, D. (1993). The importance of the role of the patient in the outcome of schizophrenia. *British Journal of Psychiatry*, **163**, 62–68.

Seidman, B. T., Marshall, W. L., Hudson, S. M. & Robertson, P. J. (1994). An examination of intimacy and loneliness in sex offenders. *Journal of Interpersonal Violence*, **9**, 518–534.

Shaw, M. L. G. (1980). *On Becoming a Personal Scientist: Interactive Computer Elicitation of Personal Models of the World*. London: Academic Press.

Shaw, M. L. G. (1981). Conversational heuristics for eliciting shared understanding. In Shaw, M. L. G. (Ed.) *Recent Advances in Personal Construct Technology*. London: Academic Press.

Shaw, M. L. G. (1989). Software description survey. *International Journal of Personal Construct Psychology*, **2** 471–472.

Shorts, I. D. (1985). Treatment of a sex offender in a maximum security forensic hospital: detecting changes in personality and interpersonal construing. *International Journal of Offender Therapy and Comparative Criminology*, **29**, 237–250.

Skene, R. A. (1973). Construct shift in the treatment of a case of homosexuality. *British Journal of Medical Psychology*, **46**, 287–292.

Slaby, R. G. & Guerra, N. G. (1988). Cognitive mediators of aggression in adolescent offenders: 1. Assessment. *Developmental Psychology*, **24**, 580–588.

Slater, P. (1969). Theory and technique of the repertory grid. *British Journal of Psychiatry*, **115**, 1287–1296.

Slater, P. (1972). Notes on INGRID 72. London: Institute of Psychiatry (Unpublished manuscript).

Space, L. G. & Cromwell, R. L. (1978). Personal constructs among schizophrenic patients. In S. Schwartz (Ed.). *Language and Cognition in Schizophrenia*. Hillsdale, NJ: Lawrence Erlbaum.

Sperlinger, D. J. (1976). Aspects of stability in the repertory grid. *British Journal of Medical Psychology*, **49**, 341–347.

Stanley, B. (1985). Alienation in young offenders. In N. Beail (Ed.). *Repertory Grid Technique and Personal Constructs: Application in Clinical and Educational Settings*. London: Croom Helm.

Strachan, A. & Jones, D. (1982). Changes in identification during adolescence: A personal construct theory approach. *Journal of Personality Assessment*, **46**, 529–535.

Sykes, G. & Matza, D. (1957). Techniques of neutralisation: A theory of delinquency. *American Sociological Review*, **22**, 664–673.

Tarrier, N. (1992). Management and modification of residual positive psychotic symptoms. In M. Birchwood & N. Tarrier (Eds). *Innovations in the Psychological Management of Schizophrenia*. Chichester: Wiley.

Thomas-Peter, B. A. (1992). Construct theory and cognitive style in personality disordered offenders. In P. Maitland & D. Brennan (Eds). *Personal Construct Theory, Deviancy and Social Work*. London: Inner London Probation Service/Centre for Personal Construct Psychology.

Thornton, D. & Hogue, T. (1993). Large-scale provision programmes for sex offenders: Issues, dilemmas and progress. *Criminal Behaviour and Mental Health*, **3**, 371–380.

Tibbles, P. N. (1992). Changes in depression and personal construing following assessment for dynamic psychotherapy. *British Journal of Medical Psychology*, **65,** 9–15.

Topcu, S. (1976). Psychological concomitants of aggressive feelings and behaviour. PhD Thesis. University of London.

Towl, G. (1995). Anger management groupwork. *Issues in Criminological and Legal Psychology*, **23**, 31–35.

Tschudi, F. (1977). Loaded and honest questions: A construct theory view of symptoms and therapy. In D. Bannister (Ed.). *New Perspectives in Personal Construct Theory*. London: Academic Press.

Tschudi, F. (1984). Operating Manual for: Flexigrid Version 2.1. August 1984. An Integrated Software System for Eliciting and Analysing Grids. Oslo: University of Oslo (Unpublished manuscript).

Turkat, I. D. (1990). *The Personality Disorders: A Psychological Approach to Clinical Management.* Oxford: Pergamon Press.

Tyrer, T. R. (1990). *Why People Obey the Law.* Newhaven, CT: Yale University Press.

Warr, P. B. & Coffman, T. L. (1970). Personality, involvement, and extremity of judgement. *British Journal of Social and Clinical Psychology,* **9**, 108–121.

Watson, J. P., Gunn, J. C. & Gristwood, J. (1976). A Grid investigation of long-term prisoners. In P. Slater (Ed.). *The Measurement of Intrapersonal Space by Grid Technique. Vol. 1. Explorations of Intrapersonal Space.* London: Wiley.

West, D. J. & Farrington, D. P. (1977). *The Delinquent Way of Life.* London: Heinemann.

Widom, C. S. (1976). Interpersonal and personal construct systems in psychopaths. *Journal of Consulting Clinical Psychology,* **44**, 614–623.

Winter, D. (1988). Towards a constructive clinical psychology. In G. Dunnett (Ed.). *Working with People: Clinical Uses of Personal Construct Psychology.* London: Routledge.

Winter, D. A. (1975). Some characteristics of schizophrenics and their parents. *British Journal of Social and Clinical Psychology,* **14**, 279–290.

Winter, D. A. (1985). Repertory grid technique in the evaluation of therapeutic outcome. In N. Beail (Ed.). *Repertory Grid Techniques and Personal Constructs: Applications in Clinical and Educational Settings.* London: Croom Helm.

Winter, D. A. (1992). *Personal Construct Psychology in Clinical Practice: Theory, Research and Applications.* London: Routledge.

Winter, D. A. (1993). Slot rattling from law enforcement to law breaking: A personal construct theory exploration of police stress. *International Journal of Personal Construct Psychology,* **6**, 253–267.

Wolf, S. (1988). A model of sexual aggression/addiction. *Journal of Social Work and Human Sexuality,* **7**, 1.

Wolfgang, M. E., Thorberry, T. P. & Figlio, R. M. (1987). *From Boy to Man. From Delinquency to Crime.* Chicago, IL: University of Chicago Press.

Yochelson, S. & Samenow, F. (1976). *The Criminal Personality. Vol 1. A Profile for Change.* New York: Jason Aronson.

Index

Index compiled by Sylvia Potter

Related titles of interest...

Offender Profiling
Theory, Research and Practice
Janet L. Jackson and Debra A. Bekerian
Explores the role of offender profiling in criminal investigations and supporting a legal case.
Wiley Series in Psychology of Crime, Policing & Law
0-471-97564-8 254pp 1997 Hardback
0-471-97565-6 254pp 1997 Paperback

Crime, The Media and the Law
Dennis Howitt
Looks at the role of the mass media in legal and criminal processes.
Wiley Series in Psychology of Crime, Policing & Law
0-471-96905-2 225pp 1998 Hardback
0-471-97834-5 225pp 1998 Paperback

Therapeutic Communities for Offenders
Eric Cullen, Lawrence Jones and Roland Woodward
Summarises examples of 'best practice' that therapeutic communities can offer to offenders in the UK, Europe and the United States.
Wiley Series in Offender Rehabilitation
0-471-96545-6 296pp 1997 Hardback
0-471-96980-X 296pp 1997 Paperback

Changing Lives of Crime and Drugs
Intervening with Substance-Abusing Offendes
Glenn D. Walters
Provides a coherent and practical model for intervention, detailed guidelines for related work with offenders, and illustrative examples and case studies.
Wiley Series in Offender Rehabilitation
0-471-97658-X 154pp 1998 Hardback
0-471-97841-8 154pp 1998 Paperback